The Next 50
Barrel Racing Exercises
for Precision on the Pattern

Copyright © 2017 by Heather Smith
Published by BarrelRacingTips.com

Cover Photograph by Kirstie Marie Photography

All rights reserved. This book may not be reproduced or utilized in whole or in part by any means, electronic, or mechanical, including photocopying, recording, or by any information storage or retrieval system, without written permission from the author.

First edition.

Disclaimer
This book is for informational and educational purposes. All recommendations are made without guarantee on the part of the author or publisher. The author and publisher shall have neither liability nor responsibility to any person(s) or entity with respect to any loss or damage, caused or alleged to be caused directly or indirectly as a result of the information contained in this book, or appearing on the BarrelRacingTips.com or 50BarrelRacingExercises.com web site(s). While this book is as accurate as the author can make it, there may be unintentional errors, omissions and inaccuracies.

Dedication

*To those who enthusiastically read this book for the exercises,
and realize –
that it's not what we do,
but HOW we do it
that determines our success...
with an exercise, and with everything else.*

Acknowledgements

Once again, to my husband, Craig:

Although building our dream life in Texas seems to have postponed opportunities for following his own passions, I know supporting mine is actually a conscious choice he makes every day.

Being my partner has meant deserting comfort zones and taking risks. I'm in awe of how you have continuously and selflessly found joy and fulfillment in caring for others.

I'll never take it for granted. Thank you.

To my Dream Horse, Pistol:

It's taken years to outgrow seeds once planted that left me doubting in his abilities.

I trusted my gut, believing not only that when I did *my part* – that you would gladly, flawlessly *and quickly* do yours, but that together we could overcome any obstacle… and *we have*.

I've never known a horse so accepting, patient and kind.

Thanks for being everything I always wanted.

Always, to my Lord and Savior:

I've learned when we renew ourselves in His truths every day that our outwardly world can actually be renewed as well.

Thank you, Lord, for shining light and making new, the conditions and situations which may have otherwise been seen as dead ends. You've given me a faith-perspective that has lit up my life.

I'm eternally grateful for the opportunity to pass it on.

Special thanks to Kirstie Marie Photography for capturing the cover photo and several others throughout this book. Thanks also to Stacy Hornberger and her gelding Wild Bill for appearing in several photos.

Table of Contents

Introduction 9
How to Benefit 11

Let's Get Physical 19
Exercise 1 – Triple "H" Program 20
Exercise 2 – Hop to It 22
Exercise 3 – Please Stand Up 24
Exercise 4 – Jet Fuel 26
Exercise 5 – Pre and Post-Ride Routine 28

From the Ground Up 31
Exercise 6 – Dream Catcher 32
Exercise 7 – Snappy Backing 34
Exercise 8 – Circle Responsibly 36
Exercise 9 – Better Biomechanics 38
Exercise 10 – Line Dance 40

Stretch It Out 42

Start Strong, Finish FAST 43
Exercise 11 – Walk to Win 44
Exercise 12 – Measured Improvement 46
Exercise 13 – Get Hooked 48
Exercise 14 – Supple Speed 50
Exercise 15 – Brake it Down 52

First Barrel Finesse 55
Exercise 16 – First Things First 56
Exercise 17 – Position Perfection 58
Exercise 18 – Mix it Up 60
Exercise 19 – Stop and Circle 62
Exercise 20 – Run & Rate 64

3 x 3 Troubleshooting Plan 66

Second Barrel Success 67
Exercise 21 – Smooth it Out 68
Exercise 22 – Lollipop 70
Exercise 23 – Reverse 360 72
Exercise 24 – Forty-Five Fencing 74
Exercise 25 – Stop the Drop 76

Thriving at Third 79
Exercise 26 – Figure 8 to Finish 80
Exercise 27 – Specific Circles 82
Exercise 28 – Double Barrel 84
Exercise 29 – Straight In & Out 86
Exercise 30 – Reverse Counter Arc 88

Do This, Not That 90

Engaged for Power 91
Exercise 31 – Triple R 92
Exercise 32 – Two Track Turn 94
Exercise 33 – Be Square 96
Exercise 34 – Break Off & Roll Back 98
Exercise 35 – Hills and Poles 100

Refined Maneuverability 103
Exercise 36 – Quatrefoil 104
Exercise 37 – Switchback 106
Exercise 38 – Pinwheel 108
Exercise 39 – Flower Power 110
Exercise 40 – Rock & Roll 112

Tack and Bit Tips 114

Need for Speed 115
Exercise 41 – Conditioning Game Plan ... 116
Exercise 42 – Fit to Fast 118
Exercise 43 – Rocket Launch 120
Exercise 44 – Get in Gear 122
Exercise 45 – Daisy Clipper 124

In It to Win It 127
Exercise 46 – Tools & Team 128
Exercise 47 – Funds for Fun 130
Exercise 48 – Wide Open Spaces 132
Exercise 49 – Life Integration 134
Exercise 50 – Heart & Soul 136

About the Author 139

*Authors Note:

Throughout this book, I have used the pronouns "he" and "him" to refer to the singular barrel horse. I have assigned the pronouns "she" and "her" to the rider. I acknowledge, however, that barrel horses and barrel racers can be of either gender.

To represent the exercises as clearly as possible, not all diagrams were drawn to scale in relation to the arena size shown.

> *Truth, like gold, is to be obtained not by its growth, but by washing away from it all that is not gold.*
>
> – Leo Tolstoy

Introduction

How This is Different

Early last year I was craving more time with our horses. However, it seemed everything I set out to do was taking longer than expected. This eventually led to a state of paralysis, unable to peel myself away from my projects, yet barely able to function so distanced from what I love most. With every milestone I reached, it seemed that the finish line kept moving. I figured it would make *much more sense* to get our horses competition-ready, when I *really* had my ducks in a row – namely the finances and time to truly give them *my all*. While I believe this a worthy route, a powerful moment occurred in the spring when I realized the gelding with perhaps the greatest level of athletic talent in our equine trio would be turning 16 years old. That put a whole new sense of urgency on *everything*. Sensible or not, something had to change.

Since publishing *The First 51 Exercises to Develop a Champion*, I've found myself on the other side of a remarkable personal transition. As a very left-brain dominant individual, I enjoy and spend an enormous amount of time learning. This isn't all bad of course, but it's led me very far down many, many rabbit holes of education in various areas – looking for missing pieces to the big puzzle. Again, this path has *also* been a worthy one, *a necessary one* to travel – but it's certainly not where I found all the answers (not that we ever find them all, anyway). In the process I *did* finally discover a personal balance which serves as the foundation necessary to support barrel racing success, and numerous other powerful and unshakeable principles I'll be sharing in this book. These are truths that don't always get talked about, but need to be. They are truths that can *also* provide *you* with the structure for achieving your own barrel racing dreams.

When it comes to structure, that's much of what my first book, the *Secrets to Barrel Racing Success* provided. It's my hope that you've enjoyed it and the others preceding this resource. Just like when it comes to educating barrel horses, there's a certain order we should follow to put the odds for success most in our favor. It's always easier (and faster) in the long run, when we understand and follow sequential steps for giving ourselves and our horses a solid start. Trust me on this vs. learning the *hard* way!

If you've also read *The First 51* I want to say a *very special* thank you. You see, I'm different now. So the *style* of *this* book is a little different too. While my quest for personal development will never end, I'm steering clear of deep rabbit holes for a while. It's way past time to get my head above ground and balance my ratio of writing vs. riding. What this means is that *The Next 50* is a bit less wordy and contains more visuals, which makes for quicker, easier reading and application. *The First 51* required a lot of thinking. Especially (and only) once you really have the basics down, is it time to THINK less and FEEL more. As it turns out, non-judgmental observation of our current habits and imagery of what *we want* to create is proven to be the best way to learn and "sensualize" our way to being the trainers and jockeys our horses need anyway. Theory is an important part of it all of course, but let's not get buried in it.

Thank you again for taking this ride with me through this ever-evolving journey as an author, teacher, horseman and barrel racer. Congratulations for making it this far – now the real FUN begins!

> *My mother used to say:*
> *It's not what you say, it's how you say it.*
> *And you know what?*
> *It's not what you do, it's how you do it.*
> *It's not what you see, it's how you look at it.*
> *It's not how your life is, it's how you live it.*
> — Sue Fitzmaurice

How to Benefit

Why Exercises?

The word "drill" is defined by the Oxford English Dictionary as *"to instruct (someone) in something by the means of repeated practice,"* or *"cause (someone) to learn something by repeating it regularly."* For me, the word "drill" brings up a negative connotation. There's a reason I try to avoid using it. While repetition is certainly part of utilizing exercises, one can assume that "drilling" our horse means that repetition alone is all there is to it. That my friends, couldn't be further from the truth. A drill then, to me, whether used as a noun or verb, isn't implied to be carried out with the timing and feel that a living, breathing, thinking, feeling 1,200 lb. animal *requires* to grow not only physically, but mentally and emotionally as well. Barrel racing certainly isn't a no-brainer sport – so we can't develop our horses as if they don't have one.

That's where *exercises* done well come in, defined by Oxford as *"to engage in physical activity to sustain or improve health and fitness."* Feel the difference? Do you think our horses prefer that we *instruct* and *repeat* OR *engage* and *improve*? Words are so powerful; we must choose them wisely. Drills can be seen as something we do *to* our horses, where-as exercises performed to *sustain* or *improve* overall health and fitness, are something we can do *with* and *for* them, with the intention not only to educate our horses and reach our goals, but also with the power to improve the quality of our horse's life at the same time.

A Review

Exercises will always be a valuable tool for developing horses and preparing them for high-level competition. However, I can't say enough that *the way* we use them is much more important than simply going through the motions. The quality of our horse's performance will always be a reflection of the quality of development we've put in, so we must be precise and intentional. Below I've shared a summary of points as a refresher, inspired by the same section in *The First 51*. Again consider these your critical prerequisites – elements necessary for gaining the most benefit out of *any* exercise. I can't stress them enough.

Prior Proper Preparation – When it comes to executing each exercise, always remember to start with a picture and sense of what it looks and feels like in your mind and body when done *with quality*. Have you ever sensed that your horse *knew what you were thinking*? Pay close attention to their eyes and ears, and there will be moments when you can *almost see it*. When a horse has just a tiny heads-up of what's coming before we offer an actual cue to them, it gets their mental wheels turning in the same direction, and may even cause a subtle shift of weight that can prepare them to coordinate each step or maneuver with much greater athleticism and speed. Remember to take a moment and use ALL your senses to really *feel* and *experience* yourself executing each exercise successfully first. Think about how you'd like your horse to carry his frame, then how the posture in your own body relates. Prepare for any transitions by raising or lowering your own energy level, based on what you'll require from your horse. Just a fraction of a second of preparation is often all it takes to help your horse perform with greater ease, quickness and success.

Do the Simple Things with Excellence – The most advanced athletic maneuvers are built on highly refined basics. When a horse isn't reaching his potential, it can almost always be traced back to gaps in the foundations. Few people want to hear that their basics need refinement, but this is where the solution to a wide variety of problems exists. Remember that an "I already know this!" attitude is one of *the biggest* roadblocks on the path to achieving success. I cannot over emphasize the importance of doing the *simple things well*. A humble, open mind, and a willingness to learn and prioritize never-ending personal development and the refinement of your own riding and your horse's education (no matter what stage you're at), will take you far in the barrel racing world. Don't settle for "above average" or "good enough," but instead commit to continuously testing yourself and raising your standards. Remember *quality over quantity* - an exercise repeated perfectly three times is better than one performed carelessly ten times.

Repetition in Moderation – As a species, horses are wired to be constantly looking out for their safety. Generally speaking, change equals danger and routine equals security. From a psychology stand-point, a horse that tends to be insecure and nervous will especially find comfort in routines and repetition. Consistency is more important, then, to an innately insecure or skeptical horse. Horses that seem more naturally calm and confident thrive with more variety. Motivate this kind of horse by mixing things up more often to keep them connected, interested and willing. Horses learn best when presented with new information for several days in a row. While consistent repetition might be beneficial for the mind, it can be hard on the body. When challenging horses physically, allow days for light riding in between harder workouts for *physical* recovery. In your individual rides, choose three areas of focus, for example, but several ways to work on each area to prevent extreme fatigue and keep your horse's mind *and* body fresh.

Consistency Builds Confidence – Because horses thrive on consistency, every aspect of how you handle your horse is an opportunity to instill greater feelings of confidence and security in them. Without impeccable consistency from us, our horses are unable to sort out what cue is causing what consequence or reward, which in turn causes insecurity, confusion and tentativeness. Your own outer circumstances will change, but your horse is not aware of this. If you allow your horse to lazily stroll behind you as you lead him for example, but then give him a harsh correction on a day you're in a hurry, then you've failed to provide clear, consistent guidelines, making yourself less trustworthy in his eyes. In a speed event such as barrel racing, there is no room at the top for a horse that is uncertain and hesitates due to a long history of inconsistent communication. Avoid changing the rules. Make it your goal to become more consistent in *all* areas; having your horse's confidence on your side can make all the difference when it matters most.

Gain a New Perspective – We're all very accustomed to analyzing videos of our competition runs, but don't underestimate the value of watching videos of your everyday riding and training sessions to study your horse's form as well as your own. So often we are completely unaware that our habits may be negatively affecting our competitive runs because we so rarely see ourselves and our horses as we ride or simply lope circles. The solution can be as simple as propping an iPhone on a fence post. Do this on a regular basis and you may be surprised by what you see as you gain a new perspective from watching the footage. In the process we learn and grow as horsemen as we develop better "vision" to see issues that we weren't previously aware of that can be affecting our horse's performance. We can't improve what we aren't aware of. This opportunity to gain awareness by watching and studying video footage is one we can *only* take advantage of, when we've actually made the effort to take a look more often, and more closely.

Meet Their Needs – A huge part of preparing ourselves for success when executing exercises means helping our horses be thoroughly prepared to learn. If a horse becomes unbalanced emotionally, this interferes with their cognitive functioning because their focus is directed toward survival, making learning difficult. In this case, make dealing with those emotions and restoring calmness in your horse a priority. Often, it's not that the horse *can't* think or learn, it's that *we* haven't done our part to *prepare him* to learn.

First and foremost, meet your horse's needs, especially for safety by offering quality leadership and they will become likely to meet yours in return. The odds for success are so much greater when you've developed your horse to be respectful, responsive, obedient and willing to stay connected to you physically and mentally. *Be* your horse's comfort zone and icon of safety. When you are, you won't have to compete with distractions for their attention, and you'll have created an ideal mental state for learning to occur.

Be Patient – Especially when troubleshooting, consider that a problem may have developed over the course of many months before the symptoms became obvious. Issues in the making for years cannot be corrected overnight. Although it takes a relatively short time to learn something new, experts believe that it takes 40 days to rewire the neural pathways in our brains. Invest the time it takes to get to the bottom of problems, even if that means putting competition on the back burner, while also understanding that simply avoiding the environment where the trigger occurs isn't a solution. We must develop *the skills* to reeducate our horses and create a healthy emotional balance in *any* circumstance. Only test your progress once you're confident you've made a significant enough positive change to avoid defaulting back to old habits. Small, but consistent improvements add up fast. Rome was not built in a day, and great horses are no different. Make decisions and ride every step and with your horse's future and longevity in mind.

Look Within – It's not uncommon to place so much focus on our horses that we lose sight of ourselves. Remember that when a shooter misses a target, it's not the target's fault. Our riding on and off the pattern for example, has so much more influence on the way our horse uses his body than many barrel racers realize. Whatever problem your horse is having, look closely at what your own body parts are doing. Are you riding in a way that makes turning a barrel *easy* for your horse, or difficult? How is your timing in a run? Our horse is our mirror in more ways than one. We get out of our horses what we put in, *the way* we put it in. Their behavior and performance is a reflection of the development we have instilled in them. It's ok to admit a horse is over your skill level, or not a good match, but the horse isn't at fault or wrong for that. Be humble and secure enough to take responsibility for what you contribute to the partnership. Make it your goal every time you saddle up to be the very best version of yourself, so your horse can be as well.

Focus on the Ingredients – When your horse isn't performing well, closely consider the individual ingredients that are important for success. So often the symptoms are not the issue; the real problem is lying under the surface unrecognized. We can't experience the satisfaction of completing a whole puzzle until all the pieces are in place. Is your horse lacking long, fluid strides? Flexion? Longitudinal suppleness through the body? Do you have an equal balance of "whoa and go?" Whatever you are missing on the pattern will also tend to be lacking in your everyday riding, just on a smaller, less noticeable scale. For example, rather than drill incessantly, teach your horse to utilize his hindquarters better at *all times*, then return to the barrels and show him this improved way of moving is also necessary *on* the pattern. Pick every problem apart, and break it down again further. It's only possible to bake a cake when we have all the ingredients. Brush up the elements, get them all going really well in isolation, then gradually combine.

Set it Up and Wait –If you find yourself having to "tune up" your horse after a few days off, or at the start of each ride, or if they seem to be lacking consistency, it's quite possible they were trained by being *put* into position. This is easy to do considering our instinct is to have control over a young horse from the very first ride. However, excellent horse training isn't about showing, putting, making or forcing. It's about creating opportunities for the horse *to think* and then make a choice that is likely to be what we had in mind to begin with, yet setting it up to be something he finds on his own. This is how lasting, authentic learning, that doesn't require constant tuning and refreshers takes place, not so much by molding our horse in to shape, which only leads to having to use our reins and legs to keep them there. Holding a horse in position doesn't allow for the mental processing that a horse's search for the right answer, for comfort, does. No matter what stage of horse development you're at, it's never too late to "set it up and wait" – and reap the benefits!

Keep it Simple – When faced with a challenge, don't hesitate to temporarily lower your standards and revert back to a place where you know your horse can succeed before presenting a more challenging request. Have a clear idea of where you're going and how you're going to get there. Don't expect your horse to move or perform in a certain way if you're not certain what you're looking for. Preserve your horse's "try" by having realistic, clear expectations. Have compassion and understanding for your horse. Imagine what it's like to have significant and rapidly increasing pressure put on you to learn something while being given very confusing signals; it would be frustrating and discouraging at best and miserable or frightening at worst. A student must understand the alphabet before she can create words, and eventually sentences. Being too demanding, making things too complicated, failing to be clear, and asking for more than a horse is ready to deliver can quickly destroy a willing, winning attitude. We must value, protect and reward this in our horses.

Release on the Thought – Especially when teaching our horses something new, it's important to make what you're looking for *very* obvious. The quicker you reward your horse for doing something right, the quicker he will learn. A reward might mean taking any pressure off, stopping for a rest, it might mean a treat, or a scratch, or softening in your energy, or it might mean a change, such as continuing on a straight line as a reward for a quality circle. Whatever form or combination of release you use, make it clear and use it often, which encourages horses to keep trying while building their desire to please in the future. That way, even if he can't reach the goal today, he'll be more enthusiastic to try tomorrow. A horse that is offered clear incentives will have more motivation. One of the biggest barriers to giving our horses relief is time constraints! Give your horse time to "soak" and wait until he licks his lips before moving on after he's done something well – this alone can be a total game changer for both horse and human alike.

YOUR Foundation – We all want to improve, but it's those who are secure enough with who they are that will ask questions, open themselves to potential criticism, and apply what they learn, that will take their barrel racing to the next level. Your belief in yourself and burning desire to succeed *must be* greater than any insecurity. However, until you seek out learning opportunities, you may never discover the missing pieces on your own. Trust yourself to sort out what works for you, but don't hesitate to ask questions; seek out professional help and pay for it when you need it. It might make you uncomfortable to do so, but that's the point. Don't let insecurity keep you stuck in a rut. Your drive to be successful must overpower any fear of failure, rejection, or of what others' think. You may look like a fool in public and that's great – embrace it! Neither other people's opinions nor your performance determine your worth. Develop a strong foundation of self-worth, and never hesitate to put yourself out there in the name of personal growth.

Be Effective and Understood – If you ever feel stuck, simply remember that it's most likely because either your horse is not in a positive mental/emotional state, doesn't completely understand what you're asking, or is not taking responsibility for doing what he does know. When making a request, always start with light pressure, give your horse time when he's learning, and appreciate when he's trying. It's just as important to be firm to reinforce something you're confident your horse understands well. This can be instrumental for creating more respect. Most riders are not soft and light enough when they first make a request, and they don't get firm enough to reinforce what has been asked when necessary, which leads to dullness.

Avoid the nagging/ambushing cycle. Consequences should be delivered in relation to the severity of the offence. When you must be firm, do so without getting emotional. Calm, connected, responsiveness is achieved in large part by being firm yet fair, and gentle yet effective, with consistency.

Good Answers Come From Good Questions – Your "How to Benefit" Checklist:

☐ Are the exercises performed in a way that educates my horse, while simultaneously improving his health & fitness?

☐ Am I pausing to visualize each exercise done with quality *first* in order to prepare my horse for success?

☐ Am I aware and willing to go back to basics, knowing it's the foundation all high-level maneuvers are built upon?

☐ Do I understand each individual horse's needs, and customize how I use repetition to help them learn?

☐ Am I a trainer that offers communication so consistent that my horses have complete confidence and trust in me?

☐ Do I watch video footage, not just of my runs but every-day riding, to constantly raise my awareness and improve?

☐ Have I empowered my horses with the education and health necessary to learn and perform with minimal stress?

☐ Am I realistic, flexible with timelines, and willing to adjust my goals to match my horse's readiness level?

☐ When faced with challenges, do I take responsibility for what I contribute to the partnership with my horse?

☐ Do I understand the difference between a problem and its symptoms, and focus on the parts to create a solution?

☐ Instead of molding and holding my horse's body into shape, do I use pressure & release to also educate his mind?

☐ When my horse doesn't understand, do I go back to what he does know, then adjust my approach and try again?

☐ Do I offer my horse a release when he does well, and have several ways to communicate when he's correct?

☐ Do I regularly put myself in uncomfortable learning situations and devote time to continued growth as a horseman?

☐ Am I committed to being "as gentle as possible but as firm as necessary" for effective and progressive training?

Horse & Rider Basics - Additional Questions to Ask as You Execute and Troubleshoot:

- Does my horse maintain gait and direction?
- Is my horse's movement forward and energetic?
- Is my horse balanced laterally, or does he lean to the inside of a circle or turn?
- Is my horse balanced front to back, with adequate weight on the hindquarters?
- Is my horse calm, connected and responsive?
- Does my horse ever push into pressure, resist, or ignore my requests?
- Does my horse show signs of discomfort or irritability?
- Does my horse show signs of anxiety or tension?
- Does my horse need to build more coordination or strengh?
- Am I looking where I want to go?
- Do I use my body (seat, legs, shoulders, weight, etc.) to direct my horse?
- Do I tend to overthink, or do I ride with feel and good timing?
- Am I leaning in the saddle, or am I completely balanced?
- Do I have an absolutely clear idea of what I want from my horse?
- Am I aware enough to notice the most subtle signs of a problem?
- Can I *really* sort out the cause of a problem versus the symptom?

More Terms, Tools and Tips

Inside versus Outside – Throughout this book, when I refer to the inside rein or the inside leg, I'm referring to the one on the inside of the circle (the side of the direction of travel). For example, the inside rein as you are rounding a barrel is the one closest to the barrel, while the outside leg or hand would be on the opposite side. The same idea applies when following the rail of the arena. The outside leg of the horse or rider, or the outside hand or rein, is that which is closest to the wall, while the inside leg is that which is on the side of the direction of travel. When traveling to the left, whether on the rail or in a left hand circle, the left side of the horse or rider is the inside, and the right side is the outside.

Make Your Mark – Some of the exercises in this book call for six or more barrels. The best place I have found to get 55-gallon plastic barrels is CraigsList.org. You might also contact your local heating and air conditioning company, car wash, dry cleaning business or laundromat. These businesses usually purchase chemicals or soap in bulk and will sometimes have leftover barrels available for a reasonable price. If you must set up and then take down your equipment after each ride, several versions of pop-up barrels are available today and offer a quicker, lighter and more portable option.

A great alternative to using old car tires for setting up patterns is to use old bicycle tires. They don't create quite as much visual reference or a physical barrier for your horse because they are smaller in size, but they add a lot of convenience due to the fact that they are much smaller and easier to move. If your local bike shop doesn't have a supply of used tires, you might ask them to keep some for you. It's likely you can obtain an assortment of them for little to no cost.

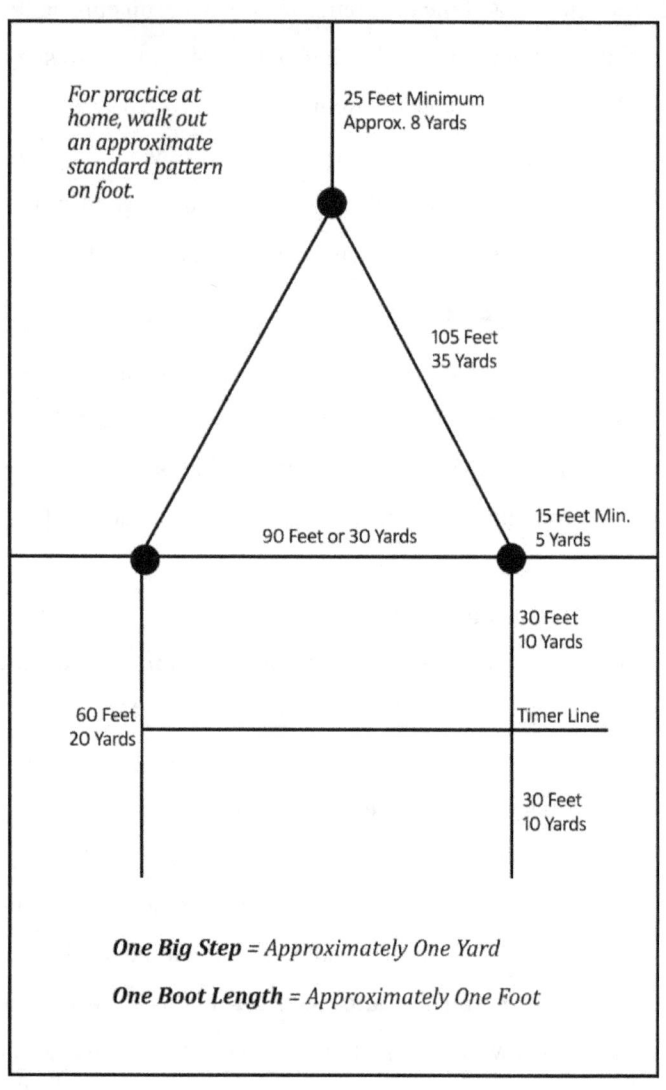

I also suggest purchasing 20 or more plastic soccer field markers/disks, which can be found online. They are small, portable, lightweight and although they don't serve as a physical barrier to your horse they are typically found in fluorescent colors and are great to use as reference points for the rider, while posing little to no danger to the horse if accidentally stepped on.

One of the quickest and easiest ways to set up markers for patterns is by walking out the approximate distances on foot. Consider one big step to equal approximately three feet or one yard. Consider the length of your boot from toe to heel to be approximately one foot. I've included a guide for setting up an approximate standard pattern. Because pattern sizes change based on arena size and set-up, be sure to vary the distances between barrels from time to time so your horse doesn't get accustomed to always making the same number of strides and is prepared for changes in pattern size.

Open the Gait – When barrel racers think of gait, most automatically think of the varience in speed between the walk, trot, lope and gallop. However, it's not so much the speed, but the actual footfall pattern that separates the gaits that deserves more of our attention. Studying and developing the quality and purity of each gait not only positively effects how efficiently our horses use their bodies in general, but follows through to the barrel pattern as well.

Each horse has tendencies to express each gait in a particular rhythm and style. In some cases a horse's gaits may not be carried out with an even cadence or strength. When utilized properly, exercises can greatly improve the quality of a horse's gait as well as his ability to transition not only between gaits but within, which is absolutely necessary for efficiency on the pattern.

Think of the straightaways between barrels as areas where we want our horses to extend or lengthen, then transition to a more shortened or collected gait in the approach to the barrel and through the turns. At a medium walk or trot, it's ideal for a horse to track up (their hind feet step in the tracks of their front feet). In a collected gait they will tend to under-track and over-track in extension. Both shortened and extended movement can be performed in the same cadenced tempo; however the extended stride covers more ground and the collected stride is more elevated. For more on this subject, see the diagram below and the "Quality Movement" chapter in *Secrets to Barrel Racing Success*.

Arena Map Key

Walk ....
Trot . . . .
Lope ───────────
Gallop ───────────
Stop □
Back • • • • • • • • • • • • • • • •
Lead Change ─────X─────

Understand Gaits

	Walk	Trot	Lope	Gallop	Back Up
Beats per Gait	4	2	3	4	2
Weight Distribution	Front/Hind 60/40%	Front/Hind 50/50%	Front/Hind 40/60%	Front/Hind 51-70/49-30%	Front/Hind 49-30/51-70%
Footfall by Gait	(4)(2) (3)(1)	(2)(1) (1)(2)	(2)(3) (1)(2)	(4)(3) (2)(1)	(1)(2) (2)(1)

> *The horse is a mirror to your soul.*
> *Sometimes you might not*
> *like what you see.*
> *Sometimes you will.*
>
> – Buck Brannaman

Let's Get Physical

If you're old enough to remember lyrics from Olivia Newton-John's once popular song, you may or *may not* get excited by the idea of "getting physical" (don't search for the video, trust me!). In the following chapter I've shared how to prepare barrel racing athletes for success on the pattern, as well as offered support in the way of *fuel*. Barrel racing is a demanding sport and it's easy to see just how much physical and mental wear & tear our horses can experience if we don't make good management choices. I personally want my horses to love their job and I want them to have longevity. I want to enjoy them and reap rewards for the time, effort and love I put forth as long as possible. When we enter the gate, I want them to think clearly, respond quickly and fire hard. This is why I put so much focus on their health care and pre-pattern development. I want running barrels to be as easy and stress-free as possible, which is why I'm so enthusiastic about offering *all* the tools necessary for success in advance, *well before* they ever prove themselves as winners and without cutting any corners.

If you're with me on this, then it's critical to also direct the philosophy toward *our own* development. I'm humbled to regularly receive heartfelt correspondence from barrel racers around the world, not only expressing their gratitude for the resources I offer but also sharing their challenges. When I receive an email expressing frustration and discouragement, often it's not a barrel racing issue at all. What I sometimes ask is that they consider what they're using for "fuel" – what are they *allowing* or *taking in* that could be *getting in the way* of success? What's missing from their personal foundation? I'm sure you realize on some level that we tend to get out of our horses what we put in. But this applies to ourselves as well. If our horses are our mirror, a reflection of us, why do we so often scrutinize our horse's diet and conditioning but overlook our own? Good question, right? I mean, we *are* jockeying race horses, after all.

With a healthy balance of quality nutrients for example, your horses can be better prepared to think clearly, respond quickly and fire hard. But if *you* are not *also* fueled for performance and functioning at a high level, they certainly won't perform to *their* absolute fullest potential. Why make it difficult for yourself, and why make it *harder* on your horses? Instead, why not make it *easy* to focus like a laser, have impeccable balance in the saddle, cat-like reflexes in a run, long-lasting and high levels of energy, plus a positive outlook? What you put *in* your body, and the environment you *put your body in,* has the power to do that. You don't have to search for motivation when you're already motivated, or go out of your way to have a winning attitude when it's there by default. That's really what nourishing food, exercise and adequate rest can do. They're the ultimate performance enhancers, they dramatically affect how we think and feel, and they can uplift our emotions and energy fast!

Are your health habits and choices a representation of how serious you are about barrel racing? If we're overlooking these aspects, we're essentially wasting runs. If you not only want to have fun but *be great*, don't send in another entry unprepared. When you know without a doubt that you've done everything possible to be at your best, it generates a huge level of confidence. Why accelerate down the alleyway without this on your side? Every moment is a chance to start fresh, wo don't start out by dwelling on what you could have done better in the past. It led you here, and the only time we have is now. Trust me when I say - whether "getting physical" is something you already enjoy *or* typically avoid, that you have nothing to lose and everything to gain by utilizing the following exercises. *That* is something to get *very* excited about!

Exercise 1 – Triple "H" Program

Description
When it comes to discipline, it seems there are folks that perceive it as limiting and those who *know* it's the path to freedom. I claim the latter. It's not an oxymoron to say there is great freedom in structure. To create a program for anything suggests that follow-through and consistency are important. The subtitle of this book states that the exercises included are for the purpose of "Precision on the Pattern." There's no denying that when fractions of a second can be life changing, it's the little everyday habits, when compiled, hat make or break us. So let's leave nothing to chance in our pursuit of barrel racing excellence!

Purpose
When we have a framework in place, we don't have to try so hard to remember what must be done to stay on track. It's done for us and becomes something we just do – *every single day*. The decisions are already made. These are your rituals, your "dailies," your non-negotiables. Whatever you call them, the standards for you and your horse's exercise regime, diet and recovery habits should be intentional, specific and high. The more you get in the habit of caring for what you value in a purposeful way, the more confidence it builds. You probably already have at least a loosely structured program for your horses. Let's take that program *and your own* to the next level, so your performance in competition can go there also.

How-to
Your Horse and Human Health Program - In any area we want to master, education and awareness are two pillars of success. If we're open and willing to implement changes in the areas below, even for just two weeks to start with, the positive differences experienced are often enough motivation to continue.

Nutrition – If you've ever started your horses on a new feed that made them "hot," you already have an idea of how powerful nutrition is when it seemingly changes a horse's entire personality. If diet changes can affect energy levels and cause a horse to either be distracted *or* focused, then we can't underestimate or forget the power diet has to help balance our horses physically and emotionally. Rather than be tempted to add supplement on top of supplement, go to the source and make absolutely sure that balanced, quality nutrients are being consumed as the foundation. However you feel, or your horse feels, consider how you'd like it to improve; do your research and make adjustments accordingly. The following exercise will assist you in doing this for your horses. Whether it's more energy or less anxiety you're after, diet has the power to support whatever qualities we need and want, in ourselves and in our horses. It's just a matter of realizing it's possible, and then learning how to create the right balance for each individual.

Exercise – It's easy to fall off the health wagon and become frustrated, then as a result become highly motivated to make a change. Sometimes the biggest transformations come as a result of hitting rock bottom. Based on the flood of gym-goers every January first, it's not unusual to start a new and improved fitness routine that's set-up for failure from the beginning because it's too extreme and throws our life as a whole off balance. I feel that specific and regular exercise to enhance our overall wellness and our abilities as jockeys is a must for every barrel racer, no matter how many hours you spend in the saddle each day. However, because of everything else our sport requires, I can say it's better to have a 20-30 minute routine 5 days a week at home (or on the road), rather than an intense but *impossible to stick to long term* hour long routine at a gym. As you can see, the rule of balance applies here as well. Find a routine that's enjoyable, fits into your lifestyle and schedule long-term, and make it a priority. Exercise isn't punishment, but a way to love and appreciate your body by rewarding it with endorphins and strength. The more energy you have, the more results you'll achieve. You and your horses *deserve* to be invested in!

Rest – If we're tired, we're more likely to experience mood swings, make poor food choices in an attempt to increase your energy, or skip your workouts. There's the common excuse of "I don't have time." But do you have time to feel and perform poorly or keep clocking a half-second off? We don't have time to *not* make rest a priority. Everything you do, you'll do better with a good night of nourishing sleep. The higher our goals and the more demanding the requirements of our sport are, the more important adequate rest is!

There will be all-night drives, there will be challenges, and there will (and should) be indulgences, in moderation. But you and your horses will be better prepared to handle and succeed despite them all with a solid and intentionally developed "Triple H Program." Most people have no idea how good their bodies and minds are designed to feel. I encourage you to find out! Join forces with your horses to *train like an athlete, eat like a nutritionist, and sleep like a baby* to *win like a champion*. Use the chart below to create an assessment, then map out your goals and post them where they'll offer constant motivation.

Your **Horse & Human Health Program** FUNsheet	*What's Working? What's Not?* What are you satisfied with in each area? What's going well? What are you good at? This leads to - what's NOT working? What could be better? What's missing? What's in the way?	*WHAT and WHY Do You Want to Improve?* WHY are adjustments important to you? What will be the result? How will you and your horse benefit? Ex: More energy and time for family, better riding, less stress/overwhelm.	*What Actions Will You Take, and WHEN?* List specific action steps you're committing to in each area, plus a timeframe or deadline for doing so. What must happen first for changes to occur and be followed through with?
Your Nutrition			
Horse's Nutrition			
Your Exercise			
Horse's Exercise			
Your Rest and Recovery			
Horse Rest and Recovery			

Exercise 2 – Hop to It

Description
Being a barrel racer also requires us to be a truck driver, groom, veterinarian and more, which means we must make our day to day routines as simple and efficient as possible. In *everything* we do, there is no time to waste! This rule applies to our fitness routines as well, because when they're targeted toward our unique needs as jockeys we can receive the greatest benefit from the limited time we have available. Many types of exercise are good for our health, but we must get *specific* to improve our ability to jockey our horses. In *The First 51* I included exercises that focused on core strength, posture, balance and agility. There are many workout programs that offer core strengthening, even outside of those directed toward equestrians. Among those fitness programs designed for equestrians, however, few include exercises to develop agility. Even fewer disciplines require the level of quickness and precision that barrel racing does! A sport with specific and unique demands requires specific and unique preparation.

Purpose
Often times I've heard from discouraged barrel racers – questioning themselves, saying "I'm not sure I'm a 1D rider." To that I have to ask, "What are you doing every day to become one?" I also have to wonder, "What else are you unsure of?" When I notice riders clocking slow, because they're riding slow, I know there's a serious limitation in awareness and therefore solutions. I'm especially perceptive to this issue, because *I've been that rider* and am anxious to help others overcome this issue as a result! Riding assertively and athletically requires that we leave hesitation and uncertainty behind, which is sometimes a mental issue. In other cases, we've been conditioned to ride in a certain way, due to past experiences, or just simply out of habit. Truthfully though, it doesn't matter so much that we understand how the patterns got started. What's important is that we realize they're there, and then commit to changing them.

How-to
It took many years, a lot of reflection, and the development of my eyes to see the truth behind my lack-luster riding in competition and develop an effective plan to get to the next level. To be totally transparent, I'm very *average* when it comes to athletic talent. But my love for barrel racing is *way above* average, meaning I don't hesitate to inspect my weak areas and embrace whatever it takes to strengthen them. Some riders lack quickness in a run because their bodies are weak or out of balance. In other cases, there's a mental component or fear issue, or just a habit of riding more passively than assertive. Regardless of exactly where you see a need for growth, "speed drills" can make even a good jockey *great*, and of course help those who are struggling for any reason. As prey animals, horses are wired to be sensitive to their environment and to mirror their herd mates. Once we understand this, we can use it to our advantage. There is no denying that the more athletically we ride, the more athletic our barrel horses will perform!

The Tools – "Speed ladders" made of rope are available online and even at Wal-mart ranging in price from $15-$50 and typically come with printed diagrams and instructions for performing exercises. Below I've shared examples of the exercises I do with a simple 20-foot rope that stays taped to my living room floor. I perform these at least once a week as an add-on to my regular 20-25 minute core or speed workouts.

Both Feet Forward and Back – Start by standing perpendicular to the rope (facing it), and with both feet jump forward and back, down the rope from one end to the other as quickly as possible until you reach the end. Do it once again in the other direction. When you feel out of breath, or the quality and rhythm of your hopping decreases, rest for a few moments before continuing. For both you and your horse, it's better to perform "speed drills" when you're fresh, not fatigued – so give yourself ample time for recovery!

Both Feet Side to Side – Start by standing parallel to *and* at the end of the rope, then jump sideways back and forth with both feet together while moving forward as quickly as possible until you reach the end. Turn around and do it again back the other direction. Aim for just barely clearing the rope with your feet, while maintaining a fast and consistent rhythm.

One Foot Forward and Back – Stand perpendicular to the rope again (facing it), and this time hop back and forth on one foot from one end of the rope to the other as quickly as possible. Then hop back to the other end on the other foot. You'll likely find that one side feels much easier than the other. To turn this into a balance drill, hop slowly, counting five seconds between each hop.

One Foot Side to Side – Start by standing on one foot parallel to the rope on one end, then jump sideways back and forth while moving forward as quickly as possible over the rope until you reach the end. Do it again, going back the other direction on the other foot. This can also be slowed down to work on balance. Spread your toes in your shoes for a better, wider base of support (do this when riding, too!).

High Knee Run – When you don't have a rope handy, run a short distance (approx. 20 feet, or back and forth/around the room) with your knees coming up as high as possible (above your waist), in quick succession. Move your arms and hands in motion with your stride. Even exercises that primarily involve our feet build all-around quickness in our upper body as well. Rest, and repeat three times.

Butt Kicks – This time, run as quickly as possible while bending your knees far enough for the back of your feet to contact, or nearly contact, your "hind end." These final two exercises are not about covering distance, but how quickly you condition your body to react and respond. Again, perform three repetitions and be sure to rest up and catch your breath as needed in between.

Forward & back.　　*Hop side to side.*　　*Repeat on one foot.*　　*Side to side one foot.*　　*High knee run.*　　*Butt kick run.*

Exercise 3 – Please Stand Up

Description

Some of us have been taught that a "good rider" is one who keeps their heels down, toes in, seat glued to the saddle, and has straight shoulder/hip/heel alignment. However, learning to hold a particular posture in the saddle so we *look* like a good rider is no substitute for actually *being one*, in a run especially (there's a difference). In fact, if we don't intentionally learn to "go with the flow" and ride securely and with fluidity at speed, no amount of knowledge or equitation lessons will help us if we don't also have *the feel*. The look alone will never be enough in a sport that requires so much quickness, balance, timing and athleticism from horse and human alike. Outside of appearances, a lot of us aren't guiding our horses as effectively as we could – not necessarily because we haven't yet followed through with that fitness program (which is a big help, see Exercise #1), or because we're not athletic enough (although this *does* factor in, but we *can* do something about it; see Exercise #4), but because we're just ever so slightly out of position. The good news is that just like any other habit that's not quite working in our favor, we can change it!

Purpose

Just because we're not judged on how well we can "sit pretty" in a run doesn't mean we should adopt a *clock as clock can* attitude. This is because HOW we get across the timer line matters. It matters especially to our horses. Barrel racing is radical enough as it is, and handling all the pressure that comes with our sport is already a stretch for them, so it's important that we do what we can to add to their confidence vs. take away from it. Remember, a great rider does not inhibit their horse by creating discomfort, hesitation and delays, but rides in a way that can actually enhance movement, build confidence *and* stop the clock.

Ironically standing UP in the stirrups helps teach your body to stay DOWN by strengthening and stabilizing the lower leg, which is essential for good communication and a secure position. Doing so trains our lower body to stay centered over the upper body with even weight in the stirrups, reducing chances of tipping forward or back. Standing in the stirrups is also effective for teaching our heels to stay down. "Heels down" isn't just a fancy equitation rule – it's incredibly important for staying secure. If you have trouble keeping your heels down, first consider shortening your stirrups. Thinking about "heels down" can cause us to stiffen our joints and push the stirrups forward, creating a pivot point that throws us forward. Instead, imagine standing on the ground and LIFTING your toes while you lengthen and flatten your lower back, allowing your weight to easily sink *through* your heel. The exercises below improve balance, strengthen the lower body, lengthen the lower leg, and most importantly solidify a proper and solid position in the saddle so it becomes muscle memory and your new default, even in a run.

How-to

Stand in the Stirrups – To test and improve your security and balance through the heel, foot and leg, stand straight up in the stirrups with your heels stretched down, first at a standstill (see A). You may be tempted to lean forward slightly, but resist taking it to an extreme. There should be a three inch or four finger (hand width) space between your crotch and the saddle. Next, move to a walk as you get a feel for the standing position. Feel free to hold the horn at first to steady yourself. Avoid locking your knees and ankles; keep them straight yet supple to absorb the movement. As you get more comfortable, progress to keeping this position at the trot for as long as you can. Take a break, then make it your goal to stand for five strides, then sit for five strides, and repeat. It's revealing at first, because if you have trouble standing at a trot, then chances are good your body isn't truly secure in general. Whatever direction you tend to fall towards tells you where your balance is. Correct this by moving your feet or weight forward or back until your lower legs stays still and you feel most stable. You can also practice standing for seven strides, then seven strides in a two-point position (B. half way between standing and sitting), then sit for seven strides, and repeat. Once you're competent at standing in the saddle for extended periods at a trot, do the same with one arm absolutely straight in the air or behind your back (C). Holding this position has the power to fix heels that drift up and helps confirm good posture as well. Dedicate at least ten minutes each ride to these exercises for 30 days and stick to it; it's one of the most efficient ways to improve your balance in the saddle.

Although we will need to get up and over our horses to hustle them out of the turns and on the straight-aways in a run, it's important that this position doesn't spill over too much into our every-day riding. Remember, leaning forward can cause our horse to also become heavy on the front end. We spend a relatively small amount of time at a full gallop, compared to the hours of training and conditioning when we and our horses benefit from correct, balanced riding. Avoid getting in the habit of looking down at your horse as you ride and train. Instead rely more on feel and keep your eyes up, looking where you're going. If you're getting tipped forward in a run, examine your saddle. You may need one with the stirrups set further forward, which can help your rear end stay down. Also, be aware of the common tendency to ride on your crotch with your lower back concave. To help your horse lift his back and engage his abdominals, do the same in your body – keep your lower back straight and your pockets tucked slightly.

While we're each gifted with varying degrees of God-given athleticism, the ability to ride *with* vs. *on* our horses isn't something that some talented riders have, and some don't. We can *all* intentionally become better riders, but it doesn't happen by accident. The riding ability we have today *can* be better tomorrow, *if* we commit to focusing on it specifically. Just because someone is not a 1D rider today, doesn't mean they don't have the ability to be in the future. It's never too late to become a great jockey! It doesn't matter how long we've been riding or how much we've accomplished; there is always room to improve. When we focus on training our bodies to ride with harmony and can guide our horses with more precision and quickness, they will be healthier, and they'll stay sounder, longer, and perform better – resulting in faster times.

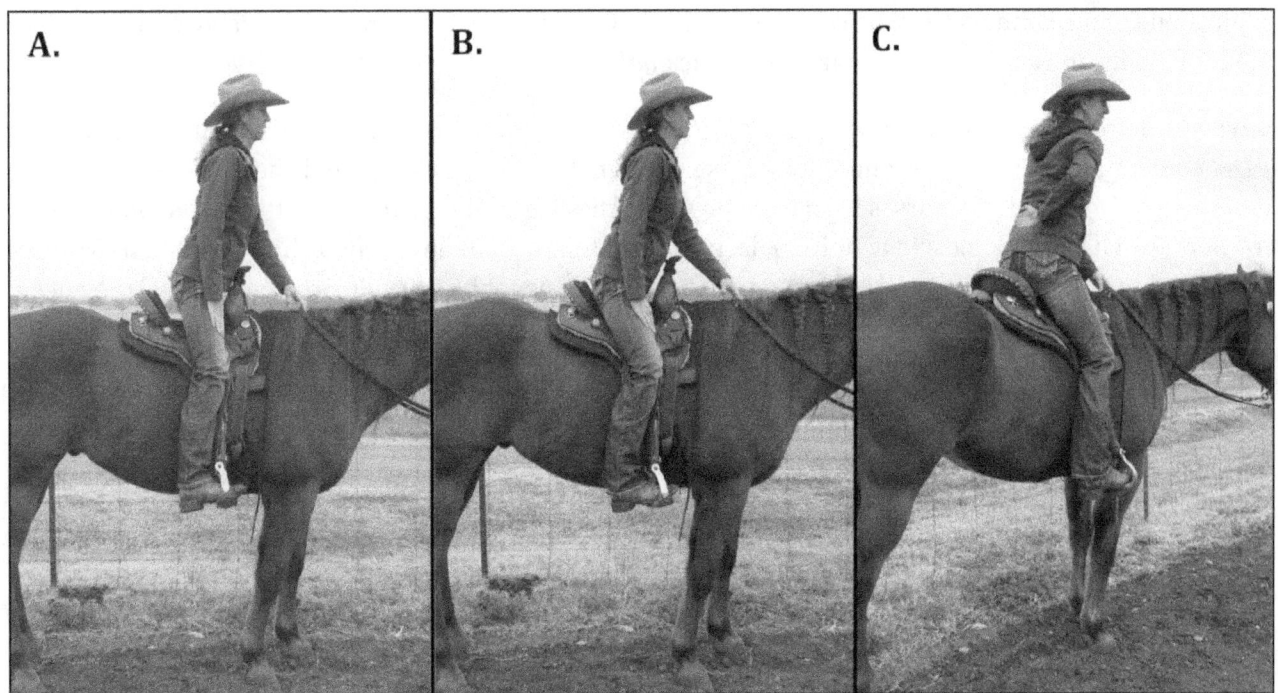

Exercise 4 – Jet Fuel

Description

Jet fuel is minimally processed and refined. It's formulated for stability, safety and predictable performance in a wide range of environments. It's significantly different than the fuel used for less critical applications, such as the fuel we put in our vehicles. How would you feel id N airline pilot came over the loud-speaker as your plane was taking off, and announced they were experimenting with a lower quality fuel in an effort to cut expenses? The plane might reach its destination safely, or it might not. It'd make you pretty uncomfortable, right? After all, flying through the air is a pretty critical application. Thankfully, this isn't likely to happen because airlines can't take that kind of risk. So why would you take a chance on putting anything but the highest quality fuel into your own or your horse's engines?

Purpose

We put so much time, expense, heart and soul into our preparation to compete. To continue with the airplane metaphor, we might be reaching for the stars, flying high with lofty barrel racing goals, only to then be hundreds of miles from home and have our horse start to cough and sputter. Of course, we might not end up in a deadly descent from the sky, but experiencing the disappointment of repetitive poor performances or being sidelined with a horse who's just not firing or even worse, is sick, is heartbreaking. The food we eat can cleanse us or clog us; it can support the performance of a finely tuned and fast flying racing machine or interfere with it. Your barrel racing dreams are *too important not* to take a chance on!

How-to

If you've ever wondered why professional barrel racer's horses often look so muscular, round, chiseled and toned? It's less about genetics and conditioning and more to do with diet. Even human personal trainers around the world are emphasizing that sculpting a fit and toned body is 80% related to diet and only 20% related to exercise. Of course, even more important than how our horse looks is how he feels and performs. We can't let appearance be our only guide, because a shiny horse isn't necessarily a healthy one. However, I can assure you that when your horse feels his best, he'll also look the part, which is just an added bonus. The physique of a champion, and the corresponding ability to fire hard and recover quickly to do it all over again repeatedly and successfully, lies largely in the *quality* of the *balanced fuel* he receives.

Analysis – Before we can be confident that our horses are getting what they need nutritionally, we first have to understand what they require, look closely at what we're providing, and then make adjustments. Often, the first sign that our horses aren't getting what they need is that they don't look like one of those "pro" horses. They'll lack muscle definition, lack a round topline and have a poor hair coat. In most cases, it's that the horse either isn't receiving enough fuel, or they may not be receiving *the specific* fuel they need.

Knowing exactly what your barrel horse requires and making sure his diet is giving him every opportunity to perform well in competition starts with a nutrient analysis of your horse's hay and/or pasture (we send our samples to EquiAnalytical) as compared to the *Nutrient Requirements for Horses* compiled by the National Resource Council (NRC), which can be read online at www.NAP.edu. The NRC states the *absolute minimums* our horses should receive to avoid deficiencies. Because we must consider both the actual amount of nutrients in addition to nutrient ratios, it's ideal to shoot for totals that are 150-200% of the NRC recommendations. Special considerations should also be made based on each horse's breed, life stage, discipline, energy requirements, etc. These guidelines are simply a starting point and a baseline.

Until we take this step, reading feed bag labels is of no use. We need to know what nutrients are being provided by the main portion of our horse's diet, which is forage, and also factor in the feeding rate. If you're ever faced with a horse health challenge, or suspect your horse could be toxic or deficient in nutrients, I also recommend horse hair analysis, which is another way of looking carefully at the source. Rather than mask symptoms of health problems or keep *adding* supplements, I believe it's ideal to ensure our horse is getting what they require at a baseline level by first providing a high quality and balanced diet.

With your hay/pasture analysis in hand, start by calculating how many pounds of total feed your horse should receive per day; which will range between 1.5–2.5% of their body weight. For example, a 1,000 lb. horse should eat 20-25 lbs. total feed (forage + any "grain") per day. When comparing nutrient percentages, average your total forage (% *dry matter* found on your analysis report) and any "grain" together. For example, if your grass hay contains 8% protein, your grain mix would need to be at least 14% depending on how many pounds you feed per day. To get the numbers hammered out precisely, you'll want to use a "weighted average." Your exercise, which you may want to come back to later, is to start by figuring out the protein and fat levels in your horse's diet with guidance from the example and instructions below:

> A weighted average is a mathematical way to calculate an average value based on proportion and importance factors. This differs from a regular average, because the importance factor gives more value or weight to the resulting average based on its importance. For example, let's say we know a horse needs 25 lbs. of feed per day. Of that 25 lbs. we want to feed one part pasture (9% protein), one part grass/alfalfa mix hay (20% protein), and one part Renew Gold™ feed (15% protein). Each type of feed contains different amounts of protein, and we want to know how many pounds of each we need to feed in order to result in 10% overall protein (8-12% is recommended for speed event horses). In this example the forage weight is our proportion and the protein value is our importance factor. To calculate the weighted average to obtain an overall 10% protein level we must first assume a weight for each type of forage. We know that the total weight should be close to 25 lbs. If we look at the current protein levels in the forage (20% in the hay, 9% in the pasture) we know it will take lots of pasture to make the average 10%.
>
> > Let's assume we want to use 20 lbs. of pasture, 4 lbs. of hay and add a half a pound of feed.
> > The mathematics would be: (20 lbs. x 9%) + (4 lbs. x 20%) + (.5 lb. x 15%)
> > This results in a value of 267.5; however, we are not done yet...
> > We then divide this number by the total weight: 267.5/24.5 lbs.
>
> This results in 10.5% protein, and is an example of our own horses' off season diet when they have plentiful access to pasture. I want a higher protein level when conditioning and competing, which would be easily achieved when they are on pasture less and eating more alfalfa hay. Further adjustments may need to be made, however, after looking at and making comparisons between other levels recommended by the NRC, what our specific horse's needs are, and what our feed analysis reports, feed bag and supplement labels tell us. I also make it a priority to calculate these figures for fat levels, which I prefer to be at 6-8% for sprinting athletes. When calculating these figures, repeat the process until you get the answer closest to your goal.
>
> Microsoft Excel is a great tool for calculating weighted averages, or to make it much easier there are also online weighted average calculators available. The weight column would be the weight of each type of forage, and the "data number" would be the % protein (or whatever you are calculating), and your result is the overall protein level based on the weights and percentages entered.

Getting specific in this way puts us a huge step closer toward ensuring our horses are fueled for the demands of barrel racing. If your brain is burning, consider revisiting and tackling the calculations above when your mind is fresh. Although it isn't the most "palatable" exercise to start with, remember success requires precision vs. guessing, and *achieving what we never have* means *doing what we've never done.*

Exercise 5 – Pre and Post-Ride Routine

Description
Whether it's the start of our day or the start of a barrel racing run, getting off on the right foot is critical. To set ourselves and our horses up to win, remember that a great pre-ride routine leads to a great ride, and great rides when compiled over time lead to great horses and great runs! We can go *even further* to say a great post-ride routine leads to a great *next* ride. There was a time early in my barrel racing years when my "pre-ride routine" (if you could call it that) consisted of a few minutes of walking. While I still recommend a slow and gradual warm up to get circulation flowing and warm your horse's tissues for maximum mobility, what I understand now (that I didn't back then) is just how demanding barrel racing *really is.* Until you've suffered through serious soundness issues with horses you deeply care about, you may *not yet* be motived to do everything possible to prevent such soundness issues (that I realize now may have been avoidable). While we can't prevent all injuries, with the help of a thorough pre and post-ride routine, we can prevent many of them! Awareness is necessary for action, and admittedly there was a time when I felt as though my horses were really "spoiled" and receiving *the best* care when I stretched them before a run, applied ice boots after, and had an equine massage therapist work on them once a month. After spending several years putting in the extra time and TLC to maintain aged horses, I am now more motivated than ever to care for younger horses in a similar way, so that in later years the odds are in our favor that it can continue as preventative maintenance vs. "absolutely necessary" maintenance.

Purpose
You probably realize that just because a horse isn't lame, doesn't mean he might not have the start of a serious soft tissue injury. Or just because he *is* lame doesn't mean he won't be ok to run in a few days. A horse can have terrible x-rays, and travel sound, or be three-legged lame with nothing significant showing up on an MRI. The reality is that most performance horses *are* subtly off if we were to evaluate them with a very critical eye. Many of the world's best performance horses aren't what we would necessarily consider 100% sound. This isn't an excuse to brush off soreness or stop pursuing 100% perfect soundness, but it's meant to be an eye-opening realization that as barrel racers we must learn more, know more and do more to support our horse's bodies and protect their wellness and longevity. "An ounce of prevention is worth a pound of cure" because the time and financial investments we make to support our horses while they are still healthy are minimal compared to "cures," *if* and *when* they are even possible at that point. While having a great equine health team is vital, I don't believe that supportive care is something we should entirely outsource. No one knows your horse better than you, and no one cares about your horse more than you, so there's *no one better than you* to closely oversee and carry out his sports therapy needs.

How-to
Every time our horses exert themselves, there is micro-trauma and stress occurring in the body. This is a normal and necessary process to build strength. However, repetitive and extreme stress (such as that from high speed turns) can cause strains, sprains, tears, and inflammation in muscles, tendons, ligaments and joints. The excessive damage that occurs isn't always shown by lameness; it's occurring all the time whether we know it or not. Obviously, the soreness or lameness *we can see* needs special attention and treatment, but so does the soreness and lameness we don't necessarily see and feel. When we provide supportive therapy, we're making an effort to prevent the occurrence and lessen the severity of soreness and lameness in the future – both tomorrow and years from now. This is why today I have a very involved pre- and post-ride routine to support our horses. Our aged geldings now *require it* to stay sound. Had I

always had an in-depth routine like the example I shared below, it could likely still be done as merely a preventative measure. In our sport, it seems it's not a matter of *if* our horses will suffer a serious injury, but when. But horses aren't disposable, and their well-being is *our responsibility* – requiring us to be accountable and go above and beyond to look even more closely at what we can do to prevent soundness issues, support our horses daily, and help them come back and make full and successful recoveries when unfortunate injuries do occur.

Equine Bodywork Goals

Dissipate muscle spasms
Soften tension (work out "knots")
Release restricted fascia
Clear stagnated energy
Balance excess energy
Reduce heat/inflammation
Increase and restore circulation
Restore mobility
Increase flexibility
Lengthen stride
Relieve pain, soreness and discomfort
Prevent injury
Create/support healthy biomechanics
Build physical fitness and strength
Improve posture & physique

I've invested in some incredible tools to support my horses physically, including cold lasers for pre-ride acupoint work to release tension and ease soreness, allowing my horses to develop even healthier movement patterns. The exercise below is designed to guide you in developing *your own* Pre- and Post-Ride and Run Routine. I share an example of what my routine consists of, which includes 10-15 minutes of red-lighting, then therapy-focused groundwork to analyze and develop my horse's movement (increase engagement, build topline, etc.), followed by stretches (see page 42) before *every ride.* While it may seem excessive, it's certainly *not* when compared to the time and expense involved in rehabilitating or replacing a horse. The extra effort is worth every minute and every penny!

Weekday Plan
Red Light, Groundwork Warm Up + Stretch Before Each Ride (15-20 min.)
- Monday – Wellness Acupoints
- Tuesday – Topline Acupoints
- Wednesday – Microcurrent
- Thursday – Ting Points
- Friday – Assessment + Acupoints

Treat + Topline Stretches, Ice Boots and/or Poultice After Ride + Magnets at Night as Needed
Weekend Schedule
Every Saturday or Sunday (2 - 4 hours)
1. Massage/Trigger Point/Myofascial Release
2. Trim Feet
3. Chiropractic
4. Microcurrent

We currently use handheld red lights/cold lasers and acupoint charts from Photonic Health, and we also support our performance horses with whole body vibration from EquiVibe, light therapy pads from RevitaVet, and microcurrent therapy from Matrix Therapy Products. Even if you aren't yet able to invest in these type of therapy tools, don't underestimate the power of using your head to learn and hands to physically support, develop and even transform your barrel horse for the better! A couple of resources I recommend to get started with use simple techniques that yield positive results by helping to release tight, restricted areas (and create relaxation) are: *Beyond Horse Massage – Introducing the Masterson Method* and *Equine Massage for Performance Horses*, both by Jim Masterson.

My Pre-Ride Routine: _____

_____

My Post-Ride Routine: _____

_____

My Pre-Run Routine: _____

_____

My Post-Run Routine: _____

_____

Additional Weekly or Monthly Therapies: ____

_____

> *How often I have found that we grow to maturity not by doing what we like, but by doing what we should. How true it is that not every 'should' is a compulsion, and not every 'like' is a high morality and true freedom. Good Horsemanship is achieved when a Horseman postpones immediate pleasures for long-term values.*
>
> – Cowboy Dressage

From the Ground Up

One of my first mentors set the course for my horsemanship journey with a powerful perspective on groundwork. In my early 20's I observed and participated in the colt starting process with several horses. At the time, it made sense to prepare a young horse on the ground first for safety reasons, but also increase their understanding and essentially make the process of being started less stressful. This mentor of mine, who was so adept at starting colts, however, also performed groundwork with his aged, finished horses as well. I remember him saying something along the lines of, *"Everything you do in the saddle can be even better with preparation on the ground."* This wasn't someone who was afraid, "couldn't ride," or hadn't done their homework, as many folks might assume, but was one of the most competent, talented and skilled horsemen I've ever had the honor of working with and learning from.

Since publishing *The First 51*, in which I made the point that for me, groundwork isn't done to "get the buck outta them" or to tire a horse physically; it has actually taken on entirely new and heightened benefits. That is, for the specific purposes of physical and emotional development and rehabilitation. Many barrel horses take on a tense, inverted posture that results in a short and choppy stride, and contributes to the development of a huge array of physical problems. Teaching my husband's rope horse gelding new *movement patterns,* for example – to stretch his topline, engage his back, and lengthen his stride, and then take responsibility for maintaining this new, healthy posture, changed his footfall. This has played an enormous part in his comeback from navicular. He enjoyed a second career as a barrel horse and will now return to the roping pen. Most importantly, he's sound. We continue to utilize therapeutic focused groundwork to keep it that way. I don't believe any of this would have been possible without changing his biomechanics in an organic way. He seeks out healthy movement on his own because he was initially rewarded for it, and he now moves more correctly in general, even in the pasture, because it's his new default. Based on how he lowers his head to blow out as he moves with quality, I know it's just as valuable to him emotionally. By softening my energy when he lowers his head and exhales, I reward his positive, relaxed state of mind. The more he experiences comfort and release for this, the more he chooses to stay in this relaxed state. In high pressure moments preceding competition, he still defaults at times to his old inverted posture; but focusing on positive movement patterns and softness helps unwind tension and remind him to think and move in ways that are calm, comfortable, healthy and balanced.

With aged or seasoned horses, groundwork is something we can do to prepare them for their upcoming ride. For me, it's not a *have to*, but a *want to* for their physical, mental and emotional benefit. Because I want to set my horses up for success, I won't start hauling a youngster until they are at the "want to" vs. the "need to" stage. If groundwork seems necessary before riding at an event, for example, the horse would likely benefit from more thorough preparation at home. I use groundwork to create a foundation of education and communication, and by the time I start hauling I'm not using it in an effort to create something that isn't there. I'm using it to make what's *already* going well, *even better.* The point of using groundwork is to *not need it.* As responsible trainers and competitors there's so much we can to do prepare our horses, and reverse the stresses that come with barrel racing to support overall health and longevity. Once riders have experienced the benefits and gained some proficiency, many find themselves really enjoying it. The following exercises will enhance your feel and timing, your horse's responsiveness, and improve movement patterns, for ultimate physical strength *and* emotional balance.

Exercise 6 – Dream Catcher

Description
You're probably aware of how critical *the start* of any barrel racing run is. When I interviewed World Champion barrel racer, Mary Walker, at the 2012 NFR, she shared that the reason for her tipped second barrel in the fourth round was a positioning issue *in the alley*. But what if your success in a run, or a ride, started EVEN before that? What *if* it started *before* you even laid eyes on your horse? Sometimes we don't realize there are things we can do to *cause* our horses to want to be with us and go to "work," and we overlook the deflating reality that our horses actually *don't* want to be with us, so we tend to write it off. When this happens, we might even dismiss how our horse feels and deny that their emotions matter, or are *that* important anyway. If you've ever been in this boat, get ready to redefine and refine the very thing that could take the relationship with your horse (and therefore your performance) to a whole new level!

Purpose
Ask yourself this: have YOU ever been cajoled into doing something you really didn't want to do? How did it feel? Did you put your very best effort forth into that task you were actually dreading, or did you just go through the motions without enthusiasm? It's hard to overrate talent in the barrel racing business, but desire can take *any horse* even further. It's all a matter of understanding horse psychology, and caring about *how your horse feels*. There is a direct connection between how your horse feels and how he performs. When we greet and halter our horse, we have an opportunity to set the tone, to set ourselves up for a good ride before we even get to the arena. A great run starts well before we get near the alley. We can choose every day to intentionally develop our understanding of horse psychology and communicate with them effectively on the ground. As we do, we'll begin to see and experience how it benefits everything we do on their backs, while creating a happier, more genuinely willing horse both in and out of the arena.

How-to
Our first opportunity to set ourselves up for success in advance of our rides and runs comes when we set foot toward our horse to halter him. Notice I said "halter," not "catch." You want to "catch" your horse's *attention*, and only *then* halter your horse (there's a difference!). As with riding, body control is just the bare basics tip of the iceberg; what we *really want* and *need* is to influence our horse's thoughts *through* his body. When we can do that, a whole new door of opportunity opens before us. Below, I've outlined steps for getting connected and setting the stage to make *every* ride and run a great one.

- Before you ride, set an intention for what you plan to work on or accomplish. At the same time be aware, flexible and willing to do what your horse needs in the moment, because it will change. Commit to making horse time, horse time – not time to catch up on phone calls, socializing, or making mental grocery lists. Honor your goals and your horses by giving yourself plenty of time and giving them your full attention. When you pick up a halter and lay eyes on your horse, smile and think positively as you focus on and approach him from a distance (start in a smaller space if your horse tends to *run* away).
- If your horse doesn't acknowledge you or walks away, follow him while focusing on his hindquarters at a brisk walk, as if you're on a mission. As you arc around toward his hind end, get more intense in your body language the closer you get, until your horse just starts to yield his hindquarters or turns to face you. Your goal is never to corner or ambush your horse, but get his interest piqued and eyes on you. Once you catch his attention, immediately stop, relax, look toward the ground, and even turn to walk the other way – take all the pressure off to reward your horse for connecting to you.

- Pay attention to your horse's body language. "FEEL" his presence or look out of the corner of your eye to determine if the timing is right to add pressure (which we do by facing them). If at any time he leaves, be quick to add pressure by walking toward the hindquarters again. Then retreat and release by turning, relaxing, and walking away if he turns toward you. Quick releases make for quick learning!
- Keep walking briskly behind your horse, arcing toward his tail (1.) until he turns toward you, even a little bit. Start small if you must, or even twirl your lead rope (from a safe distance) to encourage your horse to move and yield his hindquarters (2.). Without chasing your horse, you must make it more comfortable to be with you by increasing the *discomfort* when he's not mentally connected.

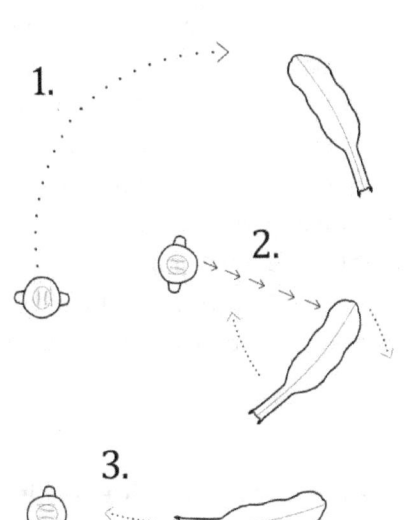

- If at any time your horse's focus leaves you or he physically leaves, walk again in a wide arc toward his hindquarters. Again release & relax when his focus is back on you and he's shifted his body to face you (3.). Remember that what gets rewarded, gets repeated. Make what you want obvious, especially at first, by rewarding your horse's curiosity and interest when he's "hooked on" to you.
- Teach your horse to lower his head by squeezing your fingers on his poll area. If this is completely unfamiliar to your horse, you might start teaching with the halter on first so you don't inadvertently reward him if he pulls away and/or leaves. Start by squeezing lightly and increase the steady pressure until he responds by lowering his head. When he lowers his head in response to the pressure, release immediately. With your arm over your horse's neck, use the same kind of steady pressure with your fingers to press on his off-side cheek to suggest that he turn his head and find the halter with his nose. Ask that he hold this position until you fasten the halter.
- Be equally as mindful when you turn your horse back into his pasture, pen or stall by asking him to keep his nose softly flexed toward you as you remove the halter. Doing so sets your next ride up for success. When you consistently approach haltering in this way, the process won't take any more time than tracking down an unwilling horse. Remember, how you begin your run, your day, your ride – *everything you do* – is more likely to go well when you have a good start. If we want a respectful, connected and focused horse on the pattern, and supple bend around a barrel, why not take every opportunity to practice the same qualities? These seemingly ordinary everyday habits lead to extraordinary results!

Exercise 7 – Snappy Backing

Description
As it applies to horse training, respect can be defined as "the appropriate response to pressure." In other words, the horse understands our requests to willingly direct his thoughts and body as our *feel* dictates. In barrel racing especially, it's important to maintain a respectful balance of "whoa" and "go" since we need both to blast full speed between barrels, then in an instant have our horses rate for the turns. If there was ever a sport that required "an appropriate response to pressure" it's barrel racing, especially considering the time our horses actually spend running vs. rating. It's easy for this ratio to get off balance!

Purpose
Perhaps one of the biggest benefits of having a dynamic backup on the ground is safety. A horse can't hurt us if we can keep him out of our space and move him in an instant. Our horse's ability to yield to halter pressure on the ground is related to his understanding of yielding to our hands when we're on his back. Although it seems elementary, judging by the number of high-level barrel horses that have learned to disregard bit pressure and body language (at the end of a run, for example), we know this is something even top competitors struggle with. A horse without this understanding is a danger to himself, his jockey, and others. It only takes one time for a horse to learn this, and the habit becomes solidified when it's allowed repeatedly. For a horse that tends to have more run than rate, or one who has learned to ignore steady pressure, or even for a lazy horse that moves with excess weight on the forehand, this exercise has the power to clarify and refine the whoa/go balance, and is also the first step in reforming (and preventing) a runaway. Outside of its importance for safety reasons, the more opportunities we take to rock our horse's weight back, the more athletically he will utilize his hindquarters in general.

How-to
Backing to Steady Pressure from the Side – This is one of the first lessons taught to a young horse before development under saddle and it's the first basic to return to when a horse gets pushy. To ask for vertical flexion at the poll *and* backward movement, start by outfitting your horse in a halter and standing by his throatlatch. Put a soft feel on the lead rope by drawing it back and down toward your horse's chest. Then raise the life in your body as you ask, just as how your energy would rise as you get ready to go somewhere (your posture straightens, etc.), before you were to start sprinting, for example. If you are facing your horse's side, send your focus in the direction you want your horse to go (which is rearward; see that my body is angled in the image). In the initial stages, release the horse instantly for just one step, then build on it. If the horse doesn't respond, increase the firmness of the pressure and bring in a secondary form such as rhythmic taps from a stick or lead rope on your horse's chest, with gradually increasing pressure over a few seconds until the horse responds. To ask your horse to only flex at the poll without moving his feet, put steady pressure on the line and wait for the first subtle give then instantly release. The goal is to have feather light, instant responsiveness to the steady pressure on the halter and for the horse to differentiate between when you ask for poll flexion and backward movement (feel *with* energy) or poll flexion only (feel with *no* energy).

Backing to Driving Pressure from the Front – Stand in front of your horse facing him, again with a halter and at least a 12-foot lead rope, and raise the life in your body as you also raise your hand to approximately the level of your horse's nose. With a slight drape in the line, focus like a laser and really send your horse's body backward with your intention. If you get a response, relax. If not, start lightly waving the lead rope in gradually increasing increments (all the way up to waving your whole arm if necessary, until the lead rope snap moves enough to provide motivation for him to yield), over the course of several seconds. Release when you get a positive, energetic response. Wait for a lick and chew before proceeding and
asking again. Your goal is always to work toward getting a higher quality, quicker, softer response with less pressure. If the horse gets crooked, use halter pressure to straighten him out and keep him facing you. At any point if your horse seems afraid or becomes afraid, casually toss the lead rope around his body with your energy low until he's relaxed enough to stand quietly again. You'll be more effective in teaching your horse once he's calm and confident about the presence of your tools. A swinging lead rope for example is not something we want our horses to be afraid of; it can have meaning or it can be meaningless, it all depends on our intention. Always start by using *your energy* as you ask, and for advanced horses don't accept anything less than a light response. Remember that if a horse isn't responding to excess action from the rope, it's because we haven't taught him that there is *meaning* behind subtle communication. When we're communicating with feel and energy, there is a float and minimal action in the rope or rein. So with advanced horses, don't hesitate to quickly jump from using just energy to extreme waving. Once you've given your horse a solid education, have high expectations for your own consistency *and* for the horse's ability to retain what he understands, and to respond with quality to what you know he has been taught.

Backing to Driving Pressure from the Side at a Distance
This variation can be performed when your horse is on a circle (such as when lunging). While circling, drop your energy and throw a subtle wave down the line with a flick of your wrist to signal a stop, or lift a stick in front of the horse as a visual/energetic block. Once the horse is stopped (ideally along a fence at first), even if you are facing your horse, "send" your focus and intention for him to move back as you toss some waves down the line with a horizontal motion of your wrist. You may even take steps backward yourself in the direction you want the horse to go. Again, release immediately when the timing is right, depending on the expectations you have. Remember, the horse's understanding of when to stop moving away from pressure is just as important as his understanding to yield from it. A horse that moves away but keeps moving and doesn't respond to us lowering our energy is essentially a runaway, *even on the ground or at a walk*. *When the life in our body stops, so should theirs.* Be consistent in using your energy and reward your horse when he gets in sync. When practiced with consistency, this newfound harmony will transfer over and benefit everything you do on the pattern.

Exercise 8 – Circle Responsibly

Description
Micromanagement is a frustrating and widely under-recognized epidemic in the horse world, causing discouragement to riders and confusion and stress to horses. Teaching horses to be responsible on the barrel pattern is something I can't stress enough. We inadvertently make "owning the pattern" even more difficult every day in little ways, when we do *for* our horses what they can (and would be even happier) doing for themselves. Lunging is also something that's typically done with the human turning with and looking at the horse. It's not unusual for the human to "need" a lunging whip to keep encouraging the horse forward. I *never* recommend chasing a horse in mindless circles, which has only limited value for exercising the body. However, lunging on a circle with mental *connection and responsibility* is indeed very powerful and beneficial. Depending on how we go about it, lunging can actually require the horse to think, and practice being mentally present, focused, and responsible for gait, direction and (at advanced levels) even shape (see Exercise #9). My goal is for the horse is to understand that once they start moving, it's their job to keep moving at that gait until given other instructions; no stopping, slowing down or speeding up. When a horse engages his mind and demonstrates responsibility, respect and obedience in this way, they are practicing and preparing to be responsible, respectful and obedient on the barrels as well!

Purpose
As a reminder, there are two types of pressure we can apply to communicate with our horses: steady pressure, which is even, and driving pressure, which is often rhythmic. Both types can be applied through our hands, body, the weight of the rein, the halter rope, a bit, or even our focus, which means that applying this pressure doesn't always require us to actually be in physical contact with a horse. The type of pressure we'll primarily use to communicate with our horses while circling us at a distance can be considered as driving. For the most part we won't have physical contact with their body. This is an advanced form of communication, one that is much more effective when a horse already understands steady pressure first.

At least a couple of times per week, I ask my horses to circle at the end of a 12-foot line (or longer) to observe and analyze their movement. I notice whether they're "tracking up" (hind feet landing in the tracks of the front feet) or whether they're "short" on one side or the other. I notice how they carry their body and how quickly they relax and stretch. I notice whether they seem free with a desire to move out effortlessly. I notice how soon they turn an ear or eye to me to check in. It's not uncommon for performance horses to get sore, but then warm out of it when ridden. I want the whole truth. This is especially beneficial because circling a horse on the ground when they're "cold" gives us the most honest gauge of their physical and mental well-being.

How-to
Start by facing your horse, with him backed out toward the end of your lead rope or line. Using your hand on the same side as the direction you intend to send, lift the line and point to ask your horse to go. As you do, use your energy and intention to suggest the speed, for example your posture might change slightly as you stand up a little straighter. Relax a bit as they get going and lower

your hand down while keeping your feet still and passing the rope behind your back. Remember circling is the horse's job. If your horse slows down or breaks gait, don't be tempted to prevent it from happening, but take quick action once it does. This means lifting the line to point and ask again, and if necessary bringing in secondary pressure with your other hand, such as lifting a stick or the end of your lead rope to add some driving pressure from behind to encourage forward movement.

Trouble-shooting

Horse Doesn't Go – Make sure your horse understands the initial concept described above, and for moments when he's not motivated to go or keep going, disengage the hindquarters (see Exercise #9 in *The First 51*) and ask for a snappy departure in the opposite direction. Keep changing direction in a lively way until your horse maintains the gate you want for an entire circle, then reward him for small victories.

Horse Goes Too Fast – If the horse is out of control or unfocused, disengaging repeatedly is helpful until the horse shows some relaxation and mental connection. In some cases, allowing a faster gait for a few minutes, or even encouraging them a bit, will result in the horse eventually wanting to stop. Play with it! Make sure to reward any effort they make to connect with you.

Horse Turns and Faces or Pulls Back – Sometimes a clever or confused horse will repeatedly turn their hindquarters away, face, and back away from you out of avoidance, or maybe because they've been rewarded for this. Keep applying pressure and direct their nose until they take a step in the right direction, then relax to reward. Do this along a fence to prevent them from backing too far away and learning to run away and avoid your requests.

Horse Puts Excess Pressure on the Line – This is a sign the horse is not mentally connected or following a feel. Slack in our lead rope can have meaning, but only the meaning we give it. Refresh your horse's response to yield off pressure and come toward you with lightness, and reward him for giving you attention (forward ears).

Horse Circles Too Close – Again, a horse that circles too close and will not move away when asked (with our energy/driving pressure from our body/lead rope/stick) may not fully understand they are to yield away from driving pressure. Add more pressure until the horse steps away then relax/stop to reward.

Circling as I've described engages your horse, not just physically, but also mentally and emotionally. It can be used for therapeutic reasons, to calm a nervous horse, to motivate a laid back one, or to get your horse in the habit of using his body even more powerfully with the hindquarters and over the topline. In addition, you're sure to discover benefits as your horse becomes more responsible for gait, direction and shape without micromanagement. As this transfers to the pattern, your job as jockey becomes more easy *and fun*!

Exercise 9 – Better Biomechanics

Description
There are certain basic characteristics of movement required for successful barrel racing, and these qualities don't change regardless of what style our horse may have. We all benefit from powerful hindquarter engagement, for example. Considering how much time barrel horses spend in an overly emotional (and often physically tense and inverted) state, or stretched out at a run (where more weight is on the forehand), it's easy to see why it's so important to deliberately focus on creating better quality movement, that ultimately leads to a stronger, healthier horse and *faster* movement!

Purpose
One thing I love about advanced groundwork is that I can *see* how my horse is tracking up while he's moving; this offers valuable feedback and gives dimension to what we feel in the saddle. Groundwork can also be a healthy way to exercise our horses without the weight of a rider on their back, making it even more valuable from a therapeutic stand point. When I consider two of our current geldings, who happen to be night and day opposites personality-wise, I know both of them have and continue to benefit from creating better biomechanics on the ground, albeit for slightly different reasons. One of them spent many years traveling with inversion and excessive tension; and the other, who is very laid back by nature, tends to move heavy on the forehand. Horses can become unsound just from being allowed to move in ways that are unbalanced and unhealthy, due to the uneven and excessive strain and concussion it places on their bodies. Creating more positive, healthy movement patterns alone has the power to, in some cases actually restore soundness, as I have experienced! Whether you have energetic, young or green horses that could benefit from the mental connection and focus, a blown up barrel horse in need of emotional rehabilitation, a horse coming back from an injury that you want to get and keep sound, or one that simply needs to learn to move in ways that are more athletic and powerful and will more directly benefit you on the pattern, there is something for every horse to gain. Even horses that have a great deal of talent, and are good movers by nature, have the capacity to be *even more successful* performers with better biomechanics.

How-to
This exercise will provide the greatest benefit once Exercises 7 & 8 are well-established. Creating better biomechanics is an ongoing process as we advance and refine our horse's ability to maintain self-carriage, yet positive changes can be achieved very quickly. This exercises uses a technique known in the animal training world as "scan and capture." Ray Hunt followers could refer to it as "set it up and wait." I like to think of it as "scan and capture, and if it's not there, set it up, wait and reward."

To begin, send your horse out on a circle with at least a 12-foot line at the walk or trot. Maintain a level of engagement in your body by rocking your weight to your heels, rounding your lower back and standing with good posture. Although circling responsibily means that we don't follow our horses and encourage them forward, for this exercise I rotate in a small circle so I can see my horse in each moment (they don't disappear out of view behind my back). This way I can take advantage of the split-second opportunity to reward a positive change in posture. The first step involves simply waiting for the horse to lower his head or blow out as he's moving forward. It may take 30 seconds or several minutes. Just putting your horse on a pattern (in this case, a circle) and leaving them there for a few minutes can be hugely relaxing as they find rhythm and consistency. Once your horse lowers his head, immediately lower your energy as you collapse your posture slightly and send a gentle wave down the line to ask your horse to stop. When they do, smile and give a verbal indicator that that's what you wanted (I often use the word "Goooood"). Using the verbal spoken word makes a bridge between the behavior you want and the reward. The more you can consistently and confidently communicate the message that they're on the right track and have them understand without a doubt, the better. Even without using a specific word, remember that *horses can feel how you speak*. Don't underestimate their ability to understand your tone, experssion, posture and energy!

The real reward for lowering their head is the rest break they receive immediately after. Even (and often especially) impulsive horses will appreciate the complete release of pressure. You might even turn your body and attention away from a very sensitive horse as you wait a few minutes for them to lick & chew. The longer it takes for a horse to find this slight improvement (lowering the head), the longer I'll let them stand and relax until I ask them to move forward again. When your horse is especially connected, he'll turn his head and look at you as if to ask "What's next?" Reward this as well to help prevent a habit of looking to the outside of the circle, which is considered "negative flexion" and will cause your horse to lean to the inside of the circle. Sometimes (not all the time), I'll bring my horse into me and let them have their rest break next to me, which builds "draw," when their comfort is received *with* their human.

As you progress, keep rewarding a lowered head with the goal for the horse to seek out and maintain this position; expect a little more as you continue while also encouraging strong, forward movement. Be aware that this includes tracking up (the hind feet landing in the tracks of the front). The only exception I make is for a very tense horse, when relaxation takes temporary priority over quality movement. Traveling in a low-headed manner isn't necessarily the end goal, but it is a valuable and beneficial *first step* toward better biomechanics for many barrel horses. As I develop horses on line, I also use a mimicry. I do in my body what I want my horse to do and wait for them to offer movement that mimics my posture, then reward it. I can do this on the ground to change gaits and build even more advanced movement, which in time will include asking for the same telescoping neck, with elevation through their withers and back. Any horse can benefit from learning new *movement patterns* that include stretching the topline, elevating the withers, engaging the back, lengthening the stride, and taking responsibility for maintaining healthy posture. This exercise is a great place to start and offers many physical, mental and emotional benefits!

Exercise 10 – Line Dance

Description

We *all* know that *real* cowboys don't line dance! Although doing it might actually be good for *our* timing as jockeys, I'll spare you that activity and instead share the benefits of empowering your horse to become more skillful and adept at managing his footfall in a fluid and athletic rhythm. Although cutting horses are trained to do a lot on their own, I'm reminded of the light bulb moment inspired by the first time I put my childhood mare on a cow. This was a horse I rode into my early 20's, and by that time I thought she was quite "broke." But back then I didn't yet know how to get a horse "hooked" on a cow. Let's just say I was pretty shocked by how ineffective and slow our communication was when I attempted to manage her with timing and quickness fast enough to keep up with the cow. What that experience revealed to me was that she wasn't broke at all. Until we test ourselves in circumstances like this, we might not fully realize we indeed *do not* have the instant connection and communication with our horse's feet that we thought. If our runs aren't coming together, it may be for the same reason.

Purpose

Instilling the understandings necessary to position a horse's body anywhere at any time can't be overstated. If we don't have this level of communication established on the ground, or going slow, there's little chance of influencing our horse's feet from the saddle, especially in a run; or even doing so effectively in slow work to fix a problem that's developed on the pattern. I not only want an instant response, but I want to move together with the horse as if their legs are mine, which is actually much faster than only pushing body parts around, and essentially chasing them and relying only on a reaction from our legs or reins. We want our horses to be soft and thoughtful and confident about positioning their feet quickly, while staying mentally connected to us. There's much more to it than just control, which is only an elementary step; what we really want and need is instant, real-time communication.

How-to

This exercise builds on Snappy Backing by adding sideways movement. In Exercise 9 – Go, Disengage, Face and Go in *The First 51*, I explained how to use your lead (rope) hand to direct your horse in a half circle, and reviewed this process for sending a horse out away from you on the ground in this book's Exercise 8 – Circle Responsibly. If necessary, refresh yourself on the instructions offered in these two preceding exercises, to make sure your horse understands how to yield his front end away from steady pressure (which is actually the very first step) and driving pressure (offered with the help of a lead rope or stick but without actually touching your horse). Before our language on the ground or under saddle can resemble anything close to dancing, it's important to learn the steps. Let's start with two ways of going sideways.

Sideways from the Side – With at least a 12-foot lead rope, position your horse's nose facing a safe wall or fence as you stand facing his midsection with a stick & string in hand. Raise your energy, then lift your stick and lift and wave it back and forth low to the ground. Your energy suggests the horse should move and the stick suggests that he move both front and rear feet. Placing the horse in front of a fence initially lessens confusion, as the horse doesn't have the option to make the mistake of going forward. It's common for a horse to move their front or hind end independently at first, or develop a habit of leading with the front end while the hind trails behind slightly. Use your energy (remember – *always ask* with energy and intention first) and then the lead rope and stick & string if necessary to influence or correct whichever part might be trailing in order get just one relatively even step. If you have to get very close to the horse to yield them, that's an indicator that he's not completely understanding and respectful of your driving pressure. In this case amplify the pressure until you get the desired result from a distance, and as usual, offer a rest reward.

Sideways from the Front - With the intention to use the same increasing phases of pressure, facing your horse and standing at the end of at least a 12-foot line (no longer at first) use your lead rope/line hand to ask your horse to step sideways again by lifting and pointing. If necessary, lift your stick in the other hand and wave it with rhythmic energy toward your horse's midsection. Since you won't be close to your horse, it's more about your intention and where you're thinking and sending your energy. At the same time, also cross over your own feet (again, using mimicry) to suggest the horse cross over and take a sideways step. If there's no response, gradually increase the motion of the stick until you get one. Even if the horse moves only the front or back end at first, give them a little rest break and wait until they lick and chew. Use your lead rope and the driving pressure you're sending to guide any part of the horse's body that is either leading or trailing, with the goal to get just a couple of nice, *even* sideways steps. Reward accordingly, and build on it!

Putting it All Together – Now comes the dance! Stand in front of your horse and back him five steps (1.), then drop your energy and ask for a stop (1a.) Again, make sure he doesn't just "run away" from your pressure but also responds (stops) when you let the life out of your body. Next, standing in the same position, ask your horse to take five steps sideways, or until you have 2-3 even sideways steps (2.), then again stop (2a.). The more difficult this seems for your horse, the more reward time you can give him when he has a breakthrough. Next, switch hands with your rope and stick to send your horse's front end away and make a ¼ turn on the hindquarters (3.); again, stop (3a.). From this position (you're now standing facing his side), ask him to back with your energy and a wave down the rope (4.), and stop (4a.). Now ask him to yield straight sideways away from you (5.), and again stop (5a.). Lastly, yield the horse's hindquarters away until he's facing you (6.), stop (6a.), then repeat. The quality of response is more important than getting the steps in perfect order. Eventually you can experiment with following all six without stopping. The goal is to move specific parts of the horse in a specific way, while changing it up and still getting soft, accurate and timely responses.

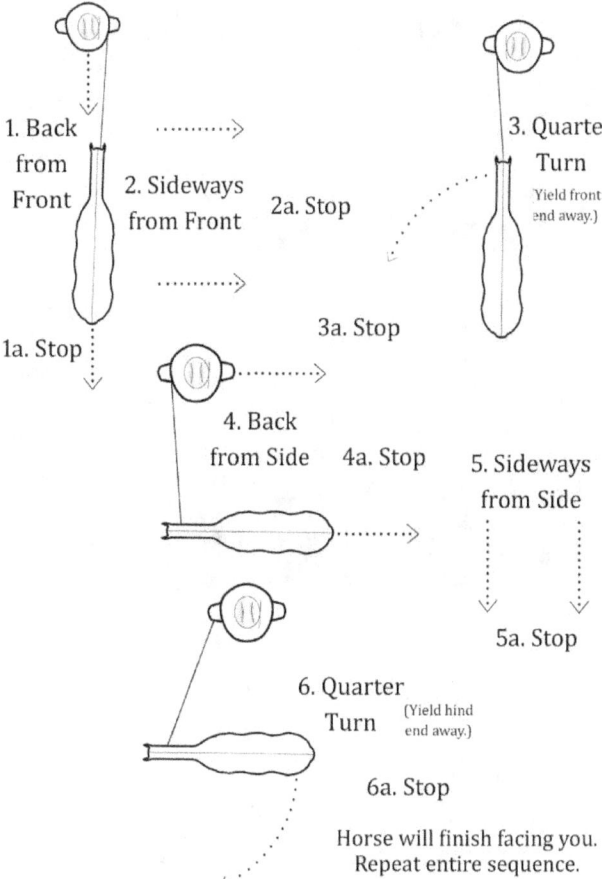

Stretch It Out

Stretching for Lengthened Stride and More Speed

Success & Safety Tips:
- Gently challenge your horse to go just outside his comfortable range of motion, without forcing
- Keep the horse's legs aligned with the body, support the joints and don't pull or hold the soft tissues
- Hold stretches for 20-30 seconds or do 3 sets of 5 – 10 seconds
- Always use caution when under, directly in front of, or behind your horse

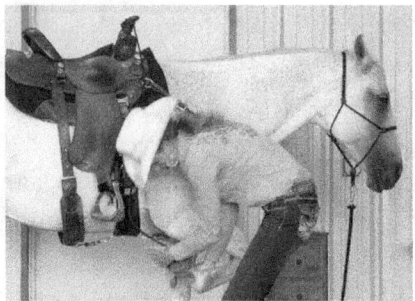

Front Fetlock Stretches Forward and back, 3 sets of 5 seconds each. Also perform stretches on the hind fetlocks

Foreleg Stretch Using your inside (horse side) thigh, bring the bottom of the horse's foot to level, and hold for 20 seconds

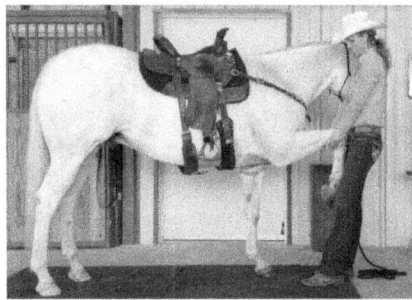

Shoulder Lift (Lift the knee to stretch the shoulder) Support just above the knee, allow the lower leg to hang

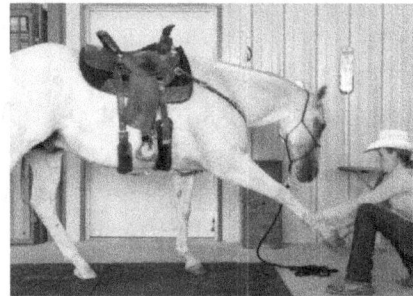

Front Leg Extension Support the foot/fetlock, gently ask to stretch forward and step down (be careful!)

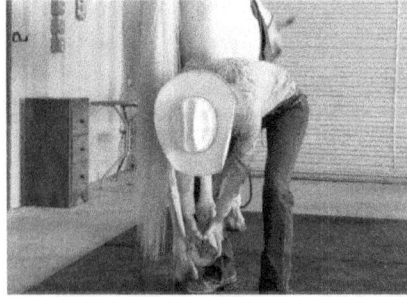

Rearward Hind Extension Allow the cannon bone to rest on your leg as you squat low and encourage the leg back. Hold up to 20 seconds, and release on relaxation.

Forward Hind Extension Pick up foot, then back up to straddle your horse's front leg. Hold stretch then gently set foot down gently so the horse will stay there for a moment.

To increase speed, we must either increase the rate at which the feet move or increase the distance covered with each step. When stretches are performed regularly after a brief warm-up before every ride, our horses become more and more supple and flexible, and are better prepared to practice traveling with quality, forward movement, which transfers to more POWER on the pattern. We have the power to greatly *influence* our horse's **quality of movement** by causing them to lengthen their stride and travel further with every step – allowing them to clock faster!

Start Strong, Finish FAST

If you're an experienced horse person who's been barrel racing for a while, it's easy to get over-confident. When we've paid our dues, been there, done that, and *won that*, we tend to become more selective about the learning opportunities we pursue and resources we take in, and for good reason. I know because I've been there. Especially as we get older and responsibilities pile up, we value our time even more and want to invest it (and our money) wisely in ways *we know* will pay off. Ain't nobody got time fo' anything else!

I often caution barrel racers, though, to be careful about thinking "I already know that," as it can be a huge mental block for many competitors. It's as if we listen without hearing – we listen to reply, to agree, or to demonstrate what we already know or can do. But this habitual response is actually less often about being selective and more often based on insecurity. To be open to learning something completely new after many years of barrel racing would be to admit that our preexisting knowledge might be inferior. Being truly open doesn't mean we don't stand firm in what we *do* know, but it *does mean* we're willing to consider a new way of looking at or doing things. So while I appreciate a willingness to advance, be forewarned that the following chapter will require reading with *eyes wide open* (not rolling).

We each have our own filters and ways that we interpret what's presented to us based on our existing understandings and past experiences. Because of this, we tend to twist new information into something that fits the mental filing system we already have, instead of making a new file or maybe starting an entire new drawer. Throughout the following chapter I'll be asking that you get *an entirely new cabinet.* The next five exercises weren't developed for you to read and think about. The value is in their application. You can't understand, know or imagine your way to the benefits ahead. They are truly eye-opening but *only if* you really put them into action and feel for yourself. You'll be shocked, surprised and maybe even heart broken, frustrated and disappointed. And that's good. That's the point. To wake you up and shake you up to what you've been skimming over, and get to the bottom, to the truth, the root of what's holding your barrel racing back and going undetected. You've got to be vulnerable and *courageous* enough to loosen your attachment to what you know and put your mind and heart on the sacrificial alter of learning.

I'm passionate about the contents of this chapter because I'm one of those folks who "did their homework." By that I mean I developed solid, educated horses, worked hard and did all the right things – but still missed the mark. I sought out opportunities to ride with and learn from the best, but what I really needed still evaded me. The following exercises were some of my turning points. Powerful breakthroughs aren't possible without looking in the right places – those that barrel racers aren't conditioned to look. They're the places where I found huge pieces to the puzzle that the barrel racing world as a whole was (and still) is largely missing. The following exercises will challenge you and they will change you.

I promised the advanced exercises in this book for "precision on the pattern" would be *fun*. Considering how heavy or distant what we've covered so far *seems* from the barrels, you're probably anxious for that part. While you *will* find many dynamic in-the-saddle exercises to implement on the pattern, remember it's the small details outside of the arena that lead to success *in it*. A desire to think and learn outside the box, and especially *our attitude* about doing so, can make or break us. If we don't start strong we'll never finish fast, or at least finish fast with consistency and longevity. Everything I've shared so far *is* fun for me. It's easy to enjoy the process and preparation when *you know* something works and are absolutely confident in where it leads. So thanks in advance for having an open mind, and confidence in where it will lead.

Exercise 11 – Walk to Win

Description

As a kid showing in 4-H, I was instructed to memorize western riding patterns by walking them. Later in my 20's when I was showing, I was still walking reining patterns. This kind of mental rehearsal isn't just for children. Knowing this, I still wasn't prepared when I attended a Jane Melby clinic in 2012, and discovered how revealing walking the pattern and going through the same hand and body motions on foot (holding reins) would be. Of course we weren't walking the pattern to memorize it (thankfully the cloverleaf is pretty simple), but to confirm we were using our bodies in *the right way* and at the *right time*. I watched in amazement as I saw students replicate on foot the riding habits they also had in a run. Then it was *my* turn. Wanting to be "correct," I drastically over-thought every step. I was stuck in my head, and my movements were a bit herky jerky and slow as a result. Let's just say many powerful insights were gained that day! The truth may be painful, but it also sets us free, so be open to discovering it in unexpected places.

Purpose

While we have to take responsibility for teaching our horses how to use their bodies correctly, both in general and in a run, we can't underestimate the power of their natural tendency to mimic what we do in our own bodies. If what *we do* is incorrect, eventually what *they do* will be also. Even if a horse hasn't necessarily been taught to pay close attention to the rider's position, his weight balance and therefore his biomechanics and direction will be influenced by ours. On top of that, it's natural for a horse to follow the rider's focus. As herd animals whose survival depends on syncing with their environment, it makes sense that horses seek out this harmony, and it's up to us to take advantage of it. Groundwork is equally as powerful for humans as it is for horses. Just like with them, the more prepared our bodies and minds are before we mount up, the better. Below I've shared several areas to analyze as you walk the pattern, both on foot and then on horseback, to change or improve your riding habits and take your runs to the next level.

How-to

Hoof It – With your barrel pattern set up and reins handy (but not connected to anything), take an even two-handed hold with your hands approximately shoulder-with apart. Head to the first barrel on foot, traveling the same path you go when mounted. When you reach your rate point, "downshift" your energy and pretend to "go to the horn" (drop one side of the rein) while walking forward into the turn and keeping your eyes up. The key to walking (or riding) through the pattern properly comes in staying balanced and aligned in your body while maintaining smooth, forward cadence in your movement. To avoid leaning too far forward or backward, your body should be balanced over your feet and just a hair forward, in somewhat of a "jockey position." Extra awareness should go to the lateral and vertical alignment of the hips and shoulders. In the turn, the entire body should gradually twist as the head, shoulders, waist and hips all rotate evenly. This should be done in one, smooth motion without any sudden, rough, or whip-like moves on the back side of the barrel. All this is done while traveling on a track that is approximately three feet away from the barrel, keeping a reasonably equal distance all the way around, except for widening that space a bit at the start and narrowing it a bit at the finish of the turn.

In addition, be conscious to weight each foot equally. In order to be in alignment for a straight, fast departure, it's important to allow time for a horse's body to finish a turn. This makes for more fluid, round, forward movement as we turn, without hesitation or extreme shifts in position or footfall patterns. If you step hard to the inside or outside it will affect your horse's balance. Just do what comes naturally at first; with expanded awareness, your habits will reveal themselves. As they do, celebrate your discoveries then make adjustments and walk the pattern repeatedly to practice *correct* form.

In the Saddle – To further solidify your new habits, it's time to saddle up. You won't need any barrels or even an arena, just your horse (preferably outfitted in the saddle and reins you compete in) and ideally 15 uninterrupted minutes per day for 30 days. Mount up, check your watch, and ask your horse to walk briskly forward while you start visualizing that perfect run, positioning your body as you would for the first barrel.

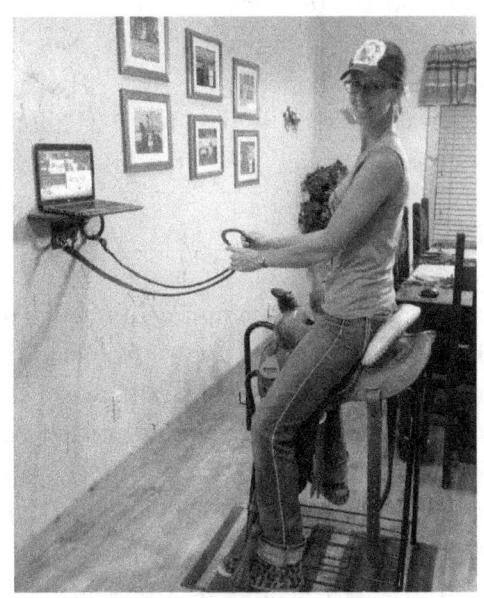

Go through the motions with your body exactly as you would like it to be in a run, except without intensifying your energy extremely. You may need to temporarily desensitize your horse if his is very sensitive and initially gets confused by your motions. There's no reason to worry about walking a certain size pattern or where your imaginary barrels are; your run must only be realistic in your mind. Be aware of the motions your body goes through as your horse walks through each imaginary run. The more aware you are of your position and how it affects your horse, the more you'll get out of the process. If you have a *very* sensitive horse and need to specifically work on amping up the intensity in *your body* in a run, do this sitting in your barrel saddle on a stand instead of horseback – even better, play videos of runs as you do!

When our bodies are properly trained, we can trust our subconscious to take over and let our body do what it's capable of and has been trained for. Remember: half-hearted efforts will result in half-hearted results. If

committing 15 minutes per day for 30 days seems excessive, consider how long you've already been challenged by riding habits that don't serve you, and how much they'll continue to affect your future. Effectively changing and improving your jockeying in a way that lasts is more than worth the time investment. Through this process, you'll create new muscle memory and new neural pathways in your brain, that will allow you to ride the way you want and need to, and achieve new heights in your barrel racing!

What we do away from the pattern impact what happens on the pattern. I'll never forget seeing signs held up by Team Melby at the NFR saying "SEE JANE RUN, SEE JANE WIN!" Instead of thinking you're "too good" to walk the pattern, have an open mind and remember that Jane RUNS and WINS, *because* she WALKS.

Exercise 12 – Measured Improvement

Description
When it comes to navigating the cloverleaf, some top barrel racers keep an even distance around the barrels. Some barrel racers still make a swooping pocket coming into the barrel, although it isn't as common as it once was. Many barrel racers come into the barrel a little wider than they leave it. Some ask their horses to follow a slightly wider or different pattern in slow work than they ask for in a run. Many barrel racers designate a "point" a certain number of feet in front of, or to the side of a barrel as the location to rate and shape for the turn. My preferred method is a combination of these concepts, and I customize the pattern slightly based on the horse I'm riding. Additional slight adjustments may be necessary in an actual run as well, depending on the conditions.

Purpose
The path we train our horse's feet to follow on the barrels can make it physically easier *or* harder to navigate the pattern quickly and efficiently. In fact, if we're approaching the barrel at a tricky angle for our horse, it can contribute to problems like going by or dropping in, which is sure to translate into slower times. By simply changing the approach, we can make it easier and faster for a horse to turn. Ask yourself: do you know exactly how many feet you are from the barrel at the start, mid-point and back side of each barrel? When it comes to distance from the barrel, you might be familiar with how many feet some barrel racing clinicians and professionals recommend. When was the last time you measured yours? It's possible that you've been barrel racing all your life and never marked it out. Considering that barrel races are won and lost by fractions of a second, this area is worth exploring and one you'll find to be especially eye-opening and revealing. Remember, what gets measured gets improved – so let's begin!

How-to

You'll need a large tape measure, white powder for marking lines (baking flour works great), a clipboard, paper and pen/pencil, some barrel racing buddies (optional), and cones or soccer field markers. Next, saddle up and walk your horse's "perfect pattern" (in freshly worked arena dirt, ideally). Then go back and measure your horse's tracks at the three points around each barrel. Draw *your pattern* on paper and write down your measurements. Your wheels will likely start turning at this point and you'll start connecting *mental dots* about the issues you're having in a run that may be related to this.

Next, mark each point on the ground, first by making a divot in the dirt with your foot, then drag a line in the dirt with your heel to connect them. Be conscious of the arcs and angles you're marking to make them as accurate as possible. With the lines somewhat visible, mount your horse again and ride those tracks. Are they exactly on the mark and matching up with what feels correct, or do they need adjustment? Remark with your boot again if necessary, then once your points and lines are *accurate*, mark them with flour.

If you're performing this exercise with friends, talk amongst yourselves about the differences in your horses and your preferences. You'll be surprised by how different each pattern is; however different doesn't necessarily mean wrong. There's plenty to learn from each other here! When you're actually able to *see* and start comparing your distances from the barrels at the various points around the pattern, really think about your horse's tendencies at each barrel. Does your horse have trouble rating at first? Does he sometimes tip the second coming in or not quite finish it? Is the third barrel a bit rough?

We must make sure the pattern we train our horses to follow allows room for their bodies to work correctly and efficiently. It's a lot like water blasting through a hose; when we don't allow quite enough space or opportunity for positioning, it's like putting a kink in the hose and our horse's bodies will tend to bind up (causing a delay) or create an energy leak (getting off track), and we won't be nearly as fast.

It doesn't seem like rocket science to guide a horse on the pattern at a walk, but doing so precisely in a run is another story entirely. If *we* don't know our pattern to the depths of our very being, how can our horses?

As you go forward, fueled to make a game plan with your lightbulb moments, keep the "three R's" in mind:
- **Responsibility** - If you plant your rein hand on the withers and guide your horse only with your focus and subtle body language, does he stay on his track or veer off?
- **Responsiveness** - Can you correct and reposition your horse in an instant (less than a second) in your slow work when necessary, primarily with your legs?
- **Riding** - Do you approach the turns and pull your horse's head around or guide with smoothness and fluidly, using your seat to encourage reach while riding the horse's *whole body* with timing and precision?

Make any necessary adjustments to your pattern and *re-mark it*. Consciously travel it over and over (on foot and under saddle), to commit it to mental AND muscle memory for you *and* your horse. Use cones or soccer field markers set just to the outside of your points by three to four feet (so they aren't in your way but are used as a guide) to keep you on path without having to repeatedly re-mark your pattern with flour.

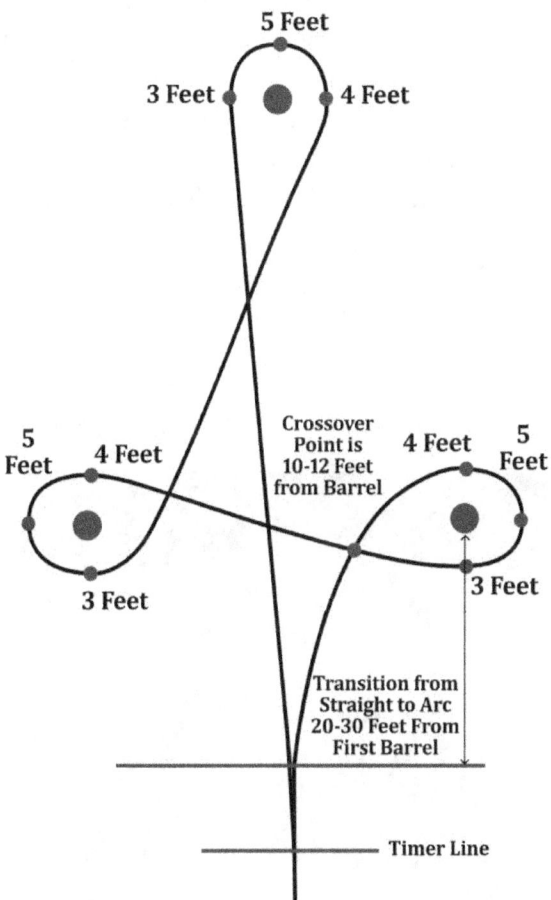

Going through this process and then committing *your exact pattern* even more solidly to mental/physical memory is just one more thing you can do to build your horse's confidence, and get around the barrels with as little resistance and as much speed as possible. I can't say enough how valuable and eye-opening the process of measuring, comparing and flour-laying is at ALL barrels – whether you're a barrel racing newbie or an ol' pro. It's easy to do, but it's also easy *not to do*. However, when you are 100% sure and confident in your own mind and body about where your horse's feet must be, *they* will better understand their job, be much more confident, and you'll *both* be able to perform more correctly and efficiently.

Exercise 13 – Get Hooked

Description
Although I've made a career out of sharing barrel racing tips and exercises, this doesn't mean I'm not still learning. In fact, plenty of failures over the years is a big part of what qualifies and inspires me to help and teach others. One example comes to mind from when I first started my husband's rope horse on the barrel pattern. Dot Com is "hot to trot" by nature, and although he was fit, due to his age and physical limitations, I didn't do much speed work during his training in an effort to save wear and tear on his body. In other words, I skipped some steps (more on that in Exercise 14), thinking that his natural talent would be enough to bridge the gap. Considering that Dot Com *already knew* how to run, looking back I should have remembered his ability to think and run *at the same time* was not quite as highly developed. I should have known then (like a barrel racing crystal ball that comes with experience), that even if his slow work was stellar, that once we bumped up the speed his brains would melt away. Sure enough, we were zooming by the first barrel with his mind in another zip code and nowhere close to being focused on the turn.

Purpose
The problem was that I had set BIG goals for us, and was still addressing this issue with only a couple of months left to achieve them. I knew I had to keep him sound, but a bigger bit, a tie down, or drilling his hiney in the ground repeatedly (and stressing his arthritic hocks further) wasn't the answer. As we were coming down to the wire, even though our videos looked pretty good, I could see he wasn't enthusiastically *devoted to turning* and knew we could be so much faster *if he was*. I had to get through to his mind *so deeply* that he knew and was committed to the core to turn, even at high speed. He had to crave it. The pattern had to be something he locked onto much more tightly, so even with adrenaline flowing and all cylinders firing to the first barrel, I could trust him to inhale it. I knew that if he could wrap his mind around the turns, that his body would follow and do so in good form (with elevation, roundness and engagement), and that it wouldn't require force, fear, intimidation, crazy acrobatics or desperate equipment changes.

How-to
If you've been following me for a while, you know I reference to the importance of creating responsibility and independence in our horses. I touched on this topic previously, but in this instance we'll be taking the same concepts to the actual pattern. The following exercise provides a powerful learning experience for the horse. However, keep in mind that if we need to do this work on the pattern, it's likely because we

failed the horse somewhere down the road earlier on. It's a form of problem-solving, and is just as important for the human as the horse. So we can't forget that the lack of responsibility in the horse is something that was our responsibility to instill in the first place. Horses learn (or don't) because they can – because of what we do or don't provide them with. With each application of this exercise must come a commitment to "do better next time."

Start out with the intention to walk the pattern by guiding your horse with your focus and subtle body language only. You can loop your reins over the saddle horn if possible, or a second option is to hold them in your hand, but "glue" your rein hand to your horse's withers by holding it there and not moving it. This is not my preferred option because it doesn't allow your body language to mimic what it would do in a run. The first trip around will be for the purpose of testing vs. teaching. If your horse isn't calm and connected enough to walk quietly on a loose rein, address that issue first. As you travel the path you so expertly defined in the previous exercise, do so with the goal of using no rein contact and no leg pressure, but lots of mental concentration and focus. When I say *subtle* body language I mean slight shifts in weight and the turning of your head, shoulders, torso and hips, not micromanaging with leg pressure. Your horse *can* feel all these small changes happening, so not using this sensitivity to our advantage, or using more pressure than necessary to get a response only slows things down. The goal is for your horse to not only maintain his footfall pattern around the barrels, but to maintain the shape/arc in his body at the appropriate times *and* maintain the gait you ask for. If you ride with a brisk walk level of energy, your horse shouldn't be lazily dragging his feet, *or* blasting through that suggestion by going faster than your body is riding. Again if these are issues, revisiting your fundamentals is necessary before benefit can be gained from this exercise.

If your horse takes a step past where he should have started turning (as dictated by your body and focus), return your hand to the reins (only to be ready to block any excess forward motion) and quickly bring in leg contact to correct your horse. How much pressure you use will depend on your horse's sensitivity. You want to create adequate motivation for him quickly search for the right answer. Without micromanaging with your reins (use them *only* to block any excess forward motion but not to direct), primarily use your legs to bother, bother, bother your horse with urgency to reposition him until his body finds its way back on the pattern. Think of your leg coming in as an extreme annoyance that your horse wants relief from. When he finds the relief by getting back on track and in position, relax and walk on, or even rest for a moment if your horse had trouble getting to this point. The key here is to *not* use the reins to micromanage the horse and physically *put him* in place. We're causing and allowing the horse

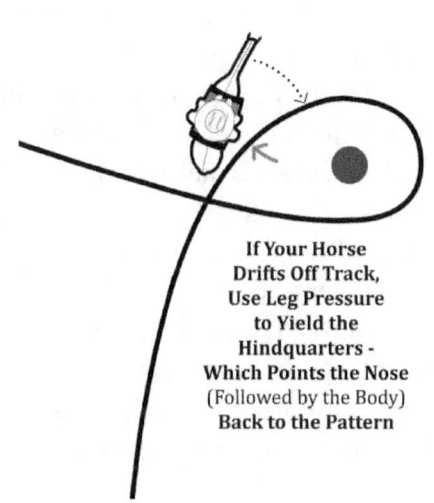

If Your Horse Drifts Off Track, Use Leg Pressure to Yield the Hindquarters - Which Points the Nose (Followed by the Body) **Back to the Pattern**

to make a choice and learn organically. You may have to release perfectionism here when it comes to perfect weight balance and shape, because we're focusing now on getting the horse mentally committed to the pattern itself, which can actually occur for the first time ever in horses who have run barrels for years but never really owned responsibility for their job. When you induce this stress with your legs, and allow a horse to flounder a little bit as they fidget around to find their own way back to the pattern with minimal rein guidance from you, it triggers their mental processing in a way that doesn't happen when we're doing it *for them*. When a horse gets comfort and relief on the pattern, they learn to hunt for those turns and *crave* being correct. You've dreamed about it and *this is how* it can be created. Once each gait is going well and your horse is owning the pattern, you're ready to test it with more speed. Really pour on the reward and appreciation for his commitment once he's on track. The more obvious we are with praise, the better!

What happens in our horse's body starts in his mind. When we can influence and shape their thoughts, the body is easy. No more wrestling matches or runaways or brute force necessary. Instead of asking "What can I do to MAKE my horse rate or turn?" instead ask "How can I CAUSE my horse to WANT to rate and turn, *then* ALLOW it to happen?" Ask the right questions, and you'll always find the right answer.

Exercise 14 – Supple Speed

Description

We all make mistakes, and there's nothing like a fresh one to deliver a heavy dose of inspiration. Another one of those came in those split seconds of urgency as I tried to salvage the first barrel turns when Dot Com wasn't "hooked," and in response, met my hands with resistance. It became obvious we'd been "riding pretty" (slowly) long enough, and that I neglected to consider all the ugliness that would still be there and not *totally* sorted through once major speed was added. It wasn't just his hot nature, a soundness issue or his previous handling as a rope horse that led to this (although they each contributed as well) – *speed alone*, even when things are seemingly going great, will show us where the holes are real fast.

Purpose

Most of us make the jump from ¾ speed to Mach 10 a little too quickly. On the other hand, I'm not a fan of exhibitioning a horse long-term, or making excessive slow runs, which can actually end up being a crutch. I do, however, feel that more horses could benefit from transitioning to speed more gradually in general. I think the reason we get our slow work good, then "go for it," is that we feel in control going slow. That's where everything feels soft and pretty and perfect, and it "looks good." When we go different speeds, many different speeds on the pattern as we progress, for example, we need to be able to adjust our own timing so we prepare for the turn at just the right place based on that speed. It's not exactly easy. My suggestion is that you take many of the exercises in this book and attempt performing them at ¾ speed and find out where things seem to fall apart and get sloppy. Where are the gaps in communication? Where exactly is the resistance, when is the timing off? How do you or your horse need to adjust? The quicker and more coordinated you can be at 1/3, 3/8, 2/5, 1/2, 5/8, 2/3, 3/4, 4/5, 5/6 and 7/8 speed, the more you will be at full speed. One reason our horses lose responsiveness and softness to bit pressure in a run, is because we've never really expected, asked for and reiterated that lesson we instilled when going slow by gradually increasing speed. It doesn't ALL transfer over. Conserving our horse's confidence means ramping up gradually, and being willing to take steps backward if necessary, all while being present and prepared to quickly, kindly and effectively remind them the same rules apply as we go.

How-to

During a run, we may use several methods of communicating with our horse, such as seat/weight, voice, and sometimes legs, but it's our hands that are the primary means of communication. A horse that lifts his head up and away from bit contact, or tenses up and resists, is giving us a big "NO" and we always want YES's from our horses. We want to be partners that work (run) together as a cohesive team. To ensure we have this at speed, we must have softness and responsiveness (in addition to whole-body soundness) very well established going slow. Then we can test and refine with gradually increasing speed at home, first off the pattern and then on it (again starting slow) and eventually in differing environments. Supple Speed is an advanced exercise, and shouldn't be the horse's first lesson in softness, vertically flexing at the poll and moving with some degree of collection or engagement.

To begin, saddle your horse and outfit him in headgear he'll respect. Assume your position by holding the reins securely with a firm fist resting at the withers. Lean forward a bit if necessary. The goal is to lope around this way with the horse yielding to and respecting the boundary of the bit contact through the reins while your position encourages forward motion. The hands will stay steady; there is no pulling, it's just a steady hold and the horse has comfort, release and freedom when he stays softly within these boundaries.

If the horse pushes against that pressure, continue holding and when the horse softens, let the horse have slack in the reins. The more a horse struggles to finally make a breakthrough, the bigger you can make the reward. This might range from a micro-release in the reins to a complete stop and rest break. You want the horse to maintain soft flexion through the poll and roundness over the topline as you use your seat, energy and legs to gradually add more speed. At some point you may hit some resistance (the same resistance that comes up in a run!). You can always release if you don't feel safe, but the idea is to hold, hold, hold until the horse can combine speed with softness.

The great benefit of this exercise is that there is little risk that the horse will learn to lean into the pressure or that he'll hit it and panic, lose confidence, get confused, injure himself, get extremely fatigued, or not receive an instant or clear release, which are all possibilities when a horse is rigged up mechanically without a human communicating at the other end. This is an even more effective alternative to bitting a horse up. I want to be involved and oversee my horse's learning, protect their well-being, and ensure they don't inadvertently learn or experience something I didn't specifically intend for. When we're right there, we get our horse's feedback and can offer real-time communication.

To add another twist to a similar concept, experiment with going forward at a walk, then stopping and backing, then going forward again, all with the same degree of soft rein contact. This helps our horse understand that it's our body and energy that determine whether to "whoa or go" in combination with the reins, and that they can collect and round their bodies, and change direction with steady contact, instead of assuming they should always stop or yield away from this pressure. Remember, pulling to stop and kicking to go are *basic* levels of communication. This a great way to test and refine our horse's education and form and teach them to be ridden up into our hands.

With practice, your horse will learn to maintain roundness, softness and responsiveness through his body at speed and through transitions. Keep in mind, this isn't necessarily natural for horses. In nature, when horses are running, for example, they are usually spooked, emotional, and their adrenalin is pumping. It's our responsibility to teach a horse how to run, move and respond while remaining soft, responsive and thoughtful, which is easier for some than others. When they can instantly yield physically and mentally to our requests, we've just significantly upped our odds for making even faster and more fluid runs.

Exercise 15 – Brake it Down

Description
When it comes to the act of preparing for the turns, if a horse is particularly talented and has learned to mentally connect to the pattern (which is not a guarantee even with plenty of repetition), it's possible to get by without heavily reinforcing the idea of "rate." Even in cases of the not-so-talented horse, it's still possible to manage a turn without really preparing for it first. But of course we don't want a "possibility" or to just "manage" or "get by" – we want *a sure thing*, or as close to it as possible! There are plenty of horses who have been thoroughly taught the importance of rate through quality repetition, but still miss the concept, and the first barrel! Why is this? I think it's similar to how you or I could know something, but still never experience it. We may know something in our head, but we don't necessarily embody it in our bones. Our horses can respond to a cue; especially well in not-so-challenging circumstances (going slow) but if you would like rate that holds up under pressure and at high speed, so your horse embodies it in a way that will be reflected in a competitive run – the exercise below is right up your alley!

Purpose
Although it's true that hustling backwards with lightness and responsiveness at or just before the barrel is one way to teach rate (and it is a good "button" to put on our horses), it's *only one* way, and not necessarily the only or best way. The more time our horse spends with his weight rocked back on his hindquarters in general, the more likely he'll utilize his hind quarters in a run. If we repeatedly transfer our horse's weight to the hindquarters, before the first barrel for example, the idea is that they will use their body similarly in a run. But if he's backed up as punishment, or backed excessively, it can turn into resentment, fear and/or soreness. It's critical then that we instill rate in a way that causes the horse *to think* and mentally *seek it* (vs. go through the motions out of avoidance), which will actually result in a healthier, rounder, more athletic posture. This is because an element of resistance will only lend to more tension, an inverted shape, and cause the horse to want to run away mentally even more, which is not at all conducive to turning.

It's important to realize that preparing for the turns is a complete way of being and thinking, not just a transfer in body weight performed at a specific spot. When any horse gallops, more of their weight will be on the forehand; there's no avoiding this. But it's all the more reason to devote more time and focus to teaching horses to be better movers, meaning in part that they move with a higher percentage of weight on the hindquarters across the board, which also promotes our horse's physical health, soundness and well-being. Mentally, our horses also need to be educated to fully respect the barriers we use, such as our seat, energy, legs and hands. This entire way of thinking, being and moving must be instilled in great depth. It can't be something we or the horse do only sometimes, or under certain circumstances, if we are to depend on the rate we instill at speed, which is critical not just for nailing the turns but also for our own safety. To have rate we can depend on, our horses need to both respond and be responsible for correct biomechanics.

How-to
Four Ways to Communicate and Educate for Rate
As we know, even when we've done our homework and put a good stop on our horses, it will be less instantaneous at speed. Again, teaching the rearward transfer of weight in a mechanical way, where the horse just mindlessly goes through the motions, won't necessarily guarantee "rate" on the pattern. To create a sure thing, there must be physical soundness and emotional fitness; then we must solidify the specific and sequential steps for the mental/educational elements that I've shared below.

Seat/Energy – If I'm riding along in rhythm with a nice walk, and I lower the energy in my body and the horse doesn't change their walk, I'm essentially on a runaway. With this awareness, we can start to fix or avoid ever having a full-speed runaway. Our body language will only have as much meaning as *we give it*. If we want to really help our horses rate at a barrel by sitting deep in the saddle (or ensure we have brakes at the end of a run), we must have high standards and reiterate this consistently. I expect my horses to respond to my seat so well that I don't actually *need* the reins to stop in my everyday riding. Of course our horses will be raring to go (figuratively not literally, ideally) before a run, but we don't want them riding around with their gas pedal stuck. Although they may take a little longer to come to a stop from a full sprint than at slower paces, I still want this understanding so well ingrained that they *should stop* (eventually) from my seat and energy only if we had no other option (in an emergency, for example). Practice teaching your horse to rate reliably by letting all the life out of your body (stop riding) and deepening your seat, and saying a relaxed, verbal "whoa," and only then smoothly pick up the reins with gradually increasing pressure. Next (if necessary), back your horse twice as far as it took him to respond to your initial request. Rest there for a length of time in proportion to how well your horse responded!

Voice – Combining the step above by adding a reliable voice cue to our seat/energy rate button is like having a back-up e-brake. Although an emergency brake is something that most folks only resort to in a bind, we want to get in the habit of always using our seat and energy *first*, only then adding our voice cue (to teach it) and only then picking up the reins – in *this order*. Of course, at advanced stages it all happens in an instant, but we have to retrain ourselves slowly to get out of the habit of always resorting to the reins first. We'll never have a truly ratey, responsive and mentally connected horse until we do!

Reins – It only takes one time for a horse to learn they can run through bit pressure or your seat. This is why we never want to ask a horse to run who hasn't first been educated to come back to us mentally and physically. While we want our high-level horses to be aggressive, there must be a respectful balance, understanding and willingness to back off our aids. The timing in which we use our hands will determine how successfully we instill this. Using our hands last in training means we have several more subtle means of communicating first, which lessens the likelihood that we will ever "run out of bit."

Commit this order to mental and muscle memory:
1. Let the life out of your body
2. Deepen your seat
3. Say a verbal cue
4. Smoothly bring in the reins if necessary.

Of course, keep in mind that these steps can and will occur within in a split second of each other at advanced levels.

> *The horse is the best judge of a good rider. If the horse has a high opinion of the rider, he will allow himself to be guided. If not, he will resist.*
>
> – Nuno Oliviera

First Barrel Finesse

After taking a long break from competition to rehab my barrel horse from an injury, bring my first three books to life, *and* get settled in our Texas home, it was time to venture out and enter up. I was in completely new territory. While we don't exactly live in a barrel racing hot spot, you *can't not* go to a local jackpot down here and not have someone "famous" enter (and usually win). I was intrigued and I watched them closely. One of the biggest takeaways was noticing the sheer energy, quickness, agility and athleticism in which these top barrel racers rode. I knew I needed more of what they had.

It's not that we haven't all witnessed NFR barrel racers have a bad run, because *it does* happen. But *what is it* that these "toughs" have that the majority doesn't? For one, it became obvious to me that these gals weren't entering on horses that were borderline ready to go; they were entering on horses ready to win and were certainly riding to win. Although these top barrel racers weren't always necessarily on aged, finished horses, they sure seemed to ride like they were. There wasn't any timidity or over-thinking as they launched toward the first barrel, and their timing was impeccable. They had obviously set these horses up for success, trusted their training, and it showed!

I know how frustrating going by the first barrel can be. When you feel like you've tried a million things, and it continues to happen repeatedly, it changes you. You start to second guess-yourself and overthink even more. It's hard to ride well when you're stuck in your head, wondering just how much you should let your horse go and when you should ask for rate. Wouldn't it be better (and a lot less stressful) to make it more automatic? To trust your horse and be confident when you head to the first barrel? *That'd be nice* – right?

Being a dedicated student of horsemanship and barrel racing, and studying the ways of successful trainers and jockeys has helped me discover and experience some "secrets" to nailing the first barrel. They're secrets largely because it's not common knowledge. Even barrel racers with many accomplishments under their belt still struggle at times with the "money barrel," so aptly named because it sets the entire run up for success. If you've struggled with the first barrel for some time, there's a good reason and you're in good company. It's perhaps one of the more challenging angles of all three barrels, with the most opportunity for error. On top of that, since it's the first turn right after the "hot spot" start at the gate, where many horses anticipate and mentally checkout, it's common for that mentality to bleed over to the first turn. There are certain identifiable patterns, though; the same handful of things that get in the way of nailing the "money barrel." What I want for you – is to have the ability to prepare a horse and give them *all* the ingredients for a successful first barrel turn, so that you can enthusiastically hustle them there and they'll *hook it* reliably. Can you just *imagine* now what that would feel like? If it still seems like a far off, distant dream – *it's FUN!*

We've already addressed the emotional, physical and mental components necessary for getting your horses focused and taking responsibility for their job on the pattern. In the exercises that follow, I've shared how you can specifically train and condition your horse for even more consistent rate, plus power and snap around the first that carries all the way to the second and beyond. To begin though, I shared a mental exercise – a checklist to go through to make absolutely certain we've eliminated *all* the obstacles in the way of a less than stellar first barrel. These are the not so obvious things, those that cause a horse to *not want* to turn, that no exercise will ever fix. There is so much more to nailing the first barrel than just getting our horse's body around it. The process requires thorough analysis, understanding and preparation. We invest our best into barrel racing; if we want our runs to pay off, the money barrel deserves nothing less!

Exercise 16 – First Things First

Description
It's only fitting to dive deep into addressing the biggest and most common problem at the first barrel, which is *going by* it. But before we attempt to fix issues here by way of training or retraining our horse's body and mind, it makes sense to first take an even closer look at what might be interfering. The six-point checklist below includes common reasons why horses have trouble turning the first barrel, which are all critical elements to review considering they are much *less commonly* recognized and addressed.

Purpose
If any of these (or other) areas are the actual culprit for first barrel issues, we only risk building more resentment and bad habits by overlooking them. This ends up creating unnecessary emotional trauma and anxiety, contributing to negative associations that can continue to affect our horses (and us) long after the initial reason they *can't* or *don't want to* turn is resolved. Let's correct and avoid that, starting now!

How-to
Your First Barrel Checklist

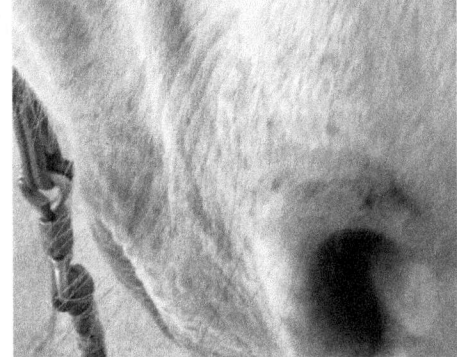
Notice the most subtle signs of discomfort.

Ulcers – It's not just hot, nervous horses that get and have stomach ulcers. You can be doing everything right to minimize stress and support digestive health, but that doesn't mean your horses are immune. Some of the most common symptoms of ulcers are not keeping weight on, poor topline, tail swishing, they may be overly sensitive to touch, cinchy or especially reactive, and tend to get quite anxious at times of stress (such as at the gate). Considering that the hind gut (while less common than stomach ulcers) is positioned on the right body wall, it might not be a coincidence that so many barrel horses especially struggle with the first barrel.

Feet & Joints – Just because a horse doesn't show discomfort when loping circles doesn't mean he doesn't experience it in a run. Just because he isn't refusing the turn (yet), doesn't mean soreness isn't causing him to go a couple strides by to delay a sting of discomfort. If you've been troubleshooting the first barrel for a handful of weeks or runs, it's well past time to work with *the best vets.* and bodyworkers – ones that embrace resolving challenging cases vs. masking them. Do what it takes to invest in troubleshooting. Be open to second opinions and management changes to ensure your horse is truly sound and free of pain.

Disengagement can be a sign of soreness.

Teeth – When it comes to eliminating resistance to bit pressure and helping a horse maximize his athleticism, proper dental work can't be undervalued. When the movement of a horse's jaw is inhibited, it contributes to "stuck" places through the rest of the body as well, which can be thought of as a system of levers and pulleys that affect each other. Anywhere there is resistance there will be compensation, and even more related resistance found elsewhere. Consider having your horse's teeth balanced once a year, with six-month check-ups when you're actively competing and absolutely need your horses at their best.

First Barrel Finesse

Freedom and comfort is necessary for rate.

Saddle Fit – I recently had the opportunity to ride in a treeless saddle. Although the one I tried didn't suit my preferences as a jockey, I appreciated the experience because I was surprised by just how much I could feel my horse's back flex, round and move under me. While even distribution of our weight is important, it was eye opening to realize just how many saddles don't allow for this freedom of movement, and also drastically restrict the shoulders. A horse won't be able to fully stretch out to run or want to gather up for the first barrel if the saddle doesn't offer a comfortable fit that allows for pain-free and comfortable, extended range of motion.

Riding – Your horse's ability to position his body in a way that makes the first barrel turn *easy* has a lot do with how he carries his weight. Due to the nature of barrel racing, it's easy for a horse to lean to the inside and on his front end. It's our job to instill habits of moving that are more elevated in the front end and balanced from side to side. The ideal position for the rider's weight in my opinion is close to equal in the stirrups or a smidge more to the outside. Your horse will tend to go where your weight is, so if you're not cranking the first barrel, expand your awareness and take steps to teach *your own body* to keep your stirrups more evenly weighted.

If we lean forward, the horse will also.

Headgear – The way a bit functions affects your horse's position in different and specific ways that can make all the difference for rating and turning. The first step in bit selection is knowing your horse and knowing yourself. How does your horse use his body, what are his tendencies? What are *your* tendencies? What do you need more of on the pattern? The right bit can help make up for some of what we and our horses lack, and there's nothing like barrel racing to put it all to the test. Combined with a high level education, the right bit can be icing on the cake that helps a well-educated horse reach peak performance.

First Barrel Checklist	Ulcers	Feet and Joints	Saddle Fit	Teeth	Riding	Headgear
***Put it to the Test** – Some Ideas for Dissolving Every Reason NOT to Turn*	Experiment by giving your horse 60 cc of Maalox 3x/day for several days. If you see a change, start an ulcer protocol.	Is your horse a little slow out of his stall, tender on hard ground, tail swishy, or bouncy in the turns? If so, see a good vet.	Is your horse's back sore on palpation? Is the pressure even under your saddle? If not, time to try something new.	Check your dentist's techniques and credentials. If your horse's teeth are overdue, make an appointment.	Trot around your first barrel without stirrups: - which way do you slide? Do you sit deep to cue for the turn in a run?	Study bit function. Does your horse tend to over-run or rate? Are you heavy or light handed? (Also see page 114.)
***Your Resolution** – Make Notes for Carrying Out Your Action Plans!*						

Exercise 17 – Position Perfection

Description

If you've ever felt that you might be doing more harm than good by fidgeting around with getting a perfect start position in the alley, you're not alone. After all, when our horse is anxious and anticipating, it's hard to know whether we should insist on perfection and potentially cause their anxiety and our position to get even worse, or just roll with it and take what we can get. It's challenging to effectively jockey a dragon as you "walk on eggshells," all while considering how your subtle actions will affect the run ahead and many more down the road. But I encourage you not to settle for poor position. Although you may have to accept what you can get as far as position in the moment, it's *always possible* to work toward better. Again, it all starts with making absolutely sure there's not a physical reason your horse is blocking you out, but that he understands his responsibilities and has every reason to yield his body and thoughts to your hands and legs at the gate. It requires a strong foundation of education and emotional fitness. When the physical, mental and emotional elements are solid, perfect position becomes simply a matter of perfect practice!

Purpose

It's not that we can't have a great run even with a poor start in the alley – it is possible! But it's *much more likely* when you're set up for success from the get-go. Why not put the odds more in your favor? When you're clear on what the ideal first barrel position is, and have dissolved any obstacles in the way, a smooth take off and crisp, fast turn is the inevitable result. That's what the exercise below will give you.

How-to

Before you expect a very specific body position in the alley, take an even closer look at the mental, emotional and physical components we started exploring in the previous exercise to ensure your horse is completely capable of, prepared and willing to deliver the high level performance you're expecting of him.

	My Horse is…	✓	My Action Steps:
Mental	*Educated, soft, understanding, confident, responsive*		
	Confused, dull, resistant, delayed, unsure, scattered		
Emotional	*Calm, connected, thinking, focused, motivated*		
	Distracted, excitable, reactive, hesitant, tense, anxious		
Physical	*Fluid, flexible, engaged, quick, supple, strong, willing*		
	Choppy, short, rough, stiff, slow, weak, argumentative		

The Ideal Body Position – As we leave for the first barrel, it's ideal to position our horse's body in a way that subtly mimics the position we'll want as we turn the first barrel. We want our horse in our hands, engaged through the hind end, slightly elevated in the front end, with a subtle lateral nose to tail arc, and to further support this position – even an angle to the body that helps keep weight in all the areas that make it easier to pick up the correct lead. We certainly won't *always* have *all* these characteristics perfect every trip down the alley, but they are *all* worth shooting for in the long run. Keep your standards high!

The Ideal Foot Position – You may notice NFR gals who go to the right barrel first, after entering from the tunnel, will go over to the far right of the alley then arc down the left side of the alley as they approach the first barrel. The setup as they come from the tunnel to the alley puts the horse in a position that is the opposite of what most want on the way to the barrel (unless they're lefties; then it's perfect!). This makes it particularly challenging because the horse's body will be arced to one side, then it must arc to the other.

There are always ways to overcome these challenging setups if you have control and connection to your horse's body and mind. Another option, for example, would be to enter the alley hindquarters first, keeping weight on the inside (right hind); and yet another would be to enter nose first then perform a spin back around to the right, again putting weight on that right hind leg to set the horse's body up for the first barrel.

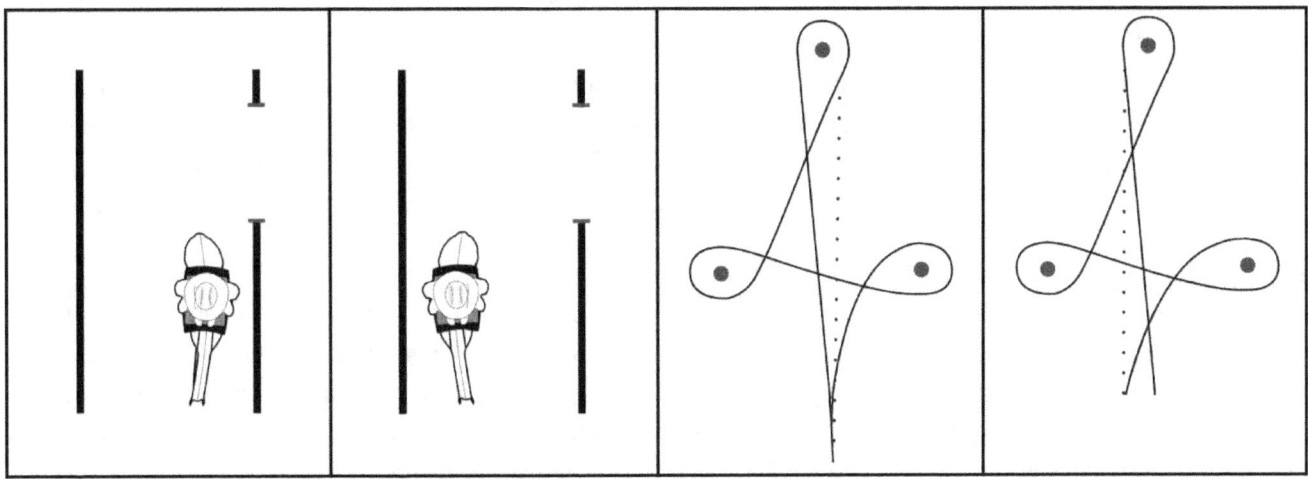

NFR entry to right barrel first.   *NFR entry to left barrel first.*   *Start position long approach.*   *Start position short approach.*

To switch gears – when presented with a long run to the first barrel, I like to start my run lined up just to the right side of the third barrel (if going right first; see dotted line). I'll run straight, and then starting about 25 feet before the first barrel (see diagram in Exercise 12 – Measured Improvement) make a smooth gradual arc as I approach. On a pattern with a short run to the first barrel, I will start further to the left, lined up just to the left side of the first barrel, giving myself a less straight and more gradual arc, making the approach easier than a sudden "button hook," which is a more physically difficult angle for a horse with so little room to prepare. Angling my horse's rear end toward the direction of whatever barrel I go to first will help lift the inside front leg and weight the hind end for the correct lead. In a perfect world, I like the idea of actually starting completely square and balanced, however, when energy is high and our horse is on the muscle, we may have to offer them a little more direction to make it as easy as possible to achieve the position we want.

Armed with some new insights and considerations, now it's time to practice your perfect first barrel setup and approach position repetitively and without the stress of a "hot spot," as shown in the diagram at right. Once your horse is familiar with responding and performing in the specific way you ask in this exercise, he'll be better prepared to make the connection and do so on the actual barrel pattern and then in competition. As with anything else, only after performing this exercise for several sessions, would you then put it to the test in slow work on the pattern at home, and gradually make your way to testing and tweaking in a run. No matter how far along your horse is, you can always improve and refine their approach to the first barrel for smoother turns and faster times!

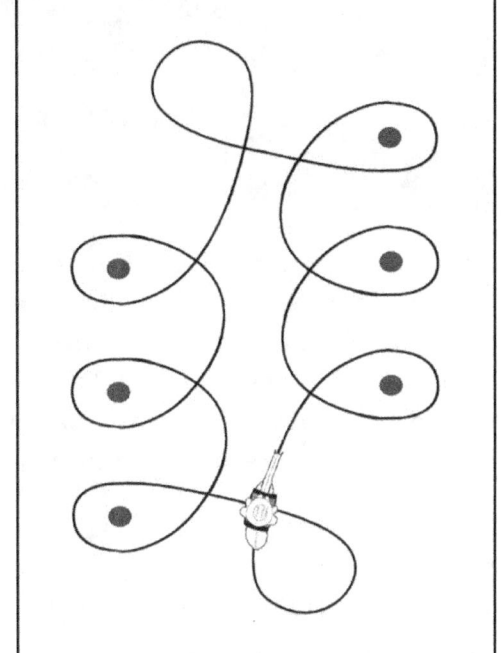

Exercise 18 – Mix it Up

Description

Part of the problem with the first barrel is what's going on in (or *not* going on) our horse's head as they sprint toward it. This really applies when troubleshooting, whether in a run or when slow working the pattern. Horses easily make assumptions, so it's our responsibility to prevent this. However, if we (or someone else) has allowed them to develop a less than ideal habit, it becomes our responsibility to interrupt these patterns. Sometimes the pattern (habit) we want to change is more mental, or it can be related to physical positioning; most times it's both. You'll find solutions to all of these problems below.

Purpose

Implementing an exercise that mimics the approach to the first barrel and requires the same kind of position but in slightly different context (such as the previous one), works by loosening up the associations our horses make in their minds, creating the opportunity to rewire the actual habits when we *do* return to the pattern. The idea is to have the simulation exercise similar and yet different. We want to get proficient enough that our horses can make a connection once we head back to the pattern in slow work, when they might revert to their old ways. Then we can communicate, *"Nope! This new way of thinking/moving/using your body applies here too, remember?"* In time, we can merge the two and leave the old, less desirable habits behind as we trade them for more powerful, correct and consistent form and function.

How-to

The UNPredictable Pattern – With your barrel pattern set up as usual, start at the opposite end of the arena and approach your "Mixed Up" first barrel to the right *or* left (see diagram A. – you can go to either way depending on how much you need to mix it up!). Approaching the pattern in this way will feel kittywampus, be potentially confusing to your horse and require extra focus on positioning for both of you; that's the point! This helps to keep your horse's attention more on you and you're less likely to deal with the positioning issues you typically experience at the first barrel. Really take the opportunity to strengthen the position and everything about the first barrel turn you want here, so that you can get it so well developed that your horse can make the connection and bridge the gap in time when you return to approaching the pattern normally. Make sure your eyes are looking where you want to go, that your weight is balanced, that your horse is driving from behind, that his shoulders are elevated and he's responsive to your feel. Keep circling your "first barrel" until you're happy with your horse's response and position, then head off and finish the pattern to put just a little bit of "real life" into the exercise so your horse realizes you are indeed working THE pattern, but with less likelihood for making assumptions.

When a horse seems to be taking over and calling the shots, it's important that we remain unattached emotionally, remembering that it was *us* who essentially failed the horse in order for the habit to develop. Also, keep a positive spin on the problem by considering that a horse's tendency for volunteering to do the wrong thing can be easily channeled into responsibility and enthusiasm for doing *the right thing.* "Mixing it up" isn't done in a way that has to include harsh corrections or force, but by simply changing the subject, and causing the wrong thing to be difficult and what we want to be easy. This doesn't mean we won't need to be quick or firm at times, but the goal is to simply loosen the mental attachment that *we* allowed them to develop. We don't have to beat ourselves up for making mistakes and having to correct them, but we should always be thinking about how to learn, take responsibility, and avoid them going forward.

In-line Pattern – With three barrels set up in a diagonal line approximately 30 feet apart, either centered down the arena or slightly offset (B.), head toward the first barrel with positioning that mimics your actual approach when on the pattern. After completing that turn, change your horse's bend and circle the following two barrels the other direction. Feel free to mix this up even further by starting in the other direction; but in each case do the first barrel one way, and the other two the other direction. Feel free to start at a trot, graduating to a lope with a simple lead change; and as you advance include a flying change in between the first and second barrel.

The focus here is perfecting your approach to the first barrel; the angles and footfall you're asking for, and the position of your horse's body. Remember that these exercises are done with the purpose of interrupting a habit that your horse has associated with the actual barrel pattern, to take away anticipation, and to create new mental and physical movement patterns. Be particular and specific, and eventually you can move the barrels further apart (C.) to more closely simulate the pattern itself, and to make the transition even easier and set yourself up for success, making it less likely your horse will default back to old habits. Avoid getting in a rush to return to the pattern, but honestly assess and test your horse's understanding and responsibility by allowing him a little more space and slack in the rein to *show you* what he's learned.

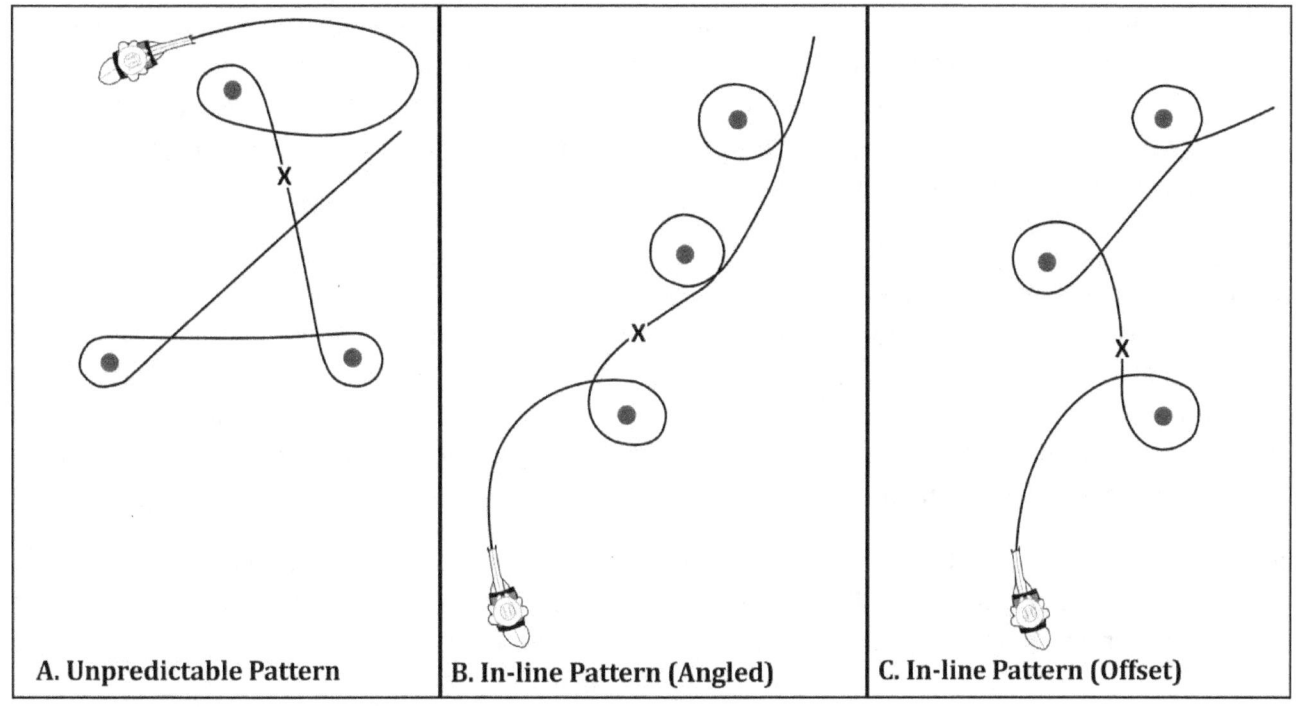

A. Unpredictable Pattern | B. In-line Pattern (Angled) | C. In-line Pattern (Offset)

Exercise 19 – Stop and Circle

Description

In many cases, horses have been allowed to run away in more ways than one (again, starting at a walk), while simultaneously over time also inadvertently taught to push through and ignore the rider's body language, *and* bit pressure; or perhaps never thoroughly educated to respond and yield to it well from the start. Some "hotter" horses are also more prone to losing their focus (and educational understandings) when speed is added. A more right-brain, sensitive horse becomes reactive quicker than a more naturally laid back horse. With their survival instincts closer to the surface, we have to devote ourselves to building their confidence and make sure that when we ask them to "get gone" (run full speed) physically, that they stay with us and don't leave mentally. It takes time, timing, patience, understanding and lots of going back and forth from speed to mental connection and back again in order to join the two together. So many horses that run off at the first barrel are long gone mentally, and their body simply follows. The exercise below is a valuable one especially for a horse with a lot of try and enthusiasm for racing to the first barrel, but not as much for staying mentally connected, and in a thinking, rating and responding frame of mind.

Purpose

In barrel racing and in life, we tend to get more of what we focus on. We get better at what we practice. The more a horse practices running to the first barrel without thinking and responding to the rider or turning with good form, the better he gets at it. The more exposures the horse has, the more time it will take to correct. The purpose of Stop and Circle is to interrupt the habit of running without thinking, making it helpful for instilling rate. After all, it's awfully hard to trust a horse to prepare for the turn when he obviously isn't thinking about it. This exercise sets a horse up to practice bringing his attention back to the rider and his job, while throttling down his forward motion a bit and shifting his weight rearward. The addition of circles will reiterate what's coming next, making for a smooth, powerful transition to the second barrel. I don't want my horses to experience a runaway even one time, so I do my best to make sure that I have respect for the boundaries I offer as a foundation, so they don't even become familiar with the feeling. I don't allow them to ignore halter pressure. I don't allow them to step into my space. Yielding their minds and bodies with softness in all areas, in all applications and circumstances is a paramount pillar in my program. However, when you've made the mistake of either not quite preparing a horse or not correcting this pushing right away, or you find yourself correcting someone else's failure to do so, the steps below are helpful for refining education and respect (the appropriate response to pressure) and bringing your horse's mind back to his job, the first barrel *and you.*

How-to

To perform this exercise have your barrel pattern set up as home as usual. After warming up, feel free to start this exercise at the walk or trot if your horse is anxious or pushy at slower speeds. Angle your horse in preparation to approach the first barrel as described in Exercise 17 – Position Perfection, so his weight is concentrated on his first barrel-side hind leg. Arc your way toward it, and depending on how extreme your horse's tendency to mentally disconnect is, you'll essentially stop, back and then circle as needed up to three or four times between your starting point and the first barrel.

How much you focus on the back up or the circle will depend on the specific issue you're facing. Is your horse not rating, not turning, not preparing for the turn with good position, not thinking, or all of the above? Use your own judgement to customize this exercise based on your needs. For example, a horse that isn't rating will benefit from more emphasis on the backing portion of the exercise. A horse that isn't turning will benefit from more repetitive circles. A horse that is getting out of position might benefit from emphasizing the positioning and weight balance, by counter arcing a few steps before circling (also see Exercise 25), and a horse that struggles mentally will especially benefit from obvious and extended rewards for a relaxed, connected and positive state of mind.

In any case, ask for the stop with your body by lowering your energy, sitting deep in your seat and saying a verbal "whoa," before then bringing in the reins. Back up twice as far as the distance it required to stop. Then let your horse breathe and relax for a moment. Reward him, and give him some peace and comfort for mentally and physically coming back to you.

No matter how firm you have to be or how much resistance you get initially, with this and all exercises, again *don't fall victim to your emotions*, which only causes a horse to want to run away from us mentally and physically even more. This isn't punishment by means of intimidation or fear. Horses do what they to do *to survive* or *seek comfort.* The boundary lines are black and white and you can be very firm without an attitude that translates into "Do THIS or else!" Your energy is neutral. There are certain boundaries that must be respected, but there are no emotional strings attached and no shades of grey, which builds respect and confidence.

After waiting long enough for your horse to relax, lick and chew, angle your horse's hips in the direction of the first barrel (don't allow your horse to lead with and fall in on the forehand) and start off loping a slightly larger than barrel-size circle right there (see diagram), in the same direction that you will turn the barrel. Loping in this direction (and not counter arcing completely off the other way) is suitable for a horse that isn't hooking the first barrel, because the repetition gets his mind thinking about and body going in the direction of the turn in advance. Repeat as space allows.

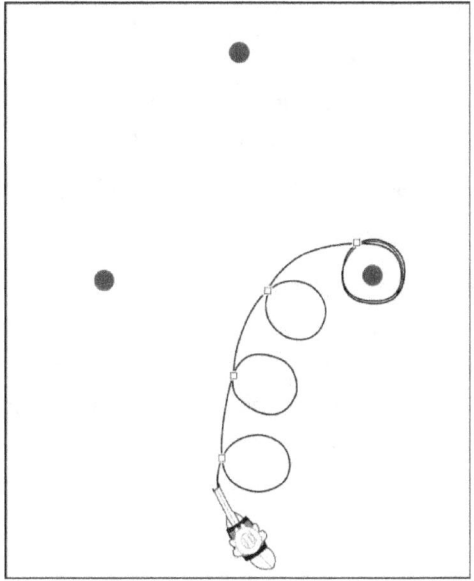

When your horse has performed a balanced, correct circle, again straighten out and head toward your first barrel and once again quickly come back down to a smooth stop. Initially, you'll just repeat as much stopping and circling to the first barrel as you have room for. As your horse begins to understand and learn, you can time your stopping and circling with the moment you feel your horse want to make an assumption and push into you, then instantly stop, rest and circle to bring your horse's mind and body back to you when it leaves. After circling the actual barrel two to five times, either finish the pattern or repeat the exercise. Remember that it's better to have too much of a good thing than not enough. Keep this in mind when considering how much repetition to use before testing your work by adding speed.

Exercise 20 – Run & Rate

Description

There's nothing more breathtaking than a horse who's rating and running at the same time. Maybe it was my first childhood experiences on my renegade pony that inspired my appreciation for this, or the many years of frustration stemming from going by the first barrel. Of course, for some horses rating comes very naturally. I don't seem to have had many of those horses! In this exercise, I'm excited to share tips for getting even more automatic and authentic "self-rate" without compromising forward motion. We've been building on "basic rate" in previous exercises and this could be considered the advanced version. Stopping or slowing down at the barrel is easy, and sometimes even necessary for extreme cases, but learning and teaching your horse to run and rate *at the same time* is more challenging, and even more fun!

Purpose

As I often emphasize, it's not so much what we do but *how*. Technically, a horse can drag their body backward without getting engaged or transferring weight properly to their hind end. Again, stopping or slowing down in our slow work on the pattern to teach rate will usually work *pretty well*, but I've also seen it cause horses to lose too much momentum; and are you after "pretty good" results, anyway? If we want a sure thing we have to think outside the box, and advance our horsemanship and ability to communicate, and instill *rate in motion*. In other words, to sum it up biomechanically, we must develop our ability to ask and clearly communicate with our horses when it's time to rate, causing them to reach deeply under themselves and prepare for the turn while still in motion and without losing power and speed. To teach this, we won't stop or change gait (we certainly don't change gait in a run, right?), we'll just change *how* the horse moves *within* that gait. Just because our horse manages to turn, or "kind of" rates, doesn't mean they are truly rating in motion. But when we make this distinction it changes everything! What makes the end result so amazing to watch and feel is that a horse will naturally round through their back, reach deeply under themselves and elevate their withers. It's beauty in motion. It feels incredible and clocks fast.

How-to

Teaching Run & Rate starts by refining even further our horse's understanding of what to do in their body based on what we do in ours. We want *our legs* to be connected to our horse's hind legs. Not only that, but the idea here is that when we elevate our "front end" by raising our chin, eyes and hands, as we sit deeper in the saddle, round our lower back, tuck our pockets and angle the bottom of our pelvis forward to ask for more hindquarter engagement in motion, that our horse should mirror this position in their body. To some degree horses do this naturally, but most of us spend a lot of time making careless movements in the saddle not realizing that we're actually desensitizing our horses to them. Refining our horse's education means teaching them to differentiate between what kind of activity is meaning*ful* and what is meaning*less*. It requires us to have impeccable awareness and consistency.

Ask yourself: "Does my horse respond to changes in my energy/life?" If you sit up a little straighter and raise the life in your body (as if you're in the starting position to run a race) does your horse feel that and get ready too? Remember an advanced education means that we don't just kick to go and pull to stop, which involves delays, but that our body and theirs move in unison. Combined with their responsibility for "owning the pattern" it's the ultimate marriage for high level performance at speed.

It's not unusual to experiment by changing your own hindquarter positon and then noticing your horse's way of moving doesn't change significantly. If that's the case, I encourage you to get even more extreme as you "set it up and wait." Over-exaggerate to motivate your horse enough that he tries to guess what you're looking for, yet not for so long that you desensitize him. Keep asking for a few seconds with your body, gradually getting more dramatic as you wait for a subtle indicator that your horse is matching you, then relax to reward, and repeat.

Starting at a standstill or walk, if you don't get a response the next step is to very lightly tap your horse's hind end with a rein or over & under in rhythm (you tap just as the hind leg leaves the ground – easier said than done!) to reinforce the idea that their hip is connected to your hip. When you adjust your "stride" by engaging your hind end, they are to also. Is your horse scared of your over & under? Remember, the meaning of our tools depends on the context, such as energy in our body. Your horse will make assumptions unless you've taught him these distinctions. As soon as you get connection, again stop and reward the slightest try. If you're still struggling, consider brushing up by reviewing the fundamentals featured in Exercise 11 – A to B in *The First 51* to teach this. Eventually move up to a trot, then slow lope and gradually up to a gallop. This will dramatically improve your stops because your horse won't have to make such an extreme change to "get ready" to stop or rate; they'll be running in a way that has their body already as prepared as possible. While in the end your horse might not run every stride of the pattern like this (they will be more "front endy" at high speed on the straightaways between barrels), it will become much easier and more natural to shift their weight just before each turn, making it quick, easy and efficient.

You can imagine as you cruise to the first barrel that instead of a horse being inverted, resistant, mentally checked out or running with too much weight on his front end, that with *your* pelvis buried and your hips "scooping" and cuing your horse's to also lower and swing forward, that he'll be mentally and physically engaged (rating) while also running. Now that you have the "how" to Run & Rate, apply it to the patterns below. When you have success there, then apply this newfound "hip connection" to *the* pattern.

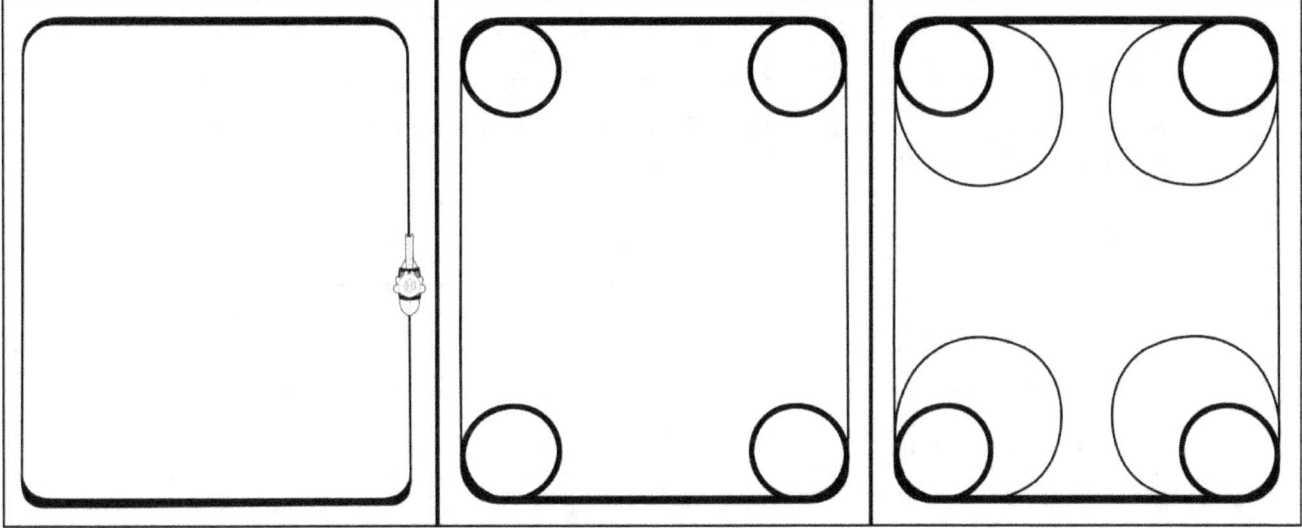

Extended gallop ("Run") on long side of arena and in large circles, collected lope or gallop ("Rate") on short side and in small circles.

3 x 3 Troubleshooting Plan

For Creating Solutions – Step x Step

For the HORSE

1. **What** is the solution you're looking for? List the SOURCE of *the problem* vs. the symptom(s).
   _____
   _____

2. **Where**? Where on the pattern is the issue occurring, *and* where on the pattern will the solution take place, or *begin* to take place? Be specific; how many *feet* from the barrel, etc.? (Mark it out).
   _____
   _____

3. **When**? What will your horse need to do, or *how* will he need to travel/use himself differently in each situation below? Make an action plan!

    a. In a run _____
    _____

    b. In slow work_____
    _____

    c. In general riding _____
    _____

For the RIDER

1. **What** must happen? As a rider, what could you be doing that is contributing to the problem? What are you willing to do (or not do) to correct this?
   _____
   _____

2. **Where**? Where exactly on the pattern are adjustments to your riding required?
   _____
   _____

3. **When**? What will you be more conscious of and/or how to you plan to ride differently in each of the situations listed below? How can you enjoy the process?

    a. In a run _____
    _____

    b. In slow work _____
    _____

    c. In general riding
    _____
    _____

Second Barrel Success

The second barrel is, not surprisingly, the most commonly tipped barrel. The fact that we're running straight toward a wall or fence, have the shortest distance between barrels, and must hook an acute angle, makes the second barrel not only challenging, but very different from the first. The exercises that follow will offer solutions for problems, such as starting the turn too soon, tipping, shouldering or dropping in, as well as tips for turning up the speed between the first and second barrels. To eliminate the frustrations associated with the second (as well as bruised knees), or just sharpen up an *already good* turn, it's critical that we take a closer look at *the way* we're navigating that corner. While it might deserve an entire chapter, examining our riding technique didn't fit in as an exercise, so I want to take the opportunity here to describe how our jockeying contributes to our second barrel success – or lack thereof!

It would be accurate to say the second barrel is also the most *looked at* barrel. After all, if we've had our knee smashed a few times, we tend to tense up and *look* to make sure that it doesn't happen again. If we need to make an adjustment, it's natural for our mind to want to know how much or how soon. Although looking at the barrel to see how close or far away we are is a natural reaction, it's not necessarily a good reaction. Looking down at our position in relation to the barrel is also a particularly common habit with beginner barrel racers. It's a lot like looking at the basketball when you're first learning to dribble, or the temptation to look at the keys when first learning to type. A primary method for resolving second barrel issues involves purposely re-routing our habits to better develop our depth perception and spatial awareness, while teaching our mind and body to rely more on peripheral vision and feel for positioning.

There's no denying that our horses tend to go where we focus. But when we look to the inside as we approach the second barrel, our body position changes as well. It's often the rider who drops their own shoulder a split second before the horse does. Their focus, weight and shoulder simply follows ours, and when we look down, the barrel often follows too! If we can focus straight ahead on where we need to go, and keep pushing into the hole, we can dramatically raise the odds for getting around the barrel more quickly, even on a horse whose tendency is to prepare too soon. Also, look at other subtleties of your own body. Are your hands high or low? How about your eyes and chin? Is your elbow bent and close to your body, or straight and far away? Are you dropping or leading with your own inside shoulder first? Is there more weight on your inside seat bone or outside? How about stirrups? Do you have supple flexion through your torso without collapsing? Is your outside shoulder coming around to rotate and finish the turn?

In addition, consider that we want our horses to be responsible and automatic. If we lift the rein and ask our horse to make an adjustment and they don't, something's broken. Remember, there should be a 51% ratio of "respond to the jockey" and 49% "know your job." We must retain the ability to reposition in an instant if necessary.

Of course, things change! The environment we're in affects how our horses respond as well. The ground conditions impact how we time the preparation for the turn. Physical issues can change how "turny" or "setty" our horses feel. Sometimes we don't know or expect these changes, or realize them until after making a run. But with experience we can begin to anticipate them. We can assume our horse will be more likely to set up and turn early in a small, dark pen with the barrels just a few feet off the wall, for example. Most important is that we do our best to prepare our horses properly from the get-go. Along with some problem-solving pointers, that's what this chapter will help you accomplish. That way it becomes less about damage control and more about truly being set-up for second barrel success from the start.

Exercise 21 – Smooth it Out

Description

While there's so much room for variation in the approach to the first barrel, there isn't much leeway to the second. While this simplifies things on one hand, it also presents a unique challenge. That being the tricky, approximately 30-degree angle we must make to complete the turn, which often translates into awkward hang-ups and less than stellar positioning at best – and serious delays and blow outs at worst. The change in direction from going straight, to making such a sharp, sudden corner can understandably be a tough one to nail without our horses getting out of position, which in many cases means leaning or transferring excess weight onto the forehand. For many horses, getting "front endy" is just a desperate attempt to make the turn happen when either the natural athleticism isn't quite there, the skill and development that helps bridge that gap is lacking, or some of both. The change in direction at the second barrel is certainly a place on the pattern that calls for advanced development, preparation and skill from both horse and rider.

Purpose

Some horses really start anticipating the turns and feel pressured to aggressively dive in, even if we just want them to lope nice, easy, collected circles. My husband's rope horse gelding turned barrel horse, Dot Com, is one such horse. I appreciate that he has so much "try," but it's been critical that he learn to match my energy and not make assumptions. The following exercise for "smoothing it out" not only helps to smooth out the awkward right angle "hook" at the second barrel to make it more round, elevated and fluid, but it also takes the excess emotion and anticipation out of turning as well (and can be applied at any other barrel). I thought it was interesting that when asked to lope around a barrel, Dot Com would really struggle, but if I loped the exact same kind of circle right *next to* a barrel there was no problem. His nature, combined with the fact that the barrel pattern is *sometimes* done with speed was enough to create an assumption that he should dig in and try his heart out, even when I really just wanted a correct, slow and cadenced, balanced circle. This exercise helps to break up that association, reminding your horse to stay slightly more connected to you than the pattern, and helps create smooth, powerful turns that might otherwise be rushed, awkward or rough.

How-to

Like many of the exercises shared in connection to the individual barrel, this one can actually be done at any or all three barrels. Use your own judgement as to which (or whether) one or more of them need it. With the barrel pattern set up, the goal will be to work circles around AND next to each barrel individually without any focus on the specific order; so feel free to do all right turns or all lefts, etc. Starting at any barrel in any direction, go into it with a good strong arc, first at a trot to test your horse's competency and

Stacy demonstrates what we don't want.

give him the idea before moving up to a lope. Make one even quality circle approximately 15-20 feet in diameter around a barrel, which is easier for a horse than a barrel-sized (approximately ten-foot) circle. From that point, make a circle about half that size right *next to* the barrel itself (see diagram). If your smaller circle feels as smooth and balanced as the previous circle, then go ahead and make the same (smaller) size circle *around the barrel*. Once you're ready for a lope, start by getting into a nice, collected, round and elevated, engaged lope to repeat the same steps performed at a trot.

When I refer to "quality circles," what I'm shooting for is a smooth, cadenced movement, where the horse is softly flexed at the poll, slightly arced laterally through their body, reaching under themselves without leaning to the inside and with elevation at the withers instead of heaviness on the forehand. To encourage this position, I make sure I keep my hands up and my eyes up, with just the amount of feel necessary on the reins to ask for the vertical flexion at the poll, ideally without having to hold the horse in place. I use my seat to encourage my horse's hind quarters forward energetically with power. I'm also conscious of my weight in the stirrups and want them close to equal, or a little bit more heavily weighted on the outside.

If the quality of that barrel-sized circle goes downhill, you're not alone! This is related to the assumptions our horse's make or the less than ideal movement (or thought) patterns they've developed for rounding the actual barrels. No problem; just go back to your one bigger circle, then one smaller, and around the barrel again – really feeling for a nice, barrel-sized loping circle with the same or similar quality as the larger circle or the side circle.

If your horse's barrel circle is not as good as the small circle, go back and do a small circle next to the barrel a second time, then move right back around the barrel again. The idea is to "bridge the gap" and communicate that "What you gave me *here*, I want *here* around the barrel." It's as if we're showing the horse it's possible to lope an anxiety-free, quality circle right *next to* the barrel, to help them understand they can do the same a few feet over, around the barrel itself. As you implement this, be sure you use your energy and body language to communicate when your horse is doing well. Even just smile or relax slightly as he lopes that nice small circle. Once the quality of the small barrel circle has improved, stop and rest to offer your horse a reward. Sometimes, there's something we're doing different to cause our turns to fall apart, so be aware of anticipation, looking down, slouching, collapsing, unbalanced weight in the stirrups, etc. You'll be amazed by how much power this exercise has for easing tension and smoothing out the turns!

Stacy and Bill showing great form at a lope.

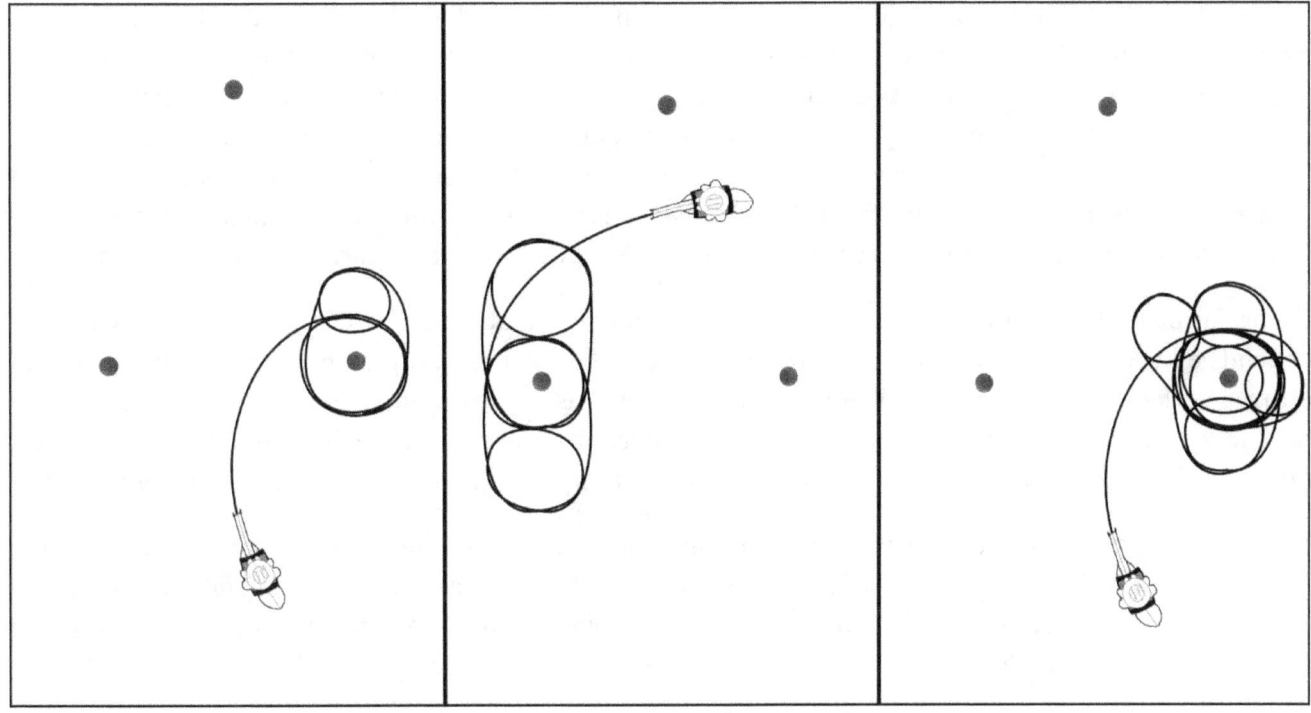

Start at any barrel or any place in the arena. Vary the location and size of the circles based on your horse's needs in each moment.

Exercise 22 – Lollipop

Description
There's probably no worse feeling than being on a 1,200 poumd unresponsive equine missile going 20+ miles per hour, heading straight in what feels like a bee-line nose dive for the second barrel. I can feel my eyes bugging out now as I catch myself looking down, trying to salvage the turn and squeak around it, then hearing the dull "dung" of the barrel crashing down, and feeling the instant twinge of painful disappointment *and* what will be a bruise on my knee! But, I always try to reframe things in a positive light. Truthfully, having an over-turny or ratey horse *can be* a good thing. It's not bad to have a horse that wants to work too much, after all. The problem is when they start calling the shots and making assumptions about timing the turn, and losing their good form and responsiveness while they're at it. So let's find some balance for our over-achieving horses and channel their enthusiasm and work ethic in a positive direction!

Purpose
Even horses that don't tend to have a lot of natural rate can fall into the trap of slicing into the second barrel. In fact, sometimes even more so, because horses with a slightly lesser degree of aptitude, quickness and athleticism for turning, means preparing won't be as easy for them, so they tend to start getting ready sooner. Again, however we know that the second barrel's position to the fence or wall, and the jockey's level of quickness, timing and athleticism, including the ability to keep their eyes up, focused forward until the very last second, all contribute as well. Of course, this can be corrected in large part with quality training, even and especially for those of us humans who have to make up for what we lack in athleticism with learned skill or simply don't have a string of horses to practice on. The following exercise is one that puts a different twist on the counter arc. It's very effective for getting a horse off the barrels if they are peeling too much paint, turning too tightly, and perhaps tipping or coming off the backside as a result.

How-to
The counter arc needs no introduction. But as a refresher, this is performed by asking our horse to arc his body laterally nose-to-tail in one direction and move his body in the other direction. In *The First 51*, Exercise 39, I shared three different versions of the counter arc that are valuable at the second barrel and any other where your horse might be "cheating," over-anticipating, making assumptions, turning too soon or getting out of position in the approach. When I say out of position, I mean that your horse might be "turning inside out" with his rib cage slightly toward the barrel. This leads to leaning and starting the turn with excessive weight on the inside front shoulder. Most horses tend to turn in this fashion to a degree, but when taken to an extreme, problems such as slipping, falls, tipped barrels, etc. are more likely to occur.

To perform the Lollipop exercise, you'll simply stop before *or* at each barrel (exactly where you stop depends on whether you want to emphasize rate or not), then roll back approximately 90 degrees to head off in a perfect circle making a "lollipop" shape. In most cases if your horse is leaning into the turn, he probably doesn't need help *thinking about* turning (hence the reason we're taking him off course), but he might need help with transferring weight to the hindquarters, which is what the Lollipop is so helpful for.

After stopping squarely at the second barrel (or any other barrel) for a moment, turn and face your horse away by doing a ¼ pivot on the outside hind leg (also known as a "cow turn" – see the following exercise for more on this). Then start off on a brisk, forward circle, with a subtle bend through your horse's body as you continue around in that circle.

Pay attention to how much bend your horse is offering in his neck. It's ideal to have yielding, subtle and supple flexion all the way from nose to tail (through the ribs) vs. only a bent neck. Horses who are stiff through the ribs will tend to over-bend at the base of the neck. If you feel this, experiment with using more persistent leg and less hands to create (then reward) the subtle degree of flexion/bend you're looking for. Change the subject as necessary to restore ample suppleness first before continuing with the exercise. Any exercise – if it can't be done with relatively good form, shouldn't be done at all. If at any point you feel your horse want to cut or drop in, use your leg to move him off and away.

You have a couple of options for closing your "lollipop circle" that are pictured in the diagram below. If you're having trouble with anticipation only at the second barrel, consider making the second half of your circle so large that you have room to come back around to where you stopped. Rest there a moment (how long you stop again depends on whether you need to reiterate rate), then again pivot and break off into another circle, up to five or so times before moving on. If your horse already has an abundance of rate in addition to drop, or if your horse tends to lean into all his turns, the other option is to perform the lollipop circle at each barrel only once. In this case, close the turn as you move onto the next barrel. Which version you use from the diagram depends on your horse and his (changing) needs – feel it out, and trust yourself!

Because so many horses seem to want to make a bubble pocket at the third barrel, use caution there with this exercise. Again, use your own judgement, and only perform as needed at each barrel. Remember, it's critical that we don't compartmentalize exercises too much but respond instantly to what's occurring in our most recent runs and from moment to moment. That might mean picking your horse up and performing a counter arc the instant you feel him drop in. Be willing to adjust to whatever your horse needs. That's what horsemen do – they feel and make adjustments as they go along vs. following a script or a list of separate exercises. Instead, it all flows together into a harmony of fluid movement. It's almost like dancing, where the horse doesn't realize he's being "trained" at all, but at the same time, he's learning a TON about where to be, when and why. Eventually, put it to the test in a run to determine how much is too much *or* just right. This is how learning and training is done, through experimentation and experience!

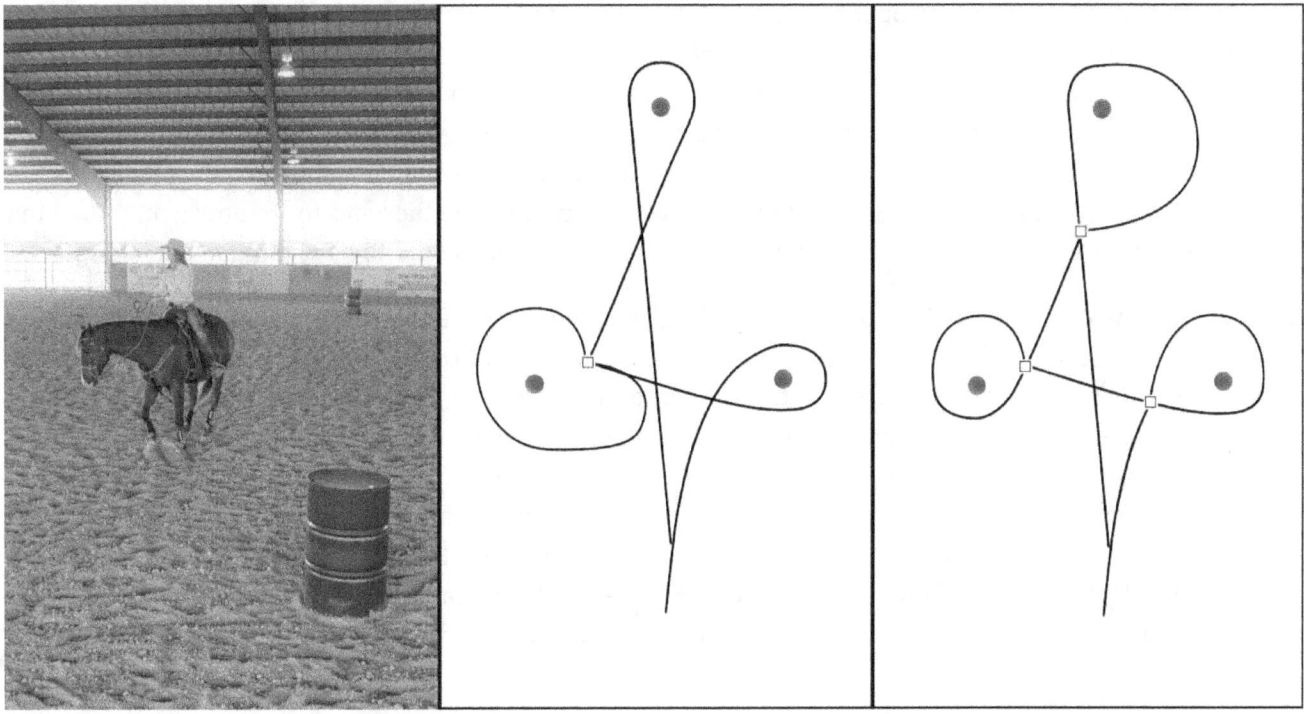

Exercise 23 – Reverse 360

Description

When teaching a horse the barrel pattern, fine tuning or correcting a problem, I personally prefer not to make extreme variations to the pattern itself if possible. If I feel the need to lope big loopy circles, I'll most likely do that around cones, bike tires, or around barrels that aren't set up as the actual cloverleaf. I want my horse to know the pattern like the bottom of his hoof! Making excessive variations has the potential to create confusion. I don't want to cause any loss of confidence or second guessing, and while there IS a time to unhook a horse from what they have inadvertently been taught (by us, whoops!), *or* if they tend to be an over-achiever that makes assumptions or takes over, these are all situations that call for shaking up what they think they know and understand. A better way to go about it, if possible, is to teach them everything in a way that is very particular and try to prevent these problems and catch them when they're very subtle. The following exercise is a "mini version" of a counter arc that helps compress a strung-out body, and keeps the margin for misunderstanding small by minimizing variations on the pattern.

Purpose

In Exercise 37 of *The First 51*, I shared a similar exercise that involves pivoting a horse mid-barrel turn *toward the barrel* with the weight on the inside hind leg for more engagement. The idea here is similar only we'll spin or roll back the other direction, and we can even further customize this to fit our specific needs. This lifts the front end out and away, and actually encourages the horse to transfer more weight to the *outside* hind leg, which is often not weighted enough when the inside front is over-weighted, which happens as the horse is leaning excessively to the inside or shouldering. It seems simple in theory, but I'll be sharing some critical "do's and don'ts" for making the most out of this exercise, which when done properly has the power to completely transform a barrel hitter, making tipped barrels a thing of the past.

How-to

The key to utilizing this exercise is *feel*. Looking back, when I was a kid and first started barrel racing, I wasn't totally clear on what a "dropped shoulder" was, or even felt like. Once I did figure it out, it didn't feel like "dropping" to me at all, but felt more like *leaning* or heaviness in a turn on the inside front leg. There's so much we can do to discourage this; again, starting with lifting our own eyes, chin and head up which changes our focus and puts more weight on the back of our seat. Also, we can move the saddle back slightly, weight our stirrups more evenly, square our shoulders, raise our hands, and use our energy to encourage more forwardness and engagement. Remember that the further and more powerfully the hind legs come under the horse's heavy body, the less likely it is for the front end to be leaning in and heavy.

Once you've ensured that you're not actually *asking* your horse to be in a poor position with your own body, as you're rounding the barrels, the instant you feel any downward suction, drop, heaviness or leaning occur – lift your reins and ask your horse to spin briskly back around away from the barrel quickly to the outside. Of course, getting the most value from this requires that you have a good handle on your horse and can pick them up and spin them around quickly and easily without resistance *off* the pattern, first. The barrel pattern isn't the time or place to teach your horse to turn around. In fact, if the horse isn't quickly, lightly and effortlessly responsive when you ask for this, it's likely there's a big part of your problem. Sharpen this element of your foundation (Exercise 17 – Separate & Combine in *The First 51* will help refine your horse's response to leg cues) is a good idea before proceeding on the pattern with Reverse 360's.

Because you're making this correction so suddenly, make sure there isn't an ounce of emotion in your mind and body. In fact, when you have to make a sudden correction, be quick but smooth, and smile! The abruptness of it might startle or surprise your horse. Although it might not be pretty, it's important that he understands this isn't punishment or something to fear, or that you're mindlessly just bumping his body parts around, but that you simply have a black and white way of communicating boundaries, that there are expectations that must be followed. We want our horses to know there's nothing to be afraid of, but that you *do* require respect and responsiveness and that they *think* and *use their bodies* in a very specific way.

As you perform the 360, shoot for making one trip around the barrel with as many spin-backs as needed, then continue forward and move on to the next one. If your horse goes back to diving in, pick him up and turn back around again. Do as much or as little as necessary. You might need to make six spins throughout one turn, or only one. It just depends on how ingrained the habit is and how quickly your horse understands. Maybe every single step the horse takes is excessively on the front end; in that case perform 360's all the way around the barrels. Also don't neglect the opportunity to teach the horse better movement patterns *away* from the pattern. Horses that don't move well on the barrels aren't likely to be great movers in general, but we can change this! Anytime your horse is making an assumption and/or dropping in, interrupt the pattern by rocking back and asking for another 360. It's as if you're asking, "Come back to me and get correct." Your horse may or may not need to perform this exercise at all the barrels. When he performs a revolution of reverse 360's with quality at the second barrel, move on to the third as normal or include 360's there, and also at the first barrel as well if needed. Also remember that the longer it takes, the more a horse struggles to make a positive change – the more relief/reward you should give your horse to make it really clear what you were after. The goal is for them to perform well physically and *also* be in a positive state of mind (although you may have to temporarily sacrifice one or the other).

Keep in mind, as you're spinning around that the hind legs should stay fairly stationary. In reining, a pivot foot that lifts up and down is acceptable but certainly not "coke bottling" or swapping ends, as if the horse's axis was in the middle of the body. Again, you want to specifically have the majority of weight on the outside hind for this exercise. Weighting the outside hind is the more practical and common way that our barrel horses use themselves in rollbacks, which requires the weight to first rock rearward. The reining horse turn/spin is a more forward maneuver with the *inside* hind weighted. As an added challenge – off the pattern see if you can specify which hind leg your horse keeps stationary when asking for a pivot.

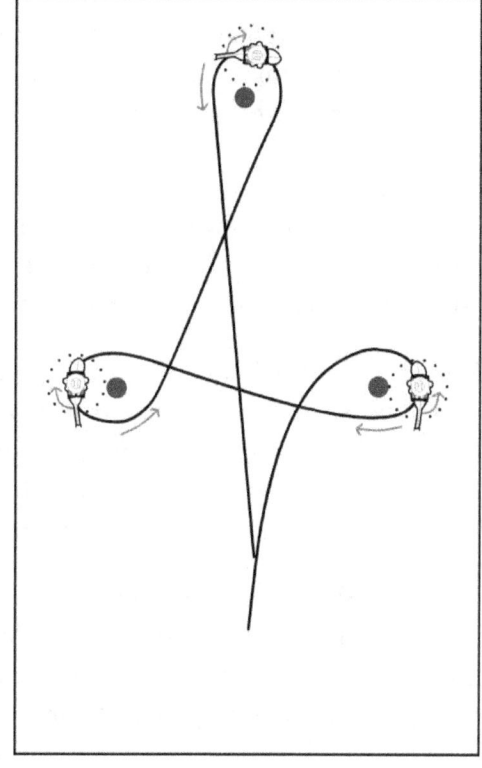

Exercise 24 – Forty-Five Fencing

Description

Recently I watched a powerful video of a karate instructor coaching a small boy to break a block of wood with his hand. There were lots of repeated "Hiiiayyaas" but the block wasn't breaking. The kid was hitting it, but not quite with the intention of breaking it; you could see he was frustrated and holding back. Finally, with some expert coaching, he sliced his hand through the air with everything he had and shattered the block! It was amazing to see the difference in the boy's energy and *really* fascinating to see the results.

I've already shared how we can train our horses to run and still be ready to rate, and certainly some horses need to work on this more than others. But what if your horse just isn't firing like you know he can, or rating and accelerating as quickly as he needs to on the pattern? It's one thing for a horse to run full out while using their body in a way that makes it quick and easy to rate; it's another to run with the brakes on, or to run half-heartedly, or in anticipation of stopping. There's a difference between all these scenarios.

Purpose

I've also mentioned that rating comes more naturally to some horses, simply due to their God-given aptitude for it. But often, our horses aren't performing at their potential because we haven't developed ourselves to *our own* potential! Maximizing and optimizing God-given talent is the name of the game. We can help our horses fill in for a lot of what they lack in athleticism with learned skill – if we're aware and deliberate. The following exercise includes several versions of "fencing," specifically adapted to fit and apply to barrel racing.

Sometimes our horses are safetying up and preparing for the turns too soon because WE can't handle going into the turn so quick, hard and fast, so this exercise is just as much for the rider as it is for the horse. In it, you'll test your horse and teach him to respond *to you* more than his environment, meaning that when you're running in small indoor pens repeatedly, for example, that you'll be able to guide your horse far enough forward to nail the second barrel successfully with little risk of tipping it. You and your horse will improve your timing and quickness in the process. It's a "quickness drill" for *both* horse and human, and can be just the ticket for shaving off that stubborn last half-second.

How-to

It's easy to avoid this work, because it's intense. I utilize it minimally and only as necessary. One reason is because it's so fast paced. I'm always taking steps to lessen the wear and tear on my horse's body, so I personally don't do any more speed work than necessary to help preserve them mentally and physically.

When I sprint my horse in an arena, I usually do so from corner to corner to have the longest stretch of ground possible. However, the object of this exercise is to blast your horse at top speed and ask him to stop at the very last minute (second) and without scotching or preparing to stop too soon. There's a tiny fraction of a second between performing this exercise in a way that will benefit you, or not. It's critical to feel for the difference, both *while* performing the exercise, *and* in your runs. Pay attention to how it relates!

This exercise also requires advanced education and responsiveness. Although I might use obstacles initially to help teach a young horse to stop, I don't recommend "fencing" a horse that doesn't already have a great stop *without* a barrier in front of them. Another few prerequisites are that the horse already stops well and with quality form in response to voice, seat/energy, *and* rein cues (See Exercise 15 – Brake It Down).

Otherwise, pushing a horse with minimal education or poor form toward a wall or fence can be dangerous, and will only confirm bad habits (always use a safe, solid fence), which is not conducive to high level performance *or* soundness. If a horse hasn't been taught to think and respond, you can't trust that they won't go *into* or *over* a physical barrier. If a horse bounces roughly in their stops at moderate speed, it's only likely to be worse and more damaging at higher speeds. This is an advanced exercise and preparation is necessary to gain benefit.

The idea is to sprint your horse from each of the four center points of the arena fences/walls to the next, to make a diamond shape. You'll do this just one sprint at a time; not in rapid succession, but in a way that allows your horse a chance to soak at each fence. Then roll back to the outside a 3/4 turn on the short sides of the arena, and a ¼ turn to the inside on the long sides, then straighten out to blast off again.

The goal is for your horse to impeccably respond to you, specifically when it comes to the precise split second you ask him to stop, rather than let the fence dictate this moment. You'll likely feel your horse prepare to stop just a hair early, and if that's the case encourage your horse forward. The degree to which your horse's timing and syncing with the fence vs. you will be *very* subtle. You must be keenly aware and quick to encourage your horse that extra step before they dribble forward and end up at the wall anyway.

I believe approaching the fence at a 45-degree angle rather than going straight toward it, takes some pressure off for the horse, making it less intimidating, physically easier and therefore less stressful for their body as well. It's as if there's a bit of an escape route, like a "runaway truck ramp" and this angle rarely results in a horse panicking or cramming and jamming into the ground on their front end.

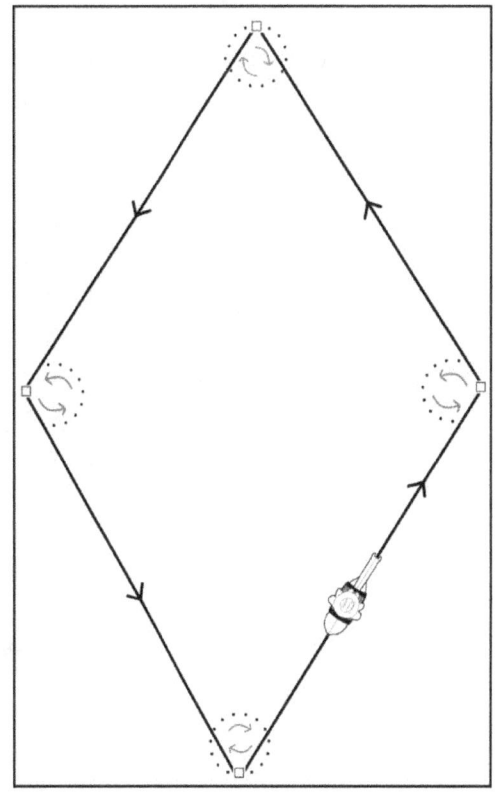

Keep repeating until your horse can go outside his comfort zone and listen to what you are asking instead of over-responding to the environment (fence). Allow him a rest reward in proportion to how well he performed, and sprint again from center point to center point at approximately a 45-degree angle. This exercise is fast and requires excellent timing on both parts. Chances are good you'll find that *you* have been safetying up and prepping to stop or turn too soon as well! If so, examine your runs and make sure you don't sit or go to the horn early: but keep hustling with your *eyes up* and save the rate for the very last moment. When this is going exceptionally well, set up a barrel positioned similarly to how and where your second barrel would be on the pattern. Plan out a portion of your diamond so that after fencing at the center point of the long side of the arena, you roll back and hustle to the second barrel – this time with no anticipation.

Exercise 25 – Stop the Drop

Description

All the importance and over-exaggeration we place on flexion and bend in our horses is something done in an effort to counteract the tendency for barrel horses to get stiff, resistant and/or "inside out" (shaped with their bodies in the opposite curve of the barrel) and drop in to their circles and turns. Most horses don't voluntarily curl around a barrel like a snake. In fact, for most horses, that extreme style of turning isn't just awkward, it's unnatural and darn near impossible. Even after all the focus spent on getting shape and bend, in a turn most horse's bodies are relatively straight with the hindquarters actually a hair to the outside. Even though this is our end reality, if we don't teach, instill and emphasize the bend, shape, flexion and suppleness through the body, we can risk losing the hindquarters too far to the outside, among the other problems I listed above. One reason I stress quality movement in general is that getting a horse balanced and collected helps keep them "under themselves" and less likely to drop their shoulder, tip a barrel, slip, fall down, have ground trouble, or disengage their hind end.

Purpose

A horse that is truly straight, aligned, balanced and forward cannot physically also lean excessively to one side or on his forehand. In fact, straightness can be described as the balance of weight on all four quarters in relation to the ground, not just the absence of flexion. The problem with excessive or improper flexion is that it causes our horses to carry their weight unevenly. And while it's a necessary part of the bigger picture, it's just a part. True straightness, something that few of us achieve and practice with our horses, is probably even more important. When a horse dives into a turn for example, and is too straight or stiff with resistance through his body, there is actually a lack of balance body contributing to this, that many mistake for a lack of bend. So just as important as moving with a proper forward, subtle arc – is teaching our horses to move perfectly straight. Seems simple enough, but how straight is *your straight?*

This is where we have to increase our awareness, pay close attention, and ask, is our horse drifting off the path we're asking them to go? Are their shoulders, rib cage or hips leading, leaning, bulging, bumping and/or falling out – even subtly? My first challenge for you is to trot from point to point and really feel just how straight and forward your horse is, meaning aligned nose to tail and balanced on all four quadrants. Straight should be like our horse's "neutral." Like a truck that's properly aligned, it shouldn't veer off when we take our hands "off the wheel." Balanced impulsion and quality forward movement plays a big part in determining how straight our horse will be. Teaching a horse to travel straight (and stay straight) is every bit as important as traveling with and maintaining bend, and is a critical part of putting a stop to the "dropped shoulder" for good! Essentially, straightness is what centers the hindquarters under our horses, giving athletic maneuvers (and turns) ultimate power and speed.

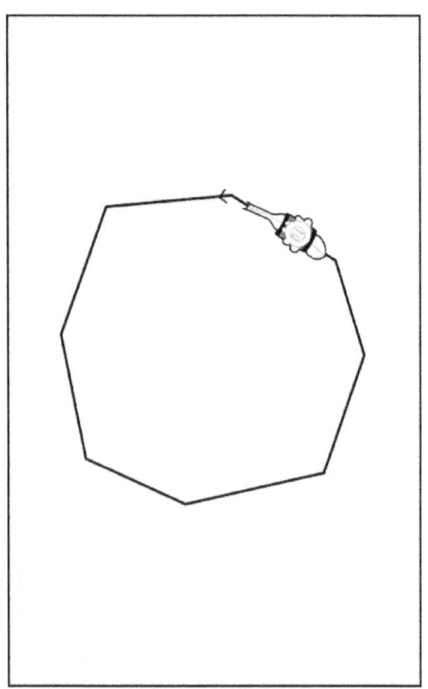

How-to

Stop Sign – The best place to start "stopping the drop" in the turns is to correct its occurrence in our circles. If a horse leans into a circle, instead of picking him up by crossing the inside rein over his neck or counter arcing, "stand up" the horse by instantly hustling him off in a straight line away from the direction he is falling in (or even the opposite direction in extreme cases). Essentially, you'll be making a stop sign shape by angling off at any point where your horse wants to fall in the circle or drop their shoulder repeatedly. It should be more work to drop in and hustle away repeatedly then it is to just maintain balance on the circle. The degree of the angle you hustle off in is based on how extremely the horse is leaning (your circle might not look anything like a stop sign at first). This is effective because a horse's feet (and therefore his body) simply goes where he is *thinking about* going.

If a horse is thinking about anticipating the circle getting smaller, it's inevitable that his body will follow by dropping and/or getting heavy on the front end. We can do the work of "picking up the shoulder" *for them*, but then they tend to fall right back in. We can get even more firm, but this often only makes horses defensive, resentful or even fearful, anxious and tense. The key is getting the horse to stop *thinking* about dropping in to begin with. By using the "stop sign" exercise the split second they lean, we're changing the subject and therefore changing how the weight is balanced over their feet. We're taking away the over anticipation by changing the subject, and thus changing their body and their tendency to lean in.

Breakaway for Lift – Next we'll take this concept to the pattern itself. This is an especially fast and effective way to correct a horse that has become very habituated and committed to dropping hard and low into the turns, which is likely to be a habit at its most extreme at the second barrel. Again, consider whether this is something you want to practice at all the barrels or not (the diagram shows the first barrel). Chances are good that an extreme "dropper" will be doing so to at least some degree in all three turns. Approach the first barrel to start your slow work as usual, and at your rate point, or at any point you feel your horse lower or drop or anticipate the turn, lift up your reins, roll back on your horse's hind quarters and hustle back to your starting point. The goal is to make it an extreme roll around right back over the path you started. If your horse is already over-ratey (not all horses that drop hard are also rating hard) you may want to implement Exercise 22 – Lollipop, which includes circling around the barrel, which helps the horse to stay more free and forward. This exercise is likely to add even more rate, but most of all will help your horse learn to prepare for the turns without dumping excess weight to the inside front.

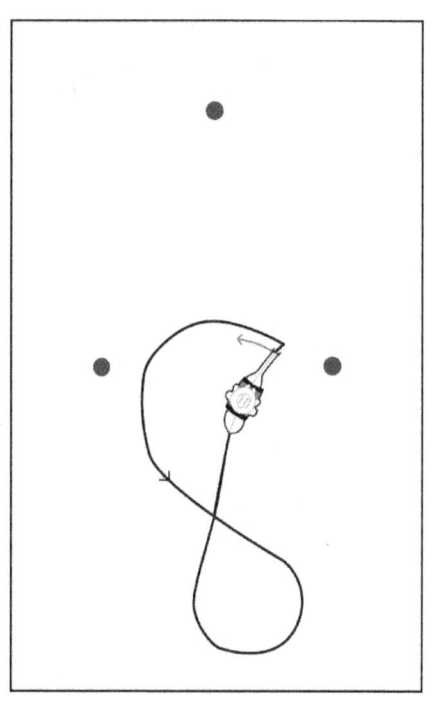

Start again to the first barrel, only continuing to the second once you no longer feel that drop. If you do feel it, keep repeating as necessary (you may need to spend several sessions on one barrel). At the other barrels, roll back, hustle off and circle the previous barrel to approach again. Again, until you no longer feel that drop, keep repeating the lifting up and rolling back around until your horse stops making assumptions. Continue going back and forth as needed, only allowing your horse the comfort of moving on once you feel a significant improvement.

> *When we listen to our horses,
> we get an education.
> When we don't, we get experience.*
>
> – Mark Rashid

Thriving at Third

Outside of utilizing specific exercises for cleaning up the third barrel, I'll take the opportunity as I introduce this chapter to first cover the common causes of problems that are often resolved, starting with our awareness vs. an actual exercise, or a combination thereof.

Considering it's such a straight shot in and out of the third barrel, for many barrel racers and their horses it's the easiest turn. One particular issue I've seen and experienced at the third barrel, however, is that the horse will sometimes seem rough through the turn, or experience a hang-up or delay on the backside. The change of direction itself takes place over a distance that's actually shorter than the length of a small horse. So it's understandable that some challenges come up as we ask our horses to quickly and smoothly wrap their bodies around the third barrel. This requires us to be very particular and purposeful about how we teach our horses to position themselves, which will be different than at the first and second barrels.

It's also not uncommon for horses to leave the third barrel too wide and not make a straight shot home. At this point you might guess that correcting this would involve over-finishing the turn, starting in slow work. This seems like a simple enough fix, but if it was that simple, one would have to wonder why so many folks still struggle with coming out wide. I believe there are a few reasons for this. One is that the rider isn't looking and riding *actively* around that turn. When this occurs, it almost appears as if rigor mortis has set in; our upper body stiffens up and is frozen in place looking, at the side fence. When this happens, it's no wonder a horse veers off. Again, I believe this happens in part because the turn just happens faster and over a shorter distance than the first two barrels. The third barrel is the quickest of all the turns, so we *almost* need to be looking toward home as we start the turn, instead of waiting for the turn to come to us, and riding very actively and athletically vs. passively.

It's also important to understand that our horse may need to utilize his hindquarters in a way that varies slightly from the other turns. It's ideal for them to slide a little through this one, considering there's hardly enough real estate to *run around* it. A horse who *runs* around the third barrel without the appropriate ratio of weight on the hindquarters is likely to feel rough and jerky with potential for a delay or hang-up, and is even more likely to come out wide. Also, just as with any barrel, if some aspect of positioning in the approach to the barrel is off, the back side of the turn will certainly be affected as well.

If we want our horses to sink down and use their inside hind leg, elevate the front end and get around this quick turn with one smooth "whoosh" move, it's critical that we also consider where we're putting our weight in the stirrups, and that we're not stepping excess weight into one side or the other. When a barrel racer's "style" includes holding their rein hand far out away from the body, it's tempting to also put more weight in the outside stirrup to counter-balance. However, when our weight is more even in the stirrups, it enables us to keep our hand, elbow and arm a little tighter and closer to our body for even more intimate communication. Keeping everything intimate and close translates, I believe, to our horse, meaning they're likely to stay more gathered up and engaged in their own body, when we are in ours. This is ideal, especially at the third barrel, where there just isn't much room to do more than quickly slide in and out in one smooth, easy (and hopefully fast) motion!

When it comes to thriving at the third – your plan should always include riding intentionally, developing proper biomechanics and awareness of rider position, and understanding how it all relates to your horse.

Exercise 26 – Figure 8 to Finish

Description

When a horse exits a turn too wide, it doesn't always have so much to do with their training as it does their soundness and emotional fitness. Sometimes a horse who is mentally checked out and just not *thinking* about the pattern can be manhandled through the beginning of the turn; but the power behind their resistance draws them off track at the exit. In these situations, it's not that they don't know the pattern, but that their emotional state is preventing them from cooperating and offering what they *do* know. It's also important that we don't underestimate the role physical soundness plays when it comes to finishing the turns tight, and pushing off straight and powerful as well. I've said before, that a horse doesn't have to be lame to have a soundness issue that greatly impacts their performance. They may only actually experience discomfort in a run itself, and not necessarily show obvious signs. Hind end soreness in the hocks and stifles is not uncommon, and in my own experience I've realized that ulcers can inhibit a horse from gathering up to turn and finish tight as well. As with any exercise, it's never about *making* a horse do what we want, but *causing* what we want to be the easiest, most obvious and appealing option. It's our responsibility to remove the reasons *why* our horses don't want to finish the turn tightly before we put our full focus on re-educating the horse to fill in these gaps.

Purpose

Figure eights are a staple in the program of most barrel racers, and for good reason. After all, our horses must have the ability to athletically and quickly (but very subtly) change the arc through their body and also the percentage of weight carried over their four quadrants. It doesn't take long, for example, to see the negative effects of a horse who carries the same arc from the first barrel all the way to the second. When the ribs aren't subtly flexed in the correct direction this usually translates into a horse that prepares for the turn too soon with a "dropped shoulder," often resulting in a tipped barrel. While we'll actually keep the same shape through the body from the second to the third (because they're both turned in the same direction) we're going to utilize the figure eight in this exercise for the purpose of emphasizing a tight finish after the third barrel, which is a strategy that can be applied to any other barrel as well.

How-to

To correct a wide exit on the third barrel, come around the backside as usual, but then over-turn the barrel keeping the same arc until you cross over the approximate area of your original rate point. Then switch the arc in the horse's body to make a circle in the other direction, approximately 10-15 feet in diameter, slightly

larger than the barrel turn itself. Cross over that point again, and switch the arc in your horse's body to go back around the barrel again, and again go over your rate point and switch the direction of bend to make another figure eight. Repeat up to three times or until your circles are smooth and forward, and then exit the turn and finish the pattern by swerving over and heading to the fence.

Most important is *how* you perform this exercise. If a horse tends to blow straight out to the side from the third barrel in a run, use version A. in the diagram at right. If your horse tends to bow out more so on the way home, use version B. This exercise is valuable at a trot and will be most beneficial at a lope, but as with most exercises, can be started at a walk. When your horse performs well going slow, transition upward in gait. Pay attention to your own body position so it's correct, especially as you come around the back side of the barrel. It's critical to keep dynamic forward motion. Keep your eyes up and shoulders back. Focus on maintaining a consistent position and an even energy level in your body so that your horse doesn't react to you, thus causing any kind of "hiccup." Again, we're training this turn to be *smooth and fluid* as we go!

After implementing this exercise for, say, three sessions in a row one week, consider adding a rest point (C.) the following week in the spot where you want your horse to *think about* going (opposite of the direction that leads him to blowing out of the third barrel). You can either stop after the barrel, off to the side of the barrel, or just make a habit of moving toward the fence after you complete each third barrel turn. Wherever you give your horse comfort (in the form of a rest break), they will be drawn to.

It's possible to over-do this exercise and actually teach your horse to veer off the other way, so proceed with caution. Test your horse by using little to no direction with the reins so he can *show you* what he knows and where he understands he should be. I have found that when things are feeling good at home it usually means I need to do a little more for the correction to hold up in competition. The ultimate test will be the next time you enter, which will tell you how much more of the exercise is needed and what version. You might not need to use the figure eights anymore, but you might always make a point on certain horses to rarely head straight home from the third barrel in your slow work, but always to the fence, or to (at minimum) change the arc in your horse's body and over-finish the turn slightly as you head for home.

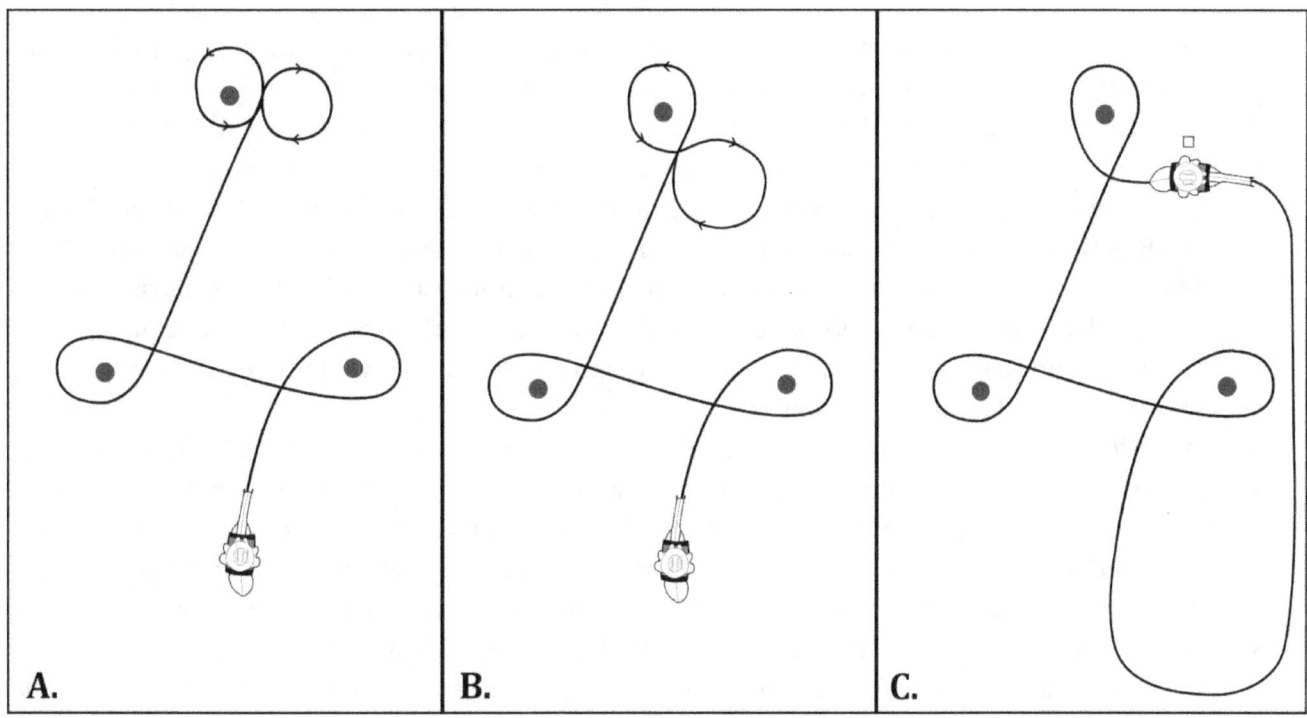

A.   B.   C.

Exercise 27 – Specific Circles

Description
It bears repeating that the quality of our horse's circles at slow speeds is directly connected to the quality of their circles around a barrel in a run at high speed. To prepare our horses to perform their best, we have to intimately know what a quality circle *feels like* and *how* to develop it, starting at a walk, trot, lope and then through a turn. This is another place where the idea of "it's not what you do, but HOW" certainly applies!

Purpose
In Exercise 22 – Perfect Circles in *The First 51*, I shared seven elements that make up quality circles. As a review, I want to include a summary of these elements below as a starting point. They are the foundation – the necessary elements and prerequisites for the "Specific Circles" exercise.

How-to
Circling is one thing, but circling *with quality* and all the elements below is another thing completely! Work toward having a perfect combination of these characteristics and you'll be well on your way to creating the fastest turns your horse is capable of.

1. **Connection** – Is your horse focused, willing, and responsive; in other words – mentally connected?
- If not, why? Can you interrupt the distracted behavior to bring your horse's attention back to you quickly and repeatedly as necessary, then reward him for the mental state you want? How's your leadership? When you have your horse's mental connection *first*, the body will easily follow.
2. **Freedom** – Does your horse easily reach, stretch and extend his stride with flexibility and fluidity?
- If not, where are the restrictions? Is it mental or physical tension, or both? Is it a soundness issue? A dentistry issue? Are you leaning or looking down, or stepping to one side in the saddle? Is it a saddle fit problem, sore feet, sore hocks? Tension due to anxiety? What's in the way of freedom?
3. **Impulsion** – Is your horse emotionally balanced with an equal amount of "go" and "whoa?"
- If not, refresh your horse on the understanding that they are to match your energy and that leg pressure doesn't always mean go, but is also for communication (your legs mean go based on your body posture & energy). Return to relaxation between speed work to improve your "neutral" gear.
4. **Precision** – Can your horse circle perfectly, and accept correction instantly without resistance?
- If not, brush up on control and responsiveness by giving yourself a visual circular line to follow (marked with flour). Direct your horse with your focus, and when or if he gets off track, quickly use your legs to get his nose then body back on track, then release pressure. Practice makes perfect!
5. **Flexion** – Can your horse *maintain* a circle, with subtle lateral nose-to-tail flexion through his body?
- If not, refine your horse's response to your leg by first moving the front end, the hind end and the ribs over, then teach him to yield the ribs only to the outside while traveling a forward circle. In the end we must combine all these elements. Develop and improve flexion alone first then ask for more.
6. **Collection & Balance** – Can your horse circle balanced, with his hind end engaged without leaning?
- If not, sit up in the saddle, put your shoulders back, lift up your eyes, and sit deep in the back of your seat. Look further up ahead on your circle, and ensure your weight is balanced. Drive with *your* "hind end;" encouraging connection to your body language, to shorten and lengthen stride.
7. **Independence** – Even if you put slack in the reins, can your horse continue loping a perfect circle?
- Does your horse have the ability to maintain all of the above with little to no help or holding from you? This is advanced, so it's something to work toward. Keep improving each element, combine

them, then expect your horse to maintain. Help as necessary by going back and forth with pressure and release to make it easier and more appealing for him to take responsibility for these qualities.

Once the prerequisites are met, take your circling to another level by putting these qualities to the test. Get the most out of this exercise by first setting up one single barrel, then marking your "perfect circles" on the ground with flour - a larger 20 foot circle around the barrel and a 10 foot circle inside that. The goal is to first walk, trot and eventually lope one and a half times on the larger circle path, one and a half revolutions on the small circle, then back on the larger circle, making three (and a half) perfect repetitions around the barrel with the flour as your guide. The idea is to make the first and last circle a little bigger and therefore easier. If your horse struggles with the smaller circles, it may be that he's not quite strong or coordinated enough to perform them well yet. If that's the case, spend more time perfecting the larger circles, making sure to offer plenty of well-timed rest breaks. Quality is always better than quantity when teaching your horses good habits and form.

As you move in and out between circle sizes, avoid allowing your horse to lead with his nose. Use your focus, body language and leg, if necessary, to move your horse's whole body in and out vs. leading with the front end only (see that my transition lines in the diagram are almost square). Remember to keep your shoulders back, eyes up, seat deep and weight balanced. Focus on where you're going, and peripherally pay attention to where your horse's feet are landing, without looking down in front of you or to the inside if possible. When you're ready to make this more advanced, set up the entire pattern and mark the same flour circles around each barrel. Then go through the pattern itself, or in an "all right" or "all left" configuration. Start each series with one larger circle, performing it not more than once if done well or more if necessary until it's correct, and then wind down to the smaller circle, and then back up to the larger circle. When you're ready to move on, look up and prepare to depart for the next barrel with good timing, shape and position.

This exercise is repetitive enough that's it's valuable for preventing a horse from making assumptions about leaning or dropping into a turn. It teaches them to stay responsive to what our body language is asking for. This helps a horse to differentiate how we ride in a run, an aggressive cruise-through at home, or a slower more cadenced and elevated loping exercise. You'll gain benefits at *all* barrels, but this will be especially helpful for smoothing out the third barrel where horses tend to get bound up, causing a delay. When you have all these elements in place and practice them with quality – tight, fluid, fast turns are the result!

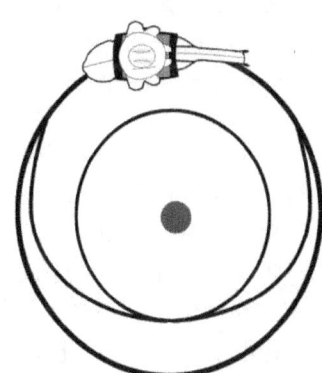

Exercise 28 – Double Barrel

Description

If you ask several seasoned barrel horse trainers about how they go about instilling rate, you're likely to get a variety of answers. Some don't believe in stopping a horse before the barrel to teach rate and others that couldn't imagine developing a horse on the pattern without stopping, yet both can achieve wild success. On one hand, it makes sense that we don't want to school our horses to lose forward motion. As an example, for this reason I don't do a lot of "scoring" in the alley. While I don't want my horse to be especially anxious there, I also don't want them to associate that area with planting their feet and not moving. When it comes to instilling more rate, it's not so much the stopping or slowing down that we really want, after all – because we *don't stop* – and ideally, we don't want to have to even slow down to make the turns, so why use or practice that, right? The goal is for our horses to prepare for the turns without losing speed, or to lose as little as possible. On the other hand, there are horses with so very little natural inclination for rate that they cause us to break any preconceived rules or beliefs we may have about what is best, and do whatever we can in desperation to instill the necessary rate and hook the turns. In some cases, losing some forward momentum becomes a better option than going by the barrel. For this reason, I suggest you always approach this with an open mind, and on a horse by horse basis.

Purpose

It's my opinion that we don't *need* to stop before the barrels to teach rate, but we *must* become masters at teaching a horse to change the way they use their bodies in motion, which is fairly advanced (and covered in Exercise 20 – Run & Rate). An easier and less advanced way to teach this is, to slow down or stop at the barrel. In doing so the horse is likely to transfer some of their weight to the hindquarters. However, it's not necessarily a guarantee. A horse can stop on their front end, move with weight on their front end, and even drag themselves in a backward shuffle without rocking their weight back properly. So yet again, it's not so much what we do but *how*. As a horse prepares for the turn in the approach to the barrel, there is a gathering, a shortening or compressing taking place. The better a horse is at doing this, the less likely it is they'll be strung out in the turn or get strung out as they exit the turns (which is so common at the third barrel). In the following exercise we'll use transitions in the turn as another method for teaching and practicing "rate in motion."

How-to

IF we feel we need to utilize stopping on the pattern to educate or re-educate a horse, the first step toward determining HOW we should use downward transitions and stops most effectively starts with analyzing our current situation. For example, if I'm rehabbing a horse who not only doesn't tend to rate for the first barrel but is in the process of overcoming a lot of anxiety, and for the first time really learning to *think* and take responsibility, I might actually head to the first barrel, and stop and back up several times in the approach – each time after backing up stopping for several minutes until the horse licks and chews or takes a deep breath before going forward.

For a horse who needs a little bit of rate, I might only stop right alongside the barrel, in fact with my leg just ahead of the barrel, and if the horse doesn't have any anxiety or unbalanced emotions, I might not stop and rest there at all. To keep from inadvertently causing the horse to lose momentum, I'll also pepper in the "double barrel" exercise, meaning that at the rate point (right at the barrel, unless re-educating a horse who needs to start thinking about throttling down sooner) I'll transition downward in gait but keep moving forward. I'll then circle that barrel a second time at the same gait I came in with and when we've performed a nice smooth turn, we'll move on to the next barrel. Stopping at the barrel to instill rate sounds simple enough. But if it was easy, we'd never go by a barrel, right? Again, I really take it on a case by case basis.

As an example, it might look like this:

- Walk to rate the point, stop, walk around barrel at least two times before moving to the second barrel.
- Trot to the rate point (with or without stopping and backing up, based on the horse's needs), transition down to a walk, walk around the barrel once, trot around the barrel the second time and trot on to the second.
- Lope to the rate point (with or without stopping based on the horse's needs), transition down to a trot, trot around barrel once, transition back up to a lope for the second time and lope onto the second and repeat.

If your horse has a tendency to prepare for the second barrel turn too soon or shoulder into it, you might not do the same routine at that barrel; it all depends on your individual horse. For example, you might decide that at the second barrel you'll keep going around the turn in the same gait and only circle it once. At the third barrel, you might keep the same gait but actually circle the barrel twice. Only perform aspects of each exercise at each barrel if it's necessary based on the results you're getting in competition. Your horse will likely have slightly different needs at each barrel!

- Smoothly slowing down and/or stopping and backing up can be good for horses who are anxious and tense. The more rate you need in a run, the more stopping (with resting/relaxing) you'll do at the rate point.
- Circling twice emphasizes to the horse to "stay in the turn and finish the turn."
- Slowing down in gait then transitioning upward teaches the horse to rock their weight back for quicker, easier preparation for the turn and more power coming through and away from it.

There are many benefits to gain from performing transitions in gait, in large part because they require a horse to shift their weight to the hindquarters (see Exercise 12 - Tremendous Transitions in *The First 51*). By performing transitions on the barrel pattern, not only will your turns be much faster and more efficient, but they'll be smoother and easier to ride as well.

Exercise 29 – Straight In & Out

Description

In the introduction, I mentioned the interesting phenomenon that occurs in the approach to the third barrel – the dreaded "unintentional pocket." Making a pocket before each turn (a bubble of excess space out to the side) was once a popular and accepted technique for all horses at all the barrels. But we've realized over the years that the fastest path between two points is a straight line. Although many of us come into barrels with more room than when we leave them, this isn't necessarily what I consider a "pocket." But I have felt even young horses with little experience on the pattern seem to volunteer to make this bubble of space or "natural pocket" at the third barrel. Because it's the shortest, sharpest turn, I believe it puts a horse's body in a bit of a bind, and this may be their way of making it a little easier. It's just surprising how quickly young horses will start doing this on their own. I always try to work with my horse's style and preferences, but the fastest path is always straight line, so swooping out at the barrel isn't something I want to allow. Because this is so common though, we can be aware and nip this in the bud before it becomes a habit and correct it if it's already become one or is adding any extra, unnecessary steps.

Purpose

I have to give credit and mention a couple of pioneers and legends in the barrel racing world, Lynn and Murray McKenzie, who were the first to highlight and share the "straighter is faster" concept in great depth. Instead of taking an outdated, haphazard approach, they brought the "science of speed" as it applies to barrel racing out of the dark ages, and many barrel racers have benefitted from their contributions that left old school "pockets" in the dust.

The idea is that by allowing more room on the back side of the barrel rather than alongside of it, and starting the turn later, it allows the horse to slingshot around a turn without losing momentum, much like a ball bouncing off a wall. This doesn't necessarily help barrel horses turn faster, but helps them clock faster by changing the turn. So although the horse might be covering more real estate; remember a barrel race isn't won by how much ground is covered, but by how *fast* it's covered. For example, through their years of timing barrel races with Shane and Lanette Pritchard's Tanner Time System, a timing machine that breaks a barrel pattern into several measured segments for comparison, they even found that if a horse does bow out of a third barrel, that it's faster just to roll with it in a run vs. attempt to correct the horse, which often slows them down. If this is happening, it may be because we're cramming them into a turn that is physically difficult for them. Performing this exercise is great for correcting and preventing the pre-third barrel swooping pocket and can help free a horse from the bunchy, binding position they take on in a traditional third barrel turn, which can also cause a horse to scramble for their footing. Once you feel the "rebound effect" of a straighter, longer turn you'll experience just how freeing, powerful and fast it really is!

Coming into the third barrel with a swoop or coming out of it wide can both often be resolved by simply giving the horse more room on the back side of the turn – by allowing them to go in deeper. This allows the horse to turn without binding up and creating restrictions in the body that lead to delays and poor position going in or out. The following exercise is also great for reiterating straightness in and out of every turn, and especially for freeing up a horse that wants to anticipate, drop in and turn too soon. As you've learned, straighter is faster at every barrel, and even if we're not having an "excess pocket problem" – the straighter we are, the faster we can be!

How-to

The Straight In and Out exercise can be done on a circular pattern of cones or barrels, or on the barrel pattern itself. The idea is that you'll approach each "turn" the same distance from the barrel or cone as you would on the pattern (with two hands on the reins, encouraging your horse to stay very straight), but then go by each cone or barrel at least far enough to catch your horse off guard and change his focus, interrupting his assumptions, and causing him to think and check back in with you. Then you'll make a half circle to come back and head off in another direction for the next barrel or cone. Be sure to stay off the barrels coming in and going out (don't cut in too close to them), so that when you make the sharp corner to turn it's not too abrupt and will still allow for hind end engagement and lateral roundness in your horse's body.

This exercise will certainly benefit a horse that wants to make an extreme pocket and also one that wants to take over and dive into the turns extremely, and is taking their responsibility to "own" the pattern a little too seriously! This would not be an ideal exercise for a horse who already tends to go by barrels, but is good for correcting a horse that cuts in too close, makes an unnecessary large pocket, or exits a turn wide.

Giving your horse the benefit of the doubt when using this exercise to make a correction might mean performing whatever version you're doing at a trot before graduating to a lope. If your horse dives in at a lope, simply line your horse out, keep a strong forward focus and perhaps taken him even further past the cone or barrel and a little faster to really unhook him mentally. As always, do your best to stay even and balanced in the stirrups, with your eyes up, shoulders elevated and lower back round.

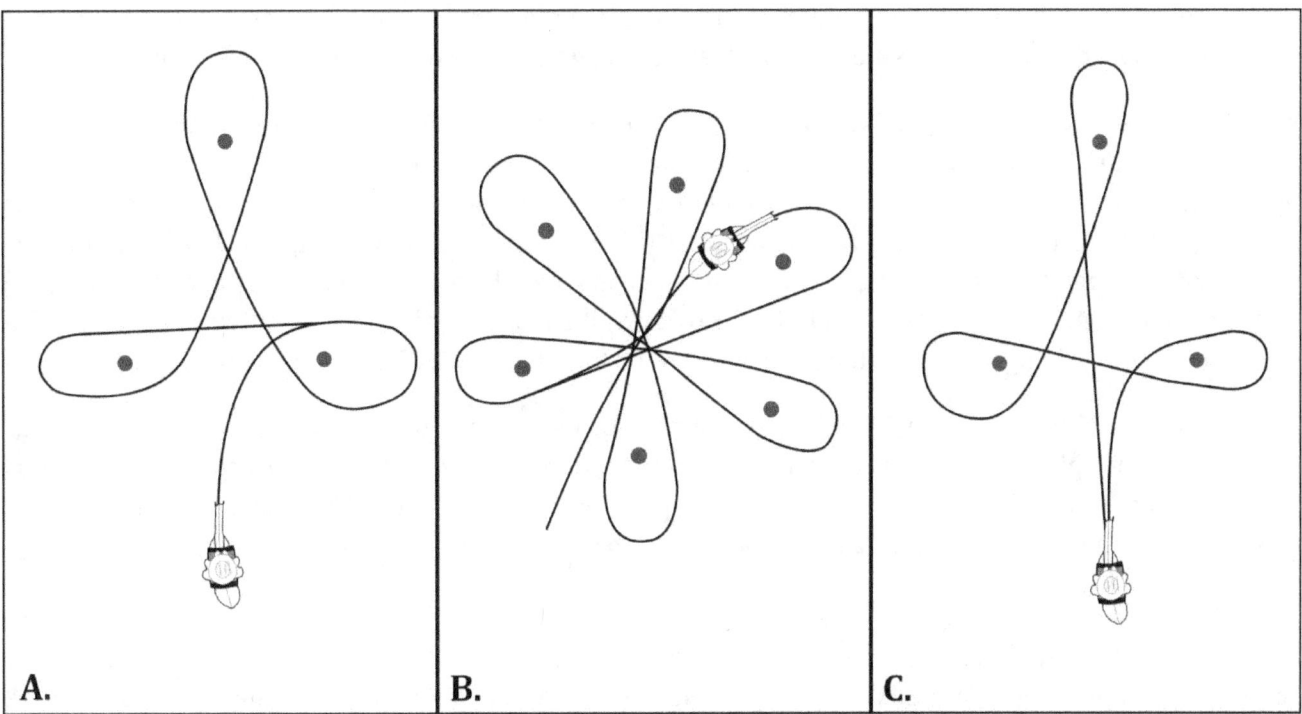

Exercise 30 – Reverse Counter Arc

Description
When a horse veers off from the path we ask him to go, it's important to sit back and consider *why*. It's easy to see why barrel horses develop the tendency to over-anticipate and drop into the turns. But correcting a horse that elevates up or pulls out and away from a turn is another thing entirely. Of course, we know that if a horse's positioning isn't correct in the approach, that they will be more likely to come out wide. A horse that turns too soon or too tight is just doing what we have taught them in excess. When they head the other direction however, they are doing the opposite of what we have taught, and this is great reason for concern.

Purpose
We train our horses to stay between our reins and legs, and expect them to do so without constantly bumping into these boundaries by making it comfortable to do so, and uncomfortable not to. When we've done our part, there are several reasons why a horse might want to oppose what we're asking and veer off in the opposite direction as what we have directed them on the pattern. Here are a few that come to mind:

- The horse simply doesn't have a good foundation. They don't firmly understand they are to follow our focus and go where we point them until we ask for a direction or gait change.
- The horse isn't emotionally fit. They're distracted, tense, anxious, distraught and not prepared yet for the sensory overload and pressure at a barrel race. Scattered mind = scattered body.
- They don't respect and trust their rider and veer off in a desperate attempt to find safety and certainty, which in their mind is likely at the trailer or the holding/warmup pen with other horses.
- Our training techniques and *way of being* with our horses have soured their attitude so much that they have a negative association with the barrels and with learning, so they attempt to check out.
- They have experienced pain or emotional trauma on the pattern and are motivated to avoid it at all costs, sometimes resulting in balking at the gate, refusing the turn or running up the wall.
- There's a physical problem occurring, such as discomfort from stomach ulcers, joint pain, muscle soreness, damaged soft tissues, sore feet, etc. causing the horse to display behavior problems.

As you can imagine, using an exercise to correct the problem in footfall and body shape on the pattern isn't going to cure any of these root causes. It's not enough to *make* a horse stay on the pattern; we have to figure out and remove every reason they have *not to*, and ask "What does he want to get away from?" and most importantly, *"Why?"* In the rare instance that this has occurred long enough for the horse to have developed a learned habit of floating out of the turns, even when the original reason has been resolved, the Reverse Counter Arc can provide a resolution. However, it should only be used when we're certain we've removed any underlying reason the horse might have for their body to drift out of the turns.

In Exercise 39 – Counter Arc in *The First 51*, I shared three versions of the counter arc that are just as effective for "stopping the drop" as they are for freeing a horse up that wants to turn too soon, including versions to add rate and improve shape/flexion and position. I also introduced the concept of the "Reverse, Reverse Arc," but below I have gone a few steps further to share advanced options.

How-to
If a horse has a habit of coming off a barrel wide or stepping out away from the turn, ask for a "reverse counter arc" in the spot where this tends to happen. Even better, be more aware in the horse's slow work

and catch him in the act to make the correction once you feel them get in a similar, but much less exaggerated position (as compared to a run). Do this by asking their ribs to yield toward the barrel, with the nose and hip to the outside. We consider this a "reverse counter arc," because the flexion in the body is the opposite of what we typically ask for, with the horse's nose and hips toward the barrel, the ribs flexed out and the feet moving out and away from the turn. Again, be aware of the subtleties of your horse's behavior and position going slow, it often reveals the truth behind why they are stepping out to begin with.

As with any other exercise, use more repetition than it seems is necessary in your slow work at home. Keep in mind that your horse is likely to default to old habits in a high speed run. The new footfall and posture must be very ingrained to hold up when speed is added again. When it doubt, do a little more than you feel is needed before putting it to the test by gradually adding speed and correcting as you go.

The counter arc is a way of performing an exaggeration of what we want more of on the pattern. This can be utilized at any point on the pattern where the horse is coming out away from the barrel, such as when you finish the second barrel (A.) and in the approach to the third (B.). You might also consider counter cantering around the barrels, if your horse is able to hold it through the turns. Remember, we exaggerate to teach something new and refine as we advance. As long as this isn't overdone, there should be little risk of your horse actually learning to get off track or out of position in a run.

When it comes to fixing problems, it's important to not allow frustrations and emotions get the best of us in the barrel pen. Changing a habit is hard enough for a horse without experiencing feelings of fear or anticipation about doing the right thing, especially considering there may have been some physical discomfort or emotional tension and anxiety that contributed to the creation of the habit we're correcting. When you condition yourself to see possibility instead of limitation, accept responsibility instead of placing blame, get curious instead of forceful, commit to learning, release judgment, and then take appropriate action, you'll be amazed by the transformations experienced in both yourself and your horse. I can assure you that your horse wants to do the right thing; it's no one's responsibility but yours to clearly communicate *what that is*. Horses are wonderfully honest and patient in helping us understand this.

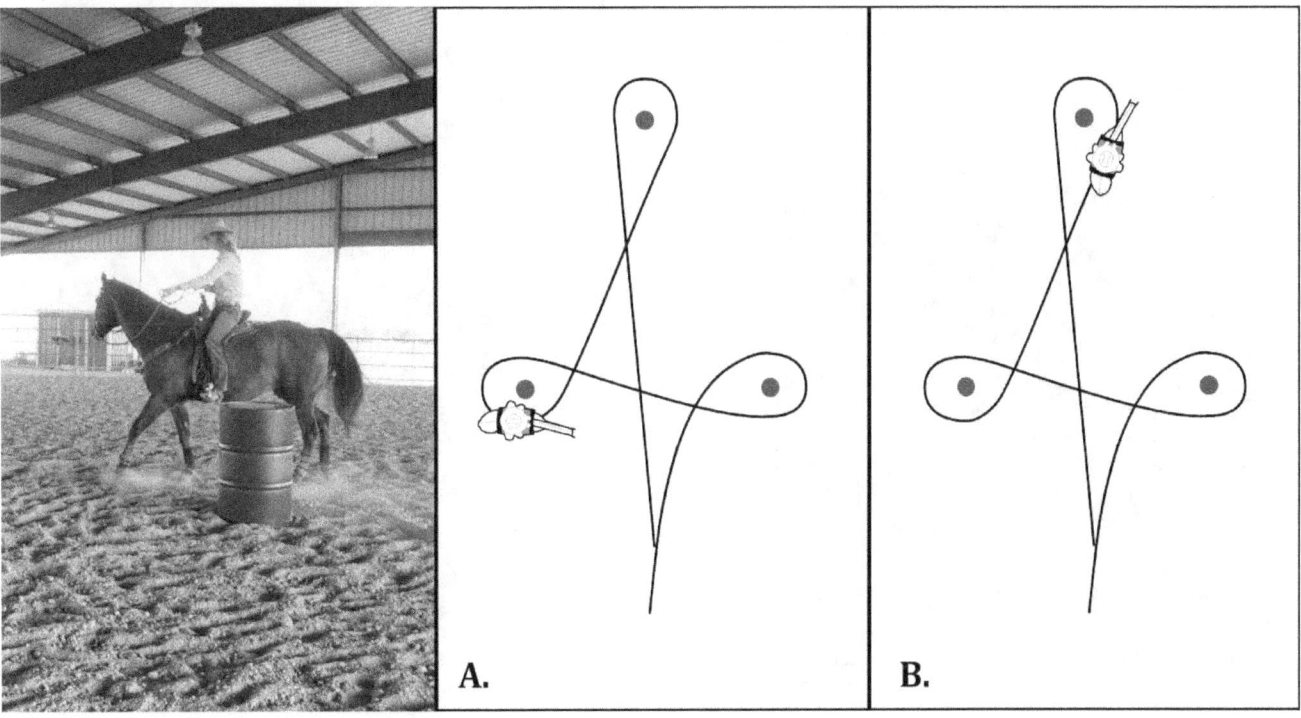

A. B.

Do This, Not That

Below I've shared images of what we commonly see (and do) as barrel racers, without realizing these habits are getting in the way of our success on the pattern, and have included visuals for better options!

Lightness, vertical flexion at the poll, and good position of the head and neck is important...

...but be sure to combine it with strong, balanced, forward movement (not lethargic schlepping).

Good posture & weight balance in the saddle and a forward focus is key for combining a subtle nose-to-tail bend, with softness, lightness AND power.

Even with a powerful stride – looking down or leaning, plus emotional tension or excess flexion, can cause a horse to be heavy on the forehand.

Even, upright weight balance on all four quadrants, hind legs that move deep under the body, a round back and elevated shoulders are keys to power.

Downhill, strung out movement, including leaning to the inside or on the forehand, as well as inverted or hollow posture inhibits athleticism.

Engaged for Power

Most equestrian disciplines require some level of *engagement* from the horse, both physically and mentally. The challenge barrel racing presents is that it requires physical engagement through the turns, however, the majority of the pattern (when performed at speed) is spent with the horse at a gallop, with 51-70% of the horse's weight on the front end; or in other words, *not* engaged. In many cases, horses are also practicing *mental* DISengagement while they're running. Combined with a horse's understandably natural tendency to remain "front endy" as they prepare for the turns, creating, developing and maintaining quality, balanced, powerful, fast and appropriately engaged movement is a continuous challenge. To introduce this chapter, I want to take the opportunity to further define and demystify terms like "collection" and "engagement." Although they're sometimes used interchangeably, successfully developing one or the other (or both) first depends on a clear understanding of their meaning.

My definition of collection is that it's simply the transfer of more weight from the forehand to the hindquarters. However, we can really consider it a complete physical, mental and emotional collection (vs. scattering) because all three must occur for authentic collection that not only heightens athleticism but is healthy and beneficial for the horse.

Engagement is the degree or depth the hind legs are moving under a horse's body, therefore changing his point of balance, which allows for even more of that weight to transfer rearwards. Engagement is required for collection, or at least it's *part of* developing it. If the horse's hind legs aren't reaching far underneath his body, you can imagine it's difficult to shift weight back. A lot of folks describe collection as a shortening of the stride, but a horse can lengthen or shorten his stride and still be collected with more weight on the hindquarters. This is actually what a barrel horse does as they prepare for the turn (shorten and transfer weight backwards) and then continue forward with as much reach possible to propel themselves through and then away from the turn.

When a horse has been carefully developed to utilize their hind legs as springs, they can come forward far enough to be used in the most powerful way to propel their heavy bodies, with more power and therefore more quickness to execute in the turns. A collected *and* engaged horse is like a crouching tiger ready to pounce, or a hover craft ready to change direction in an instant. The more we develop engagement and collection, the more athletically and quickly our horses can perform!

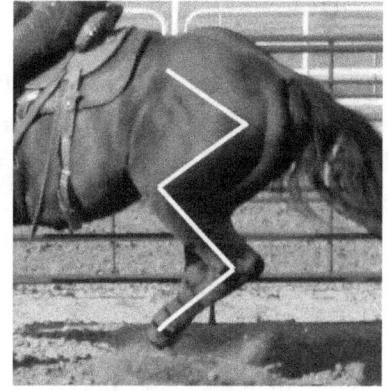

Not only that, but when our horses are using their bodies in a way that doesn't put repetitive unbalanced stress on their joints and soft tissues, they hold up better and longer. Quality movement patterns set our horses up to stay sound and enjoy careers with fewer injuries and greater longevity. Creating this opportunity for the horses we love is no accident; it must be done carefully, purposefully and with intention. I can say with confidence that even horses who manage to clock and win with poor movement patterns, could clock faster, win more and last longer with better ones – so let's get started!

Exercise 31 – Triple R

Description

Developing quality movement in horses is always an ongoing process in my program. There's a reason why some of the best horsemen in the world take several years to fully develop a horse. While this journey may seem shorter with especially gifted and elite equine athletes, there's no getting around the fact that doing it thoroughly and correctly takes time. However, there are quick and easy changes we can make to our riding that can make a world of difference in a hurry. Something as simple as pausing for a fraction of a second longer as we rise in a posted trot for example, or lifting our eyes and focusing higher or further ahead are just a couple of examples of simple things that make a big difference. As we accept what a time investment it is to develop a horse, at the same time, let's not overlook ways we can "fast forward" our progress.

Purpose

For power on the pattern we must meet several prerequisites. Refining these areas takes time, but in the long run will take *less time*. This is another area where performing the exercises alone, without the awareness and development of the preceding elements first (although the horse would show some improvement through the exercise alone) isn't going to yield nearly as many positive results. There are certain patterns when followed in a certain order that will lead your horse to success. Skip these areas and it becomes a gamble. Backing a horse, for example, will help a horse transfer more weight to the hindquarters, but the magic is in *how* the horse backs up. Let's also make sure we get the most out of the exercises in this chapter by first revisiting Exercise 16 – First Things First. After all, there's a difference between a horse that "can't" engage his hindquarters because of a physical restriction and a horse that "won't" because he lacks education. It may also be that the horse simply needs more time to develop strength and balance. By following the checklist below and giving each area the focus it requires, you'll be well on the way to creating power and strength on the pattern!

How-to

The Prerequisites

Relaxation and Connection: A relaxed, supple horse has reach. Although a worried horse will tend to "square up" his hind legs in preparation to flee if necessary, his quality of movement is poor because it's done with tension in the mind and body. Tension isn't part of what we want, because it's doesn't build strength in a healthy way. A horse that is anxious and tense will tend to raise his head, brace his body and move with a short, choppy stride, stressing their nervous system and joints, and inverting their entire topline, *preventing* the very engagement we want and need. Don't settle for defensive, tense or distracted. Make it a priority to develop a relaxed horse that is calm and confident, and willing.

Restore Relaxation: Asking a horse to bend through their ribs, disengage the hindquarters a bit or even move sideways (laterally) is very effective for interrupting emotional behavior patterns. This is because when a horse is in flight mode, their body becomes tense and rigid. When we softly ask for bend and keep redirecting their attention, it engages the horse's mind and helps the anxiety melt away. It's difficult to softly bend *and* be rigid and prepared to flee at the same time. Reward your horse with a rest break, not just when you feel a positive physical improvement, but also when you feel a change in their state of mind.

Responsibility Checklist

Responsibility for DIRECTION: Practice walking, trotting and loping from point to point. If your horse gets off track, stop and back a few steps, then rotate on the hindquarters to realign with your focal point, and start toward it again. To make the right thing easy and the wrong thing even more difficult, stop and back *briskly*, then pivot to point your horse back toward your destination. Another option is to use your legs to steer your horse's hindquarters. If your horse starts drifting to the left, use your right leg to push the hindquarters left so that the front end is once again facing the desired direction, then release. Repeat as needed, using the reins sparingly and only temporarily to block any excess forward motion.

☐ **Direction** – My horse follows *where my eyes* focus without micromanagement, and is respectful and instantly responsive to adjustments without resistance.

Responsibility for GAIT: What is *already* in motion is more likely to stay in motion. This also goes for the weight transfer from front to back; it's difficult to shift a horse's body weight when the body is not already in motion. To refine quality movement, our communication resources (seat, legs, energy, etc.) can't be tied up in keeping the horse going forward (micromanaging). Ask your horse to go once and expect them to keep going at that gait based on the energy you're riding with. If they don't maintain, remember to use the steps for teaching and reinforcing go: 1. Raise your reins and life, 2. Ask with slight leg pressure (add an optional verbal cue), then 3. Tap your leg with your hand or rein, 4. Then tap your horse's rear. Also make sure your horse can keep moving forward even with light rein contact. Just as using your leg doesn't always mean go, using the reins doesn't always mean stop; it depends on our focus, weight, seat, energy.

☐ **Gait** – My horse maintains forward motion without micromanagement with impulsion, balance and rhythm on a straight line and in large to medium sized circles.

Responsibility for SHAPE: For longitudinal shape over the topline (something there are very few resources available for in the barrel racing world) see Exercise 44 – Long & Low in *The First 51*. For improving lateral nose to tail bend, refresh your horse's response to leg cues in a side pass without holding them with your reins to block excess forward motion. When your horse's ribs, shoulders and hips can yield freely individually from a standstill, put the full body bend into action starting with a walk. Set an obstacle in the arena as a focal point to circle around or laterally move toward. With your horse traveling with soft bit contact, use your inside leg to yield the ribs to the outside while in motion. Keep the same position in your body with your focus and your leg, but loosen the bit contact and expect your horse to maintain. If he drops the bend, pick up the reins again, then put your horse back on his honor. The more he drops responsibility, the firmer you can use your aids to encourage the horse to seek the lightness and what is easy – which is to maintain bend.

☐ **Shape** – My horse understands and can maintain (at least for a few strides) three types of flexion:
- Longitudinal – Over the topline, nose to tail
- Latitudinal – Lateral bend through entire body
- Vertical – From the base of neck to poll

When your horse is **relaxed, mentally connected** and taking **responsibility** for **direction, gait** and **shape**, you're officially *prepared for more power!*

Exercise 32 – Two Track Turn

Description
Once we have the prerequisites nailed down and are able to ride our horses with beginner engagement and collection in straight lines and large circles, it's time to move toward asking for this quality movement in smaller circles, which is more challenging for horses. It requires an advanced education, higher levels of impulsion, balance and strength, and is something we develop over time. Even if you have an aged or seasoned barrel horse, it will always pay off to revisit, redevelop or maybe even develop this degree of quality movement for the first time. Regardless of a horse's style or current habits, more hind quarter engagement and collection will always result in more power, and therefore more speed on the pattern.

Purpose
Consider how a speed boat motors powerfully across a lake with its engine engaged down in the water as its front end elevates. The goal here also, is to create more weight transfer to the hindquarters and elevation in the front end in order to dissolve the tendency many barrel horses have, which is to dive excessively low on the forehand, causing their hind quarters to disengage. As this occurs, their center of gravity moves forward, losing power. In the following exercise we'll be using specific lateral positioning and bend to encourage the horse to do all of the above around a barrel with softness and suppleness.

How-to
Start by setting up one cone or barrel and marking two circles around it with flour, one ten feet in diameter and one 20 feet. After a proper warm up, begin trotting your horse in the arena along the rail or in a large, approximately 30-foot circle, with dynamic, quality, collected and engaged movement. Feel free to post to this trot to really encourage your horse to move forward powerfully, remembering to post on the correct diagonal ("rise and fall with the leg on the wall"), which helps encourage your horse's inside hind leg to reach powerfully forward. Now move into trotting a smaller, approximately 20-foot circle (not the double circle you marked - save that for later), with the objective of maintaining these qualities as you do.

Your Body Position – In the smaller circle, sit the trot instead of posting to really feel every engaged step your horse takes. Use your energy and focus and a driving, dynamic seat to really sit deep, raising it lightly with each stride to drive your horse forward in each step. Keep your shoulders back and eyes up. Keep your lower back round and your abs engaged. Keep your hands high, but not so high that it causes your horse's nose to raise excessively; test your horse's softness by making more soft contact with the reins. The goal is for your horse to mirror your position and do in their body as you do in yours. We exaggerate to teach, so don't be afraid to take your own position to extremes to help your horse get the idea.

Your Horse's Body Position – Again what we're looking for in the smaller circle is to feel more weight shifted to the hindquarters, meaning the withers and shoulders will elevate. You'll feel the forward momentum slow down slightly but at the same time feel more powerful. The movement might seem more vertical and dynamic and quite possibly totally unfamiliar, but this is what helps prevent our horses from going to the extremes that barrel racing naturally leads to, which again is leaning on the forehand with disengagement. Your horse's head might be higher than you're comfortable with, but as long as he isn't resistant when you offer contact, allow the head to be carried a little higher than you'd normally prefer as they learn to elevate their withers and shoulders. A higher head carriage is ok to a degree, as long as their neck and back isn't also tense and inverted. A horse can lose the vertical flexion at the poll because of the difficulty of maintaining the suppleness through their entire body. When you gain correct position in one place, in the early stages you often lose it somewhere else! When this happens, simply go back and forth making corrections with the goal of capturing it all at the same time – the engaged forward steps without a loss of momentum, the subtle lateral flexion through the body from nose to tail, and softness to bit contact and vertical flexion.

Now that you've practiced your position, take it all to your marked barrel or cone with the intent to use your focus and seat/leg to angle your horse's hips slightly closer to the barrel. Your horse's front legs will follow the outer track and the back legs will be angled toward the inside track while encouraging elevation in the front with weighted hindquarters – all while maintaining subtle full-body bend and softness. Remember, our horses can't be athletic and forward when they are bound up, so there should be freedom and suppleness vs. tension and resistance. This angle helps to discourage your horse from anticipating the turn around an actual barrel. It's helpful to remember that the barrel should stay "behind your leg." If your horse is leaning in and putting more weight on the front, your leg will tend to seem behind the barrel and your horse's front end closer to the barrel than the hind end.

If it doesn't feel correct, consider which elements are missing and work on those areas individually before putting them all together again. When you feel the legs coming further forward, the withers elevating, or their weight coming back, relax and offer your horse a rest or give micro releases as you go. The key is to go back and forth, rewarding for effort without fatiguing your horse so they keep trying for you.

While this exercise doesn't actually include much sideways movement, lateral yields are especially helpful for developing collection and engagement. In relation to the lateral maneuvers of the dressage world, this exercise could loosely be considered a "Haunches In On a Circle." For reference, I've included a diagram to better understand and experiment with these movements, shown from most elementary to most advanced.

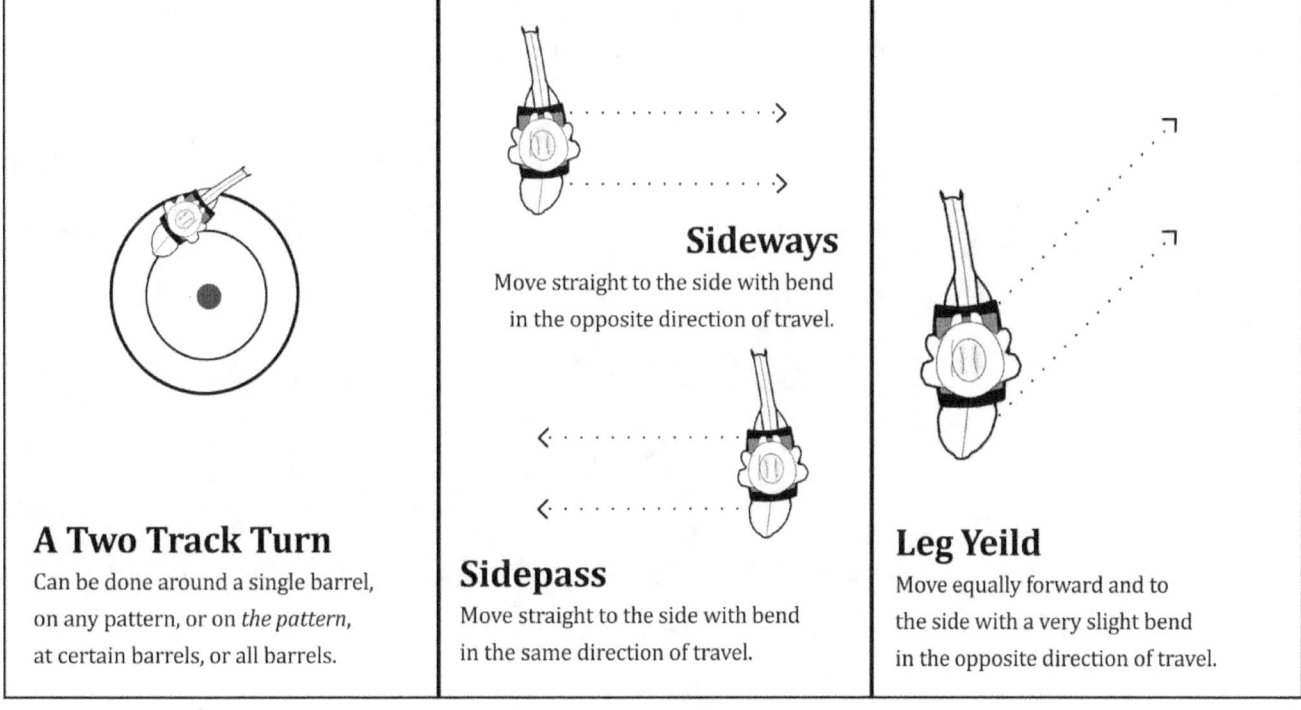

A Two Track Turn
Can be done around a single barrel, on any pattern, or on *the pattern*, at certain barrels, or all barrels.

Sideways
Move straight to the side with bend in the opposite direction of travel.

Sidepass
Move straight to the side with bend in the same direction of travel.

Leg Yeild
Move equally forward and to the side with a very slight bend in the opposite direction of travel.

Exercise 33 – Be Square

Description

Outside of the geometry world, the word "square" has additional definitions. According to Wikipedia, *"Square used as slang… is often used to speak of a person who is regarded as dull, rigidly conventional, and out of touch with current trends. In referring to a person, the word originally meant someone who was honest, traditional and loyal."* These descriptions aside, there's certainly nothing dull about the square exercise as it applies in barrel racing! First developed and shared by multiple time NFR qualifier and World Champion, Connie Combs, it's been a staple in the programs of many top barrel racers. We already know that the fastest and most powerful path between two points is a straight line. Even though there are circular turns between the straightaways, our horse's body must stay even and engaged without getting unbalanced in the four quadrants, causing a physical kink in the forward motion and subsequent delay on the pattern. The squares exercise helps develop this positioning, keeping your horses honest, loyal and successful!

Purpose

Emphasizing straightness is critical for engagement and collection, as shared in Exercise 29 – Straight In and Out. When we focus on bend too much, or practice it incorrectly without also asking our horses to move with complete straightness, we risk sacrificing power. In addition, many barrel horses that are struggling with engagement or collection aren't maintaining direction well. Before we can ask for engagement and collection, we must have responsibility for straightness (direction) on their footfall path, and before we can ask for straightness on the barrels, we should have it well established off the pattern.

Remember – *bend can bind*, so performing squares solidifies the footwork and positioning we want and need for ultimate engagement, power and speed. This exercise is especially helpful for a horse who anticipates turning, effectively teaching the horse to stand up in the turns. When the hind end is collected and engaged, the front end can't lean in and drop down, which allows a horse to stay in four wheel drive and keep pushing through the entire turn in a way that is most powerful. Practicing squares helps remind a horse to keep his feet and weight up underneath his body vs. scattered with the shoulders slinging to the inside or the hind quarters to the outside. When the back legs are following the front, everything is in balance and the hind springs are loaded, creating movement that is strong, smooth and fast!

How-to

First Things First – Let's be sure to differentiate the various ways our horse can pivot to change direction.

Coke Bottle Turn/Swapping Ends

Rearward Cow Horse Turn on Outside Hind

Forward Reining Turn on Inside Hind

In a **Coke Bottle Turn** our horse spins like a glass pop bottle laying on its side - from his center with both hind legs disengaged as he also pulls himself around with the front legs. This isn't what we want, but it's common when we haven't developed the education and feel to teach and ask our horse to isolate and yield specific parts of their body, such as sweeping the front end around while keeping the hind end stationary.

The **Rearward Cow Horse Turn** is what you'll see when a reined cow horse races down the fence and turns a cow back the other direction. In this rollback move, the weight is primarily on the outside hind leg and the weight of the horse rocks backward to propel and launch the horse off in the opposite direction.

The **Forward Reining Turn** is what you see on a reining pattern. The inside hind leg might come straight up and down off the ground, but it doesn't move all over the place or to the side extremely. It's the pivot or rotational point the horse puts his weight on while his front end steps around it in a forward motion.

A barrel horse uses both hind legs, the inside more at the start of the turn and the hind as they finish. As an experiment, see if you can turn your horse around while specifying which hind leg they pivot on. To correct a problem with leaning in the turn, focus on asking your horse to specifically weight their outside hind leg.

Below I've shared diagrams highlighting two variations of the squares exercise. Diagram A. indicates complete straightness in every step of the pattern, which is ideal for a horse that is leaning and unbalanced even between the barrels. It's likely this horse isn't rating well and might be going by barrels because their approach is so unbalanced. If that's the case, it's best to stop with the barrel at the horse's shoulder and rest for a couple of minutes before taking two steps forward then pivoting to start the turn. Feel free to place cones or soccer field markers for reference, making sure they are set as guides just inside the path where you intend to travel, which should be 3-5 feet coming into the turn and 2-3 feet leaving it depending on your horse. To perform the pivot, sit a little heavier in your seat and be sure to execute the change in direction by turning your eyes/head/shoulders as you ask your horse's front end to sweep around with your outside leg at the cinch. If your horse gets out of position, correct with your rein or leg to block any movement in the wrong direction. Use your outside leg just behind the cinch and/or outside rein as necessary to discourage disengagement or swapping ends (Coke bottling).

The other version (B.) allows for a subtle arc between barrels and is best for a horse that is struggling in the turns. For this horse (who may be rating well), stop further forward with the horse's hip at the barrel. Again, it's beneficial to stop and rest at each point. Squares can also be used instead of circles in any exercise. The key is in not allowing the horse to lean or fade into the pivots or start the square turn with their nose by leaning to the inside, but pivot with elevation in the front and engagement in the hind end.

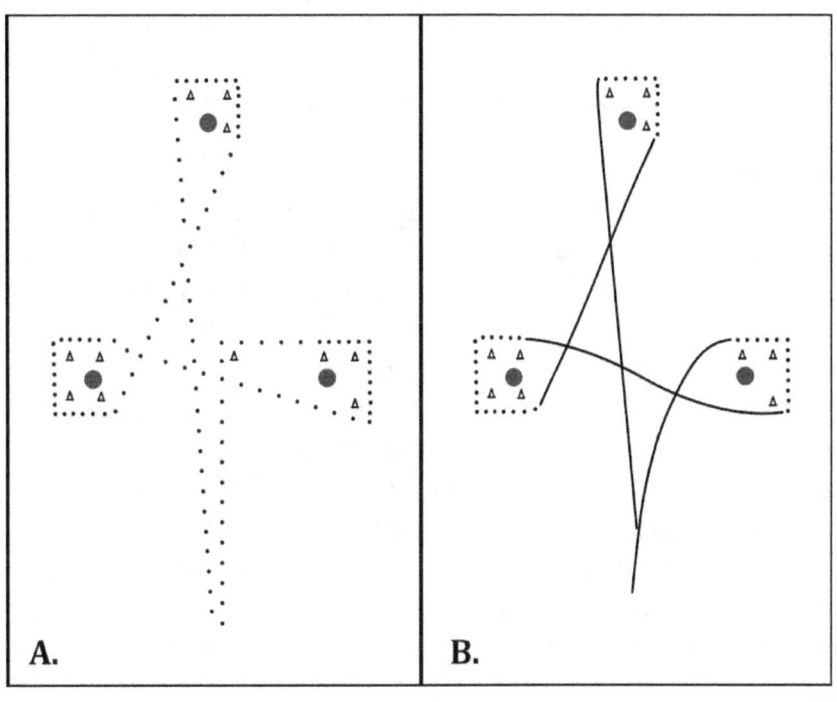

Exercise 34 – Break Off & Roll Back

Description

Speed is an amplifier. The problems that occur in a run are often problems that exist otherwise, but are just more subtle, so they go undetected and unaddressed. Typically, a horse that loses engagement in the hind end will be a horse that doesn't have a habit of traveling with great quality in general. Remember – speed and the pressure of competition puts everything under a magnifying glass, emphasizing everything! A problem that is barely noticeable will suddenly become glaringly obvious in a run. This is why it's so critical for barrel racers to understand what quality movement really is, and *how* to develop it – so there are fewer surprises! Doing so would solve many issues on the pattern, which is why I dedicated an entire chapter to the subject of quality movement in my first book, *Secrets to Barrel Racing Success*. Let's say, however, that you have very skillfully developed the quality of your horse's movement and were absolutely positive they were using themselves correctly, with impulsion, collection, flexion and all the elements that make up quality movement – and your horse STILL was not engaging his hindquarters on the barrel pattern? If that *seems* to be the case, the exercise below is right up your alley.

Purpose

If you find yourself needing to close the gap between awesome practice and lackluster barrels, you're not alone. In fact, being that I'm somewhat of a "stayer" with my horses, means that their training improves and changes as I improve and change over the years. What they initially learned on the pattern in the past, they may need to relearn and do differently! Of course, keep in mind that when operating at speed, there's not much time to consciously think things through (for the horse *or* for us), which is why it's so important to build a foundation of correct movement patterns from the get-go. It's easy for a horse to get stuck in a rut, wanting to move in a certain way on the pattern exactly like they were originally shown and have practiced. So sometimes we need to take steps to shake things up and "unhook" those old patterns, habits, associations and muscle memory in their minds and bodies. The first and best way to start rewiring the muscle memory is to first STOP allowing the incorrect movement to occur. This means not even attempting to make a run until you're confident you've solidified new, more positive habits. To do this we must create new movement patterns over the course of time, using quality repetition. I shared numerous ways to apply this concept in Exercise 38 – Close the Gap in *The First 51*, and below I've gone into greater depth for applying it on the pattern for more engagement through the turns.

How-to

Let's say that your horse uses his body really well in rollbacks but lollygags his way around the barrels somewhat disengaged. To bring qualities from one area to the other, start by placing a barrel in relation to a wall where you plan to practice roll backs. Position the barrel approximately 30 feet from the wall, then lope a circle, roll back on the wall in the opposite direction, then lope around the barrel like you would a turn – really using your posture and body to sit deep yet hustle your horse around that barrel utilizing his hindquarters just as he did in the rollback. If the turn doesn't feel good yet, again perform another rollback or two then again lope around that barrel. You should start to feel your horse moving  with more quality around the barrel, with more weight balanced in his hind end like he does in the rollback.

You can roll back to the outside, meaning you'll circle the barrel to the outside, or rollback to the inside and therefore circle the barrel to the inside, since your rollback will dictate the lead (A.).

Once that's going well, you can also set up two (or three if you have room) barrels in a row (B.) and perform an occasional rollback to let your horse know that the posture he uses on the fence is similar to what you're looking for around the barrels. By doing so, you're essentially closing the gap between the two and creating a new habit by letting your horse know that this way of moving is not just necessary in a rollback, but it applies around a barrel as well.

Don't get greedy at this point. When your horse starts making the connection, improves and performs a nice turn, be sure to stop and give him a good rest reward. Only when you can lope around a series of barrels along the fence would you go back and attempt to put it all together on the actual pattern (C.). You would only add speed to the pattern once your horse is moving with quality at a slower pace. As you do, don't hesitate to leave the barrel pattern and perform a rollback or two and then return to remind your horse that what applies on the fence, applies on the pattern as well.

The longer your horse has had a habit of using himself incorrectly, the longer it's likely to take to completely rewire this tendency. Be patient; you may even need to plan on spending at least a month or more creating the new mental association and physical muscle memory. How quickly your horse learns will depend on your ability to feel and correct the movement you don't want and then reward the movement you DO want. Either way though, quality takes time. It doesn't do any good to rush this process. If you test things out at high speed too soon, it's likely a horse will just revert to the same old habits. Only go forward when you're confident things are going well at the speed you're at.

When we understand how the brain and body develop habits, it makes total sense that it can be challenging to create completely new ways of moving at speed once movement patterns are already well established, but it CAN be done! It all goes back to knowing what quality movement is, how to develop it, preventing the bad habits from reoccurring and having the confidence and patience to create new ones.

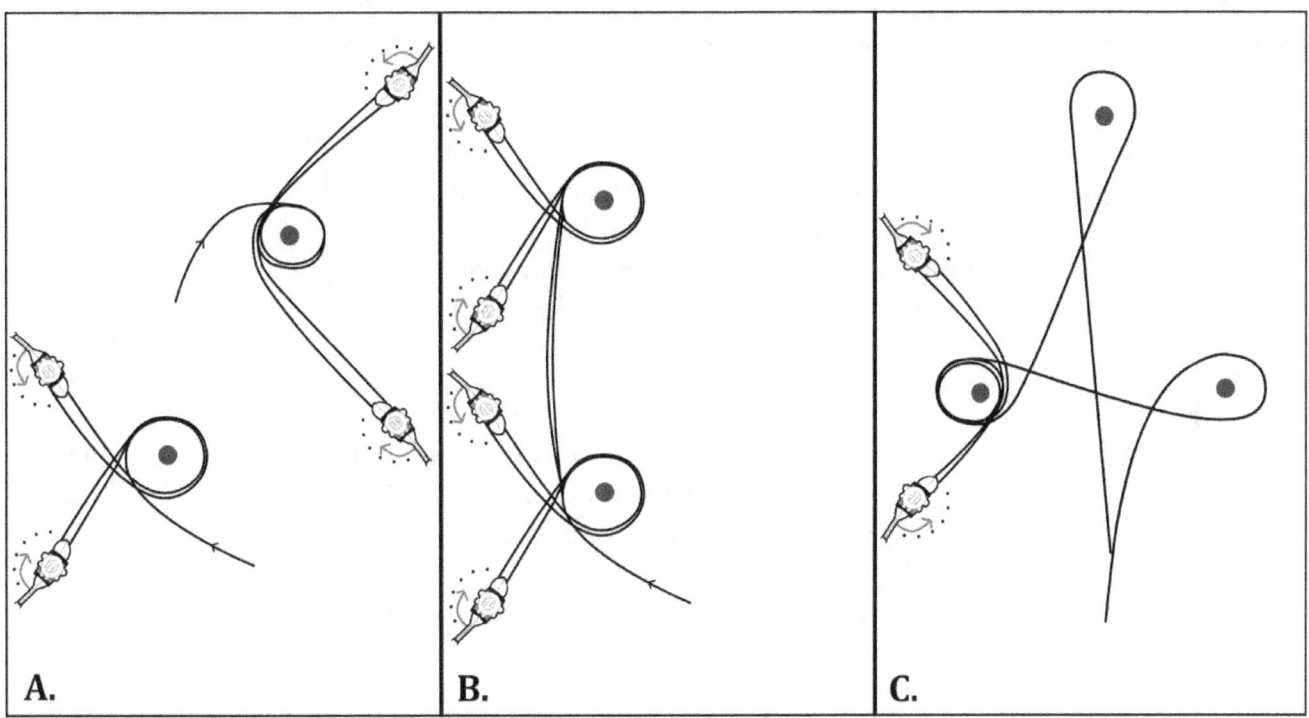

A. B. C.

Exercise 35 – Hills and Poles

Description
While it's important to remember that one of the best ways to build strength for barrel racing is to actually barrel race, or perform exercises that mimic the use of the anatomy that is used in a run (even at slower speeds), it's also beneficial to include cross training that targets *very specific* muscle groups. When it comes to developing strong hind quarters – the spring for accelerating away from the turns, there's possibly no better way than to utilize "Hills and Poles." I'm grouping these exercises together because not everyone has hills, but working over ground poles offers similar positive results.

Purpose
There are many benefits that come from hill and pole exercises that go well beyond physical development. A horse that is asked to move over varying terrain needs to think about where to place his feet. This is well suited practice for all barrel horses, who tend to spend excess time running and often limited time thinking. Another benefit is that it builds sure-footedness and confidence by improving proprioception and coordination, also making these excellent exercises for rehabilitation following injury. The more a horse concentrates on placing their feet and gets comfortable on varying terrain, the more relaxed and secure they will become in general. Horses are very protective of their feet by nature and when asked for refinement may get tense and nervous about positioning them precisely and handing over that control, which in their minds can be equal to losing their very life. A horse without control of their feet in the wild is not a safe or alive horse; so it's our job to soften these instincts for a lower stress transition into the pressures of being a performance horse. In addition, hill work and pole work strengthens both postural and gymnastic muscles, which are important for fast barrel runs, not to mention soundness and longevity.

How-to
Carelessly pulling our horse backward up a hill, or letting them fall on the forehand going down-hill, or trotting lazily or sloppily over poles isn't going to create the results that asking a horse to collect, round, and frame up will. These are advanced exercises for horses that have already been introduced to moving with quality, and will take their movement to another level.

Weave Over at a Walk – Place poles end to end in a long line, at least four poles long, but even more is ideal if you have them. Ride in a narrow weave back and forth over the poles with your horse's body straight. This is a good introductory exercise to get your horse more aware of his feet and more accepting of the poles. For a more advanced version, weave with subtle nose to tail counter bend, switching bend each time you cross over the poles.

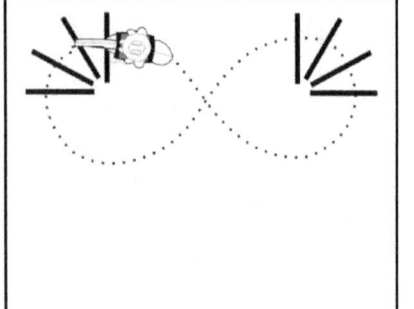

Corner Fans at a Trot – In the short end of your arena set up four poles in a fan shape, with one end touching (or near touching) and four feet apart in the center. Set up four more poles in the other corner the same way. Trot over one set, circle around to the fence then straighten out to go over the next set to form a bow tie pattern (with more space between the fans, you'll have room for a straight line, making a bow tie).

Four by Four – Set up two sets of four poles, four feet apart (a little more or less depending on your horse's size and stride length) with 12 feet between the two sets. Ride a steady, big, posting trot over the two sets of poles with the goal to keep the same rhythm between them. Keep your eyes up, and think about and prepare for where you're headed. Once your horse is comfortable and confidently performing this exercise, narrow the space between poles to no more than three feet, and use a block to prop up alternating ends of the poles for a greater challenge. The lifting action required is especially beneficial 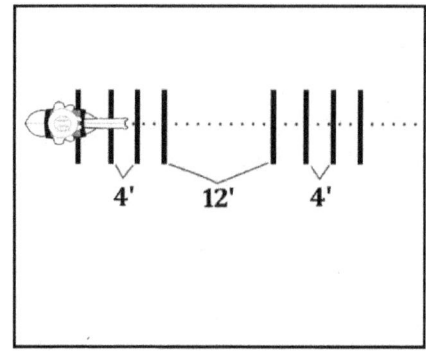 for strengthening and conditioning the stifles and hocks. Eventually you can lift both sides of the poles to a height of six inches. You can also remove two poles from each series of four to make two sets of two to go over at a lope with the poles placed six to ten feet apart. This is even more challenging and the goal is for the horse to stay calm about footwork and form when going faster. Take your time, and remember that the benefit comes not in just going over the poles, but in doing so with quality, calmness, balance and rhythm.

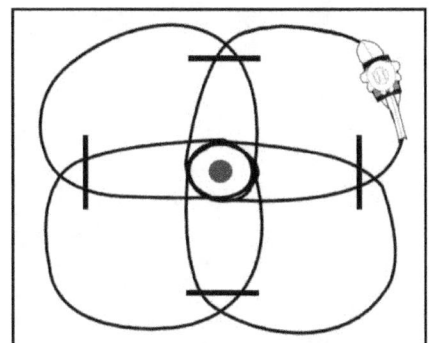

One Barrel Square – Set up four poles 60 feet across from each other forming a square, with one barrel in the center. Introduce the exercise at a walk by entering the square over a pole, then go around the barrel and out the opposite side. Next travel around the outside of the square to enter again, circle the barrel in the middle and exit out of the other side, crossing over the pole. Move up to a trot with the goal to keep an even cadence over the poles and around the barrel without slowing down, speeding up, shortening or lengthening stride. This exercise is excellent for bridging a powerful, extended stride with calm relaxation. The poles serve as a physical obstacle causing your horse to think for himself as he connects his mind to his feet. While you have this pattern set up, you can also remove the center barrel, turn the poles 45 degrees and ride a cloverleaf pattern through them. As you do, concentrate on total straightness between the circular portions.

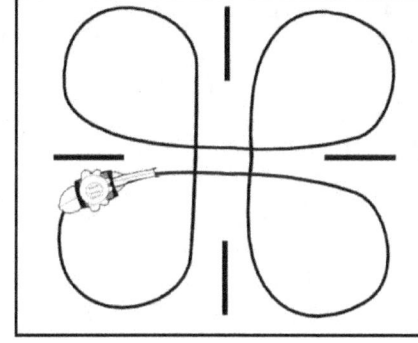

Backing Up Hills – If you have a pasture with gentle inclines at home, spend ten minutes of each ride trotting up and down the hills (it's a good idea to walk first). Next, focus on backing up the small hills. Consider adding a neck string to ask your horse to back, which helps a horse learn to shift his whole body weight rearward rather than just compress his neck in response to the reins. Hill work is great for building topline and hindquarter strength, but as always, be aware of *how* your horse is moving. The *way of going* is much more important than the task itself.

By using pole work to pay special attention to footfall and stride length – both maintaining the same cadence and also lengthening and shortening – you'll find less need for stopping or backing your horse up to teach rate. You may even find that this is no longer necessary, further minimizing physical stress while enhancing athleticism!

> *Fast is fine,
> but accuracy
> is everything.*
>
> – Xenophon

Refined Maneuverability

FreeDictionary.com defines maneuverability as: *To make a controlled series of changes in movement or direction toward an objective.* The exercises in this chapter will focus on developing a more athletic, educated, coordinated and responsive horse – one that can change direction in an instant, with healthy, fast, powerful form and a good attitude – with the *objective* of winning barrel races!

It's amazing to think how well horses adapt, adjust and even win in spite of us. It's not uncommon to get into horsemanship habits that completely contradict what we need in a competition run. But every day we have opportunities to practice and build on refined maneuverability *if* we're aware enough to take advantage of them. In many cases it doesn't take any more time than what is required for solidifying the more harmful habits that distance us from our goals, which many of us do regularly without realizing it. Even if you're happy with the foundational education your horse has, do you think it would benefit you both if he was *even more* advanced? Advanced, as in – more athletic, more educated, and more responsive? If developing this didn't require a huge time investment from you, would you be willing to pepper in the small action steps to make it possible along the way? Of course. Who wouldn't, right?

Well there are a few timeless principles that when understood and practiced, lead right in this very direction, which I feel are important to share as I introduce this chapter. Refined maneuverability isn't something we put in a box or in an exercise. We don't just start training once our horse is warmed up in the arena, or once we throw a leg over them. We're developing them in every single moment we're even remotely in their presence, for the better or worse.

It's easy to train a robotic horse that yields their body parts without fail. But if our communication only goes one way, it ends up being a shallow, mechanical and superficial conversation. We don't just want our horses to react, or only respond, but to think. So first, in the initial training stages or when teaching a horse something new, don't underestimate the necessity and importance of "set it up and wait." If we don't allow them processing time, especially in the learning stages, they won't *learn* to think; they'll just learn to react, survive and avoid. Of course, on the other end of the spectrum is the trainer that is too patient, allowing horses to be "too wrong for too long," and in the process horses get good at doing the wrong thing (or nothing). Allow horses processing time, yet limit their "guessing games" when whatever behavior they offer is excessive or dramatically far from correct (and especially if it's dangerous).

Second, remember that a horse can only become one with us, and move with fluidity and grace consistently, *if* we offer the opportunity consistently. So many riders use their reins or legs first and neglect to use their energy, subtle body language, weight and focus *first*. Therefore, the horse will never respond to a lighter, more subtle cue than what's first presented. For example, a split second before you neck rein your horse to the left, raise your energy and start turning your eyes, shoulders and torso to the left. The horse should already be turning at this point, so *only then* use the reins and then legs when and if they *don't* turn. Reins aren't the first point of communication. Our horses won't advance if we fail to use the subtlest forms of language to communicate with them. It all happens in a fraction of a second, and most of us have to get in a practice of re-learning and re-teaching ourselves, due to habits developed from well-meaning parents or mentors who offered the best of what they knew at the time, and taught us to kick to go and pull to stop.

When *we* make the commitment to start thinking, communicating and riding with refined maneuverability, our horses will start moving, running, *and winning* with refined maneuverability.

Exercise 36 – Quatrefoil

Description
When I set out to name the exercises that follow, some research brought up a geometrical shape called a "quatrefoil," which is an outline made up of four symmetrical and partially overlapping circles. It's a pattern commonly used as a decorative framework in both graphic design and architecture. The word quatrefoil means "four leaves," due to the way it resembles a four leaf clover. It only seemed deserving that these exercises would bear the name of the shape that inspired them!

Purpose
There's no denying the importance of forward momentum in a run. In fact, in my experience simply driving more with my seat in slow work has yielded incredible results in competition. As I added more of this forward drive, I tried my best to not just increase speed but to increase my horse's stride, and it made a big, postitive difference in a hurry. The three variations of the Quatrafoil I've shared allow us the opportunity to practice "forward" in a dynamic and powerful yet easy way without unecessary stress.

Really amplifying our horse's God-given athleticism requires simulating what actually occurs on the pattern, but in moderation. We can't over-do it or be careless about performing speed work at home. It's easy to stress our horse's minds and bodies, leaving them even *less* prepared to perform well when it matters most. It's also easy to lose some precision and finesse when we add speed. But if we do it gradually and intentionally with consistency, our horses can be prepared to give their best without any negative pressure of being "trained" along the way. When we take this gradual, intentional and consistent route, we make it eaiser on ourselves as well, ensuring we have the time necessary to practice our own precision and accuracy for guiding our horses effectively. In barrel racing and in life we get what we focus on, and we get better at what we practice.

Another way to look at it, is that we get out of our horses what we put in. The more simple and fun we can make our sessions, the better. The more we can do "serious" training without the horse even knowing it, *even better!* If we put in the necessary ingredients – such as the quick combination of forward power and lightning fast rate – and put it in *in a way* that is easy, free of pressure and easy for the horse, we get a higher level performance with more relaxation and reach. The result is that when it counts, they'll just simply do what they've practiced, in a natural kind of way, with plenty of fluidity and little anxiety.

Each of the progressive options I've shared on the following page are slightly more challenging than the previous one, allowing your horse to become more prepared to stetch his body to it's max and eat up the ground in a run, yet very quickly gather up and rock back for the turns. Similar to the Exercise 27 – Four x Four in *The First 51*, the distinctions below are more challenging because they offer more variation, especially in circle size.

Depending on how long you choose to set the pattern (the end barrels), you also have the opportunity to help your horse prepare for the quick transitions in speed and position between the first and second, along with the slightly longer distance to the third barrel as well. Between the large loops, mixed with smaller, more intense circles and straight stretches in between that vary in length – you and your horse have the perfect opportunity to practice a balance of consistency and variety, helping you both to improve your quickness and timing, as well as confirm good form, enabling you to have all of the above in competitive runs as well!

Refined Maneuverability

How-to

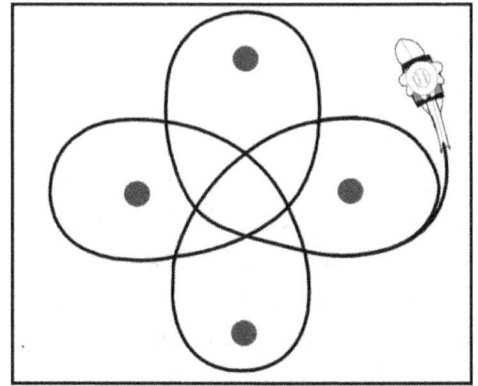

Quatrefoil Option One – Begin this simple version by setting up four barrels forming a 60 foot equal-sided square shape, *or* set the middle two 90 feet apart to make a cross. True to the quatrefoil shape, starting at a trot, arc across the center to make your first large, loopy, slightly teardrop-shaped circle around your first barrel. In the same direction, move to the next barrel with one large, free-swooping circle, approximately 30 feet in diameter, which is significantly larger than an actual barrel turn. Go in both directions, and also perform at a lope.

Option Two – On the same pattern, start at a trot and make one similar, large, approximately 20 to 30 foot teardrop circle around the first, top barrel, then make a second balanced and even tighter ten foot (barrel-sized) circle. Going in the same direction, move to the next barrel and perform one large looping circle; then move down to the third barrel for one large swooping circle, then again tighten your second circle to resemble a barrel turn. Also perform at a lope, first going in one direction, then the other. Be sure to make a subtle change in your body language and focus without getting overly aggressive, so your horse knows when to narrow.

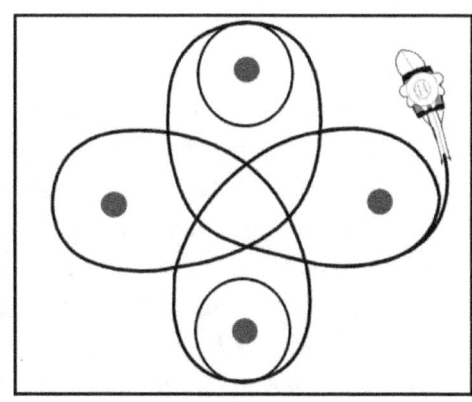

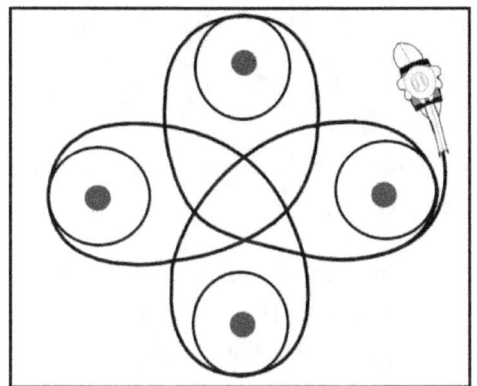

Option Three – On the same pattern, again start at a trot and make one similar, large looping 20 to 30 foot circle around the first, top barrel; then make a second even, balanced, tighter ten foot or barrel-sized circle. Going in the same direction, move to the next barrel with one large swooping circle, then again tighten your second circle to resemble an actual barrel turn. Repeat this at each barrel. Also, perform in both directions and at a lope. Encourage a free, forward pace, even in the smaller circles. Really encourage your horse to elevate and reach powerfully, keeping the qualities of the larger circles as you continue into the smaller ones.

Exercise 37 – Switchback

Description

If you look closely, the most athletically talented horses will seem to have more freedom in their gaits. It's more than youth or soundness, although those things no doubt play a part as well. It's as if the higher degree of flexibility they possess adds to their aptitude for organizing their bodies in an athletic instant for performance endeavors. If the conditions call for it, there seem to be fewer limitations to how they can contort their bodies in whatever way it takes to make a phenomenal turn or run happen. It's amazing to witness and even more amazing to ride. This heightened suppleness and flexibility, while innate in part, is even more largely something that we, as trainers and jockeys can create, enhance and preserve over time, depending on how we develop and care for our horses.

Purpose

So many aspects of our sport contribute to resistance, so it's not enough to just develop a thorough foundation in a young horse. We have to be continuously conscious of *keeping* our horse's minds and bodies soft, supple, fluid and free-moving. Where there's understanding, there's peace, which is the best gift we could give our horses. Ask yourself, *does your horse know he has body parts, or is he like one big seized hinge?* Does he trust you with the placement and position of *all* his parts? While straightness is critical, it's not created by allowing existing rigidity, but by loosening up all the parts and then teaching the horse to move them together in a structured way. We go about this by instilling a quality education, providing the best physical support possible and by removing any reason *why* our horse might start to feel resistance or experience a "kink" in his movement.

Beyond that, we can't forget to include exercises in our program that simulate the level of athleticism necessary on the pattern. If a horse takes three strides, for example, to switch the bend in his body between the first barrel and second, that's not nearly fast enough. We have to be ready for the first barrel before we leave for it, and positioned for the second barrel ideally as we leave the first – the sooner the better. What we get in competition is a result of what we and our horses practice, so aspects of our preparation also need to be quick and intense. When sitting on the sidelines, or watching a run on video, it's easy to underestimate the level of quickness and athleticism our horses truly need to excel. When there are no stuck spots, no kinks, no resistance, and complete freedom of motion, there are fewer limits on the pattern and therefore on the clock. That's what the exercises that follow are for: developing a new level of suppleness and pliability throughout your horse's body, for the quickness and coordination it takes to win.

How-to

This exercise calls for a total of eight cones or tires, set up in a circle as large as your arena has room for – sixty feet or more in diameter if you have the space. Unless you have plenty of room or are sharpening the edge of an already very advanced and athletic horse, plan to spend the majority of time at a forward, rhythmic trot. The repetitive change of direction and shape would require simple or flying lead changes if done at a lope, which you're welcome to perform as well if your horse is ready for it.

Switchback Option One – It's a good idea to start this exercise at a walk. Perform a weave in and out between each of the eight cones, leaving an even distance around each of them. Focus on even, rhythmic cadence and tempo, switching bend in the short straightaway portions between inner and outer curves. Be conscious that your horse's whole body has a subtle nose-to-tail bend, not just his neck or hips alone. Keep your eyes up, focusing ahead, preparing and positioning for the next change in shape. For more of a challenge, consider moving the cones to make the size of the circle smaller, which offers even greater benefit for increasing coordination and quickness!

Option Two – Begin by trotting one barrel-sized circle around the first cone, then switching bend to swoop to the inside of the neighboring cone. Again, switch the arc in your horse's body for one complete circle around the next cone, repeating this pattern all the way around the circle. Essentially, you'll be trotting a complete circle around every other cone, with a half circle yielding to the inside of the cones in between. Switch and perform the exercise in the other direction as needed, being sure to spend the most time in the direction your horse most needs to improve on. Perform this primarily at a trot, but experiment with loping your complete circles and trotting in between. This version offers exceptional practice for horse and human to think ahead, and get physically prepared for the upcoming changes, just as we must do in a run.

Option Three – Now things get really dynamic! Using the same pattern, start by trotting around your first marker two and a half circles before switching bend, and moving on to circle the neighboring marker in the opposite direction, this time one and a half times around, before moving off to the next and again circling two and a half times, repeating this pattern around the entire circle. Perform this primarily at a trot, but feel free to mix in some loping as your horse's readiness dictates.

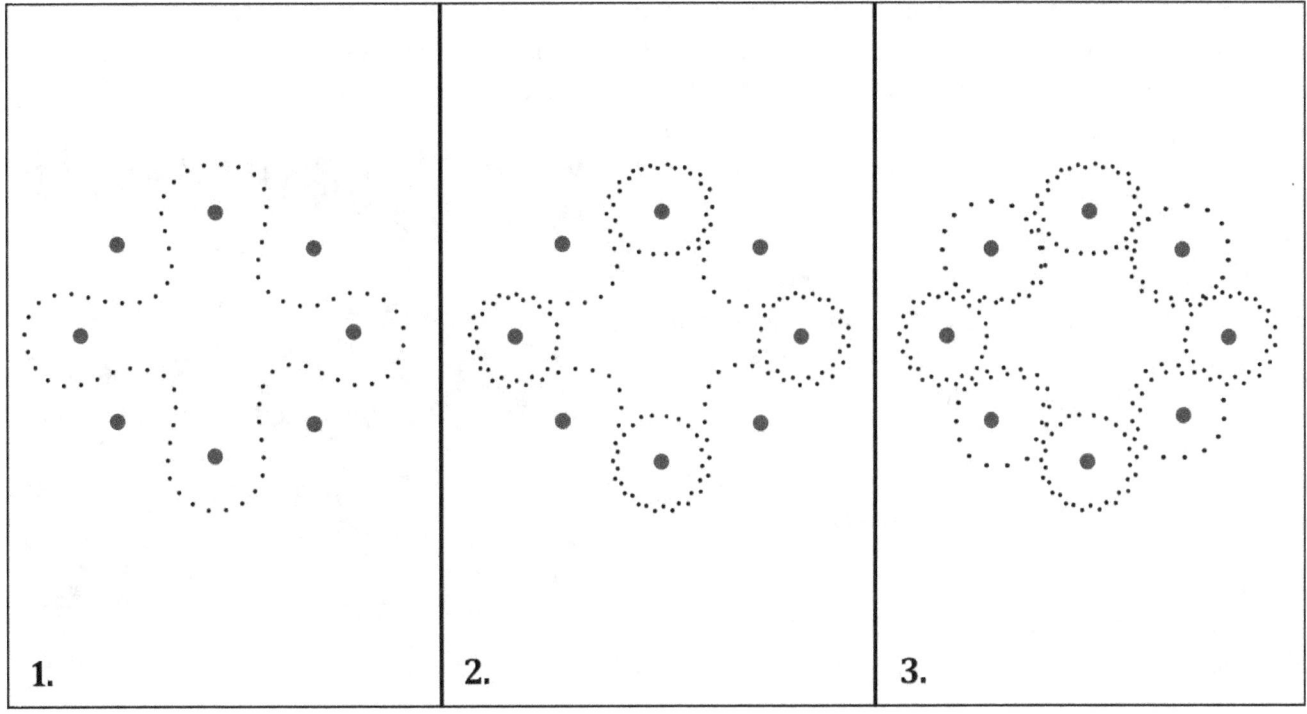

1.   2.   3.

Exercise 38 – Pinwheel

Description

When it comes to increasing maneuverability by means of increasing suppleness and flexibility, we really need more than one type. By that I mean we must execute these exercises to stay supple, and be willing to yield *ourselves* – specifically in our minds. Admittedly, I'm a sucker for structure. If I could plan every step of my barrel racing program and training sessions and carry them out precisely on track and on schedule without a hitch, I'd be one happy cowgirl. But alas, these are horses we're dealing with. Much like children, their changing needs often determine the courses of action we take day-to-day. It's great and even necessary to have goals and plans of course, but don't latch onto them too tightly. To do so is only setting ourselves up for disappointment, because we'll never consistently reach our targets. Tony Robbins said it best by suggesting, *"Stay committed to your decisions, but stay flexible in your approach."* There are certain values and beliefs we must stand firm in as we strive toward our goals. But the route we take, the timeline, and the "how" is always subject to change.

Purpose

The pinwheel exercise presents an opportunity to confirm good posture and form, while also practicing the soft full-body bend we've been building on a pattern that includes a barrel, and therefore more realistically simulates *the* pattern. I believe including actual barrels in our exercises is important and should be done intentionally by first considering the horse's needs. For example, does the horse seem to use his body one way around a barrel, but not around a tire or cone? Does the horse get anxious in exercises that involve barrels due to a negative association they've developed? In some cases you might make sure the horse is working correctly around tires or cones first. Then add in just a couple of barrels to emphasize the same form without the horse making assumptions. It's a gradual way to "break up" those pesky mental and physical associations. While we're on that topic, the pinwheel is an exercise, like many others, that presents plenty of options for variation. It's important that we don't over-compartmentalize our training. The fact that "barrel racing exercises" are so popular and enthusiastically sought after is an indicator that barrel racers in general are compartmentalizing too much, and not relying enough on their feel in the moment. We are the leaders in our herd of two, but it's *the horse* that determines how we go about it in each moment. This may require completely abandoning plans to work on certain exercises, while being willing to get creative and make adjustments as you go along.

How-to

Set up one barrel in the center of your arena, with four cones or tires set around it to form an oblong diamond shape, with the far cones or tires being 30 feet from the barrel and the shorter side being approximately 10 feet away. You'll want to start performing this exercise at a trot, but do advance to a lope in certain versions or portions based on your horse's readiness.

Pinwheel Option 1 – Execute this version of the exercise by circling the short side cones (closest to the barrel), then continue to the long end cones in a reverse arc. You won't circle the far end cones but just go around them, keeping the same bend in your horse for the entire duration of the exercise (until you go the other direction) as you move on to the next close cone and circle it again before continuing the pattern.

Pinwheel Option 1b – A slightly different option includes following the same pattern described above, only making a complete turn around the long end cone in a counter arc position. This option is excellent for a horse that over-weights his front end, drops in, shoulders or even elevates and fades out of his turns. Really encourage your horse to stay soft to your inside rein by insisting he shape his body around your leg.

Pinwheel Option 2 - The second option involves circling the barrel and is the inspiration for this exercise's name based on how the path you travel resembles a pin wheel. Again, start by making a barrel-size circle around one of the short end cones, then figure-eighting to the inside to circle around the barrel in the opposite direction you started in. Move on to the opposing cone, which will be on the long side, before again figure-eighting to the center then moving on to one of the side cones. The difference in distance between the cones keeps your horse responsive, and at any point you can mix things up by counter arcing around the cones instead. Also, feel free to add some loping, which is best done as you leave the barrel and head

out to approach one of the long end cones, giving your horse adequate time and room to prepare.

If your horse suddenly performs a certain maneuver exceptionally well that he'd previously struggled with, or starts moving, thinking, or behaving in a way that you especially appreciate, *stop right then and there* and offer some verbal praise, time for a deep breath, lick & chew, and "soak." Smile and relax in your body when you're pleased. Remember, your horse is a *master* of communication without words, and can *feel* and *sense* this. Horses are so much more sensitive than we realize – use it to your advantage!

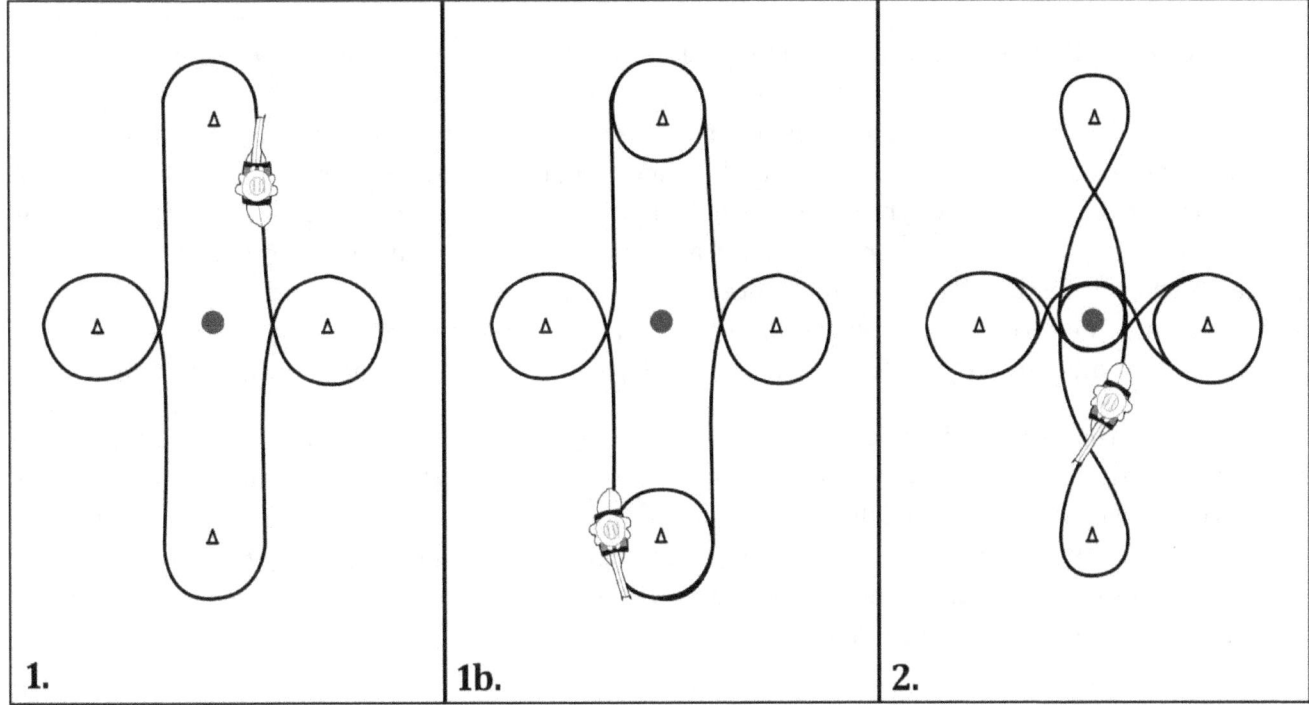

1.   1b.   2.

Exercise 39 – Flower Power

Description
In the 60's and 70's "flower power" became a slogan used by protestors to show resistance to violence and war. I like to think of the following exercise as serving a similar purpose. By utilizing it, we'll certainly inspire less opposition in the relationship with our horses. Because the exercise is dynamic and large in size, including both long straight lines and small, collected circles, it has the power to shift our horse's perspective while also increasing their fitness and coordination. The barrel pattern will seem like a walk in the park in comparison, and exercises like this are sometimes just what we need to educate our horses without them feeling like they're being "drilled," thus inspiring and maintaining a "pro peace" attitude!

Purpose
Since the Flower Power exercise is repetitive and on-going, it especially requires our horses to find balance and rhythm out of necessity. This is a unique exercise, in that the pattern practically does the work for us. We'll be turning things up a notch with the intent to perform this one primarily at a lope. The longer your horse lopes through the pattern, the more he'll realize the importance of carrying himself well. This is because horses find it difficult to maintain imbalanced posture for long periods, and will often find more balance on their own if motivated to do so with enough time spent loping (a rest reward is in order when they finally do!). This way of going about it makes it the easy choice for the horse. It's another way of using psychology to passively get the horse to choose to do what we have in mind.

How-to

Using a total of eight cones, barrels or tires, set up a large circle at least 60 feet in diameter. A quick and easy way to do this would be to first set up a square with four markers an even distance from your short side arena fences, then simply spacing out and placing the remaining four markers half way between each one to form a perfect circle, making it very likely to be even without measuring.

Flower Power Option One – It can be helpful to start out at a trot, just to get your own timing and special awareness for the exercise sharpened up. Start by going straight across the middle of the large circle, then arcing your way around to make a half circle around your first marker; then angle your way straight across your tracks to make another half circle around one on the opposite side. Each time you come across you'll be crossing over your lines when you come over the center. Next, aim back straight across the circle to the cone (or tire/barrel) just next to the one on that side you rounded previously, going back and forth across the circle, moving one over each time. Perform this once going in one direction around the circle. Let your horse rest, then perform it in the other direction before moving up to a lope where it can be done going in both directions.

Option Two – The idea is similar here, but in option two you'll perform a complete circle around each outer marker before making your way back across the center to the opposing one on the opposite side. Again, with each trip across the middle, lope around the marker just next to the last one you circled, making straight lines across the center each time. It's important that you keep your own energy up, as this exercise can get tiring for both horse and rider. Make "quality over quantity" your motto, and keep pushing forward until you complete one entire revolution around the pattern.

Refined Maneuverability

Option Three – For this version, mix things up and make it more challenging by adding a barrel to the center of the large circle. Start by loping a circle around the barrel, then branching out to either arc around as in option one, or do a complete circle around the outer markers (only do what your horse's fitness level allows) before returning to the center. Remember, it's best when performing this or any other physically intense exercise, to not overdo it before giving your horse a good rest or break at a walk to catch his breath. It's always better to perform exercises when your horse is fresh vs. practice them in a weak, fatigued state. When a horse is breathing heavily, the quality and quickness of movement will decline, and they will be more at risk for injury. When your horse is rested up and has caught his breath, repeat again the other direction.

There are a couple of specific points in this exercise where the horse and rider's position is critical and can make or break the benefits available. One is the transition in direction that takes place from the straightaway to the arc or circle portion around the outer markers. As with any time you're sharply transitioning from a straight line to a circle, keep your shoulders back, eyes up, and shift the weight in your seat down and back a bit. This discourages your horse from leaning or diving into the intense change of direction, which will be quite common. If left to their own devices, many horses will transfer extra weight to the inside front and in the process their hind end lightens up, creating some disengagement. With young horses, or those just learning the barrels or quality movement for the first time, I'll support them more with feel and give from my hands, without constantly or firmly holding them in place. I'm right there, with two hands, keeping my own shoulders even and square, helping *only as much as necessary* while offering micro correction and releases that test the horse's responsibility for staying correct on his own. When I feel a horse hold good position while on a "micro release" (slightly loose rein), I'll be sure to reward it with a BIG release!

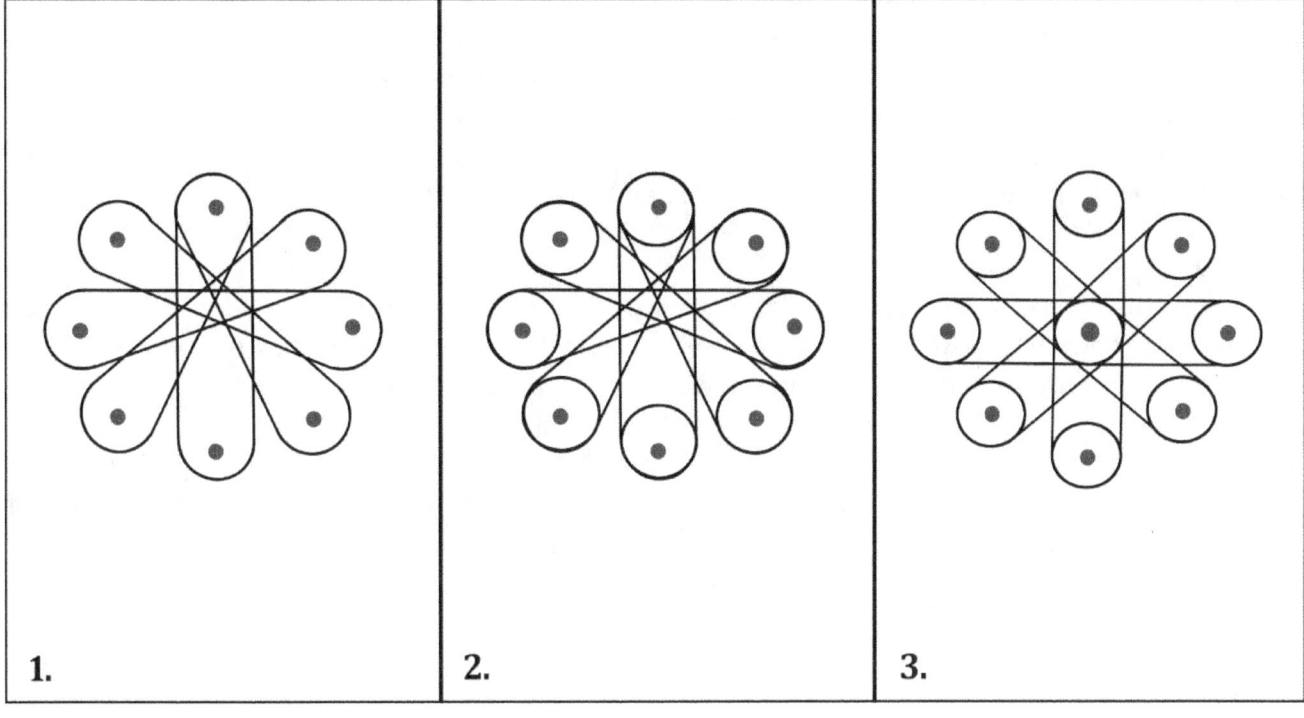

1.   2.   3.

Exercise 40 – Rock & Roll

Description

During the home stretch of writing this book, I peeled away from my office long enough one fall evening to ride Dot Com. A new saddle I ordered weeks earlier had arrived, so I was anxious to try it out. I didn't have an agenda that evening, other than just to ease around the arena and allow both DC and I to get a feel for our new "wood" (fiberglass, in this case). It was that time of year in Texas when the temperature and humidity had subdued just a bit to make an evening ride comfortable for a change. As the sun started going down, everything seemed right with the world. I loped and loped and loped more circles, so grateful that Dot Com was nowhere near the fire breathing dragon he'd been in years past, making him a *true joy* to ride. As the sun slowly started to set and I cruised around the arena, I felt like I could do it forever – just ride and ride and ride. Later I asked my husband, "Do you know what I love most about horses?" He replied, "What?" "*Riding them*," I said with a cheesy smile. While I certainly utilize intense rollbacks and sprints in our training, and the kind of riding I *love most* is indeed fast paced, powerful and exhilarating – there was something special about the low-key loping that day. It's an amazing feeling to be over the horse training hump, and to just enjoy myself, my horse, the environment, and simply riding. If you've made it this far, it's cause for celebration! Now the fast-paced fun *really* begins.

Purpose

The preceding exercises have offered several options for improving your horse's handle and coordination. All the changes of direction and transitions really require a horse to be connected to you, responsive and dialed in. If your horse wasn't quite there all the time before, by performing the Quatrefoil, Switchback, Pinwheel and Flower Power, he will be soon! It's all practice for the mental and physical requirements in competition. As a little warm-up for the "Need for Speed" chapter, in this exercise we'll be combining dynamic roll backs with powerful high loping diagonally across the arena, followed by gathering up for small, dynamic barrel-sized circles. In the process we'll confirm all the critical elements of the pattern, by first putting all our hard work to the test *off* the pattern. It's fun at this stage because we're moving away from teaching and more toward conditioning and practicing, always with a little refining as we go. Our horse should be using himself well now, and we're just sharpening their edge and ours to create the next level of balance, coordination, quickness and timing.

How-to

When executing any of the three versions below, I can't emphasize enough how critical it is to *stay conscious of our own body position*. I, for one, used to have a bad habit of leaning my way into roll backs instead of sitting back and allowing my horse to carry me. It's awfully hard for a horse to sweep his front end around with a "closed door" (leaning jockey/excess weight) in his way. Second, if at this point something doesn't seem quite right when you ask your horse to launch off – if there seems to be an awkward hitch in his giddy up – by all means take a close look at video footage, and consider seeing a vet. If a horse seems to bounce in his hind end, holds his tail high, or and doesn't seem to reach deeply and offer to fully compress his hind legs (springs) with ease, he may be sore. Get this addressed and resolved before springing forward!

Refined Maneuverability

Spring Loaded Option One – Start by loping on a right lead down the long, left side of the arena. Three quarters of the way down, stop smoothly and quickly roll back into the fence and hustle out on the left lead. As you near the corner, slow the rocking motion of your seat and gather up your horse to perform a small, upright ten foot circle in the corner. Continue at a collected lope along the short side to the next corner and lope another collected circle before launching off down the right side arena rail, still on the left lead. Again, stop and perform a rollback back *into* the fence, now picking up the right lead as you lope off down the rail, back to the corner for another circle to repeat the exercise.

Option Two – Start loping on the right lead straight down the long, left side arena rail. Again, three quarters of way down stop and roll back into the fence. Instead of circling at the corner, just gather your horse to ride through it with a balanced lope, maintaining collection to the next short side corner, where you'll gather in advance, then ask your horse to do a 45 degree turn, to head at a high lope diagonally across the arena to the opposite corner (still on the left lead). Once there, stop, back up, and settle for a moment, then do a rollback to the right, picking up a right lead to go back to the opposite corner, where you'll make a collected 45 degree right  turn. Continue in a collected frame back to the other short side corner and again do a 45 degree rollback to hustle diagonally across the arena. Stop in the corner, back up, settle, rollback to the inside/left and repeat.

Option Three – Start by loping a small ten foot circle to the right in the bottom long side corner of the arena. Continue in a collected lope to the top long side corner for one and a half circles, then rock & roll back 45 degrees again to hustle across the pen to the diagonal corner. Stop, back up, then rock & roll back again to the inside, picking up the left lead. Head back to the corner for a collected and dynamic left small circle, then on to the next short side corner for another circle and a half before rock & rolling yet again across the diagonal for another stop, backup and rollback. Repeat!

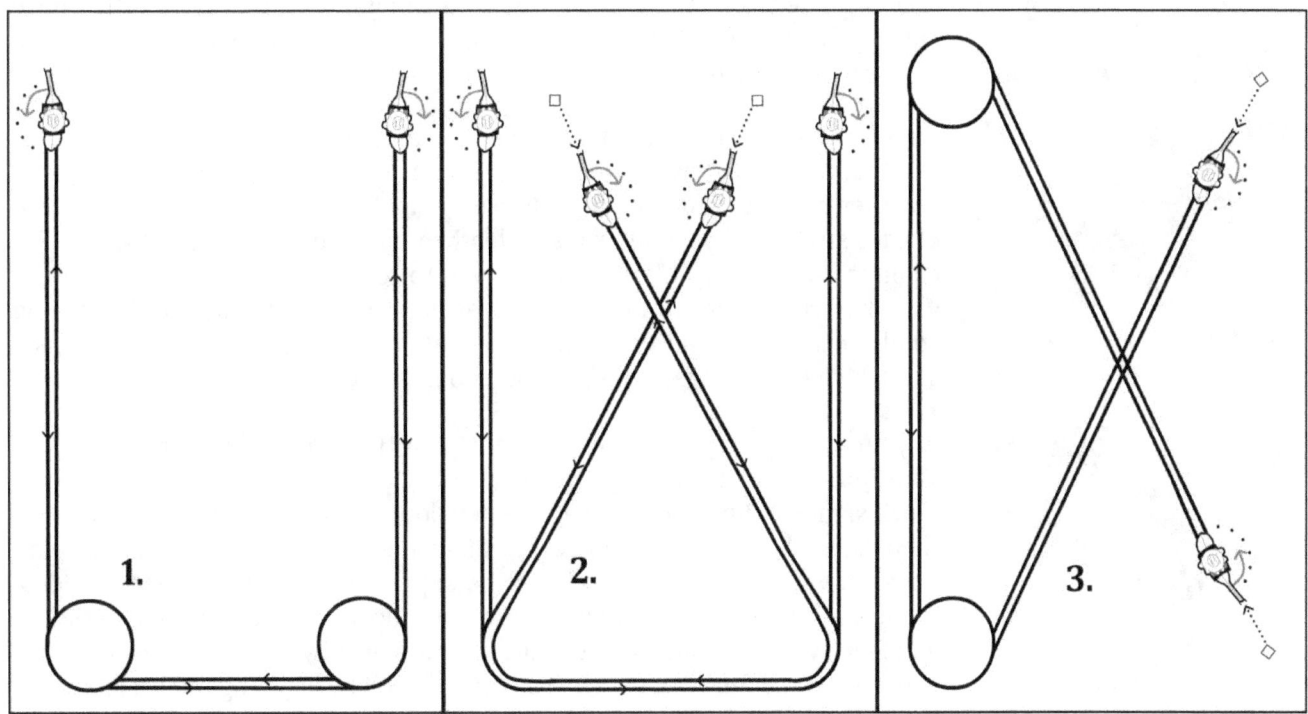

Tack and Bit Tips

The bits and tack we select and how they're adjusted has a significant effect on how we jockey and communicate. Much of it's personal preference, so it's important to know yourself and your horse, yet always strive to learn and improve so your performance is *enhanced* by these tools vs. dependent on them.

With your horse's head in a natural position, adjust your reins to loop on your pinky with your thumb touching the horn; this is a good competition length. From there, shorten or lengthen depending on your horse and your own preferences. Shorter reins result in quicker, closer and more intimate contact, ideal for a horse who likes "hand holding" and a rider with great feel and timing. Too short can cause a rider to lean forward. Longer reins may be better for an automatic horse that doesn't need or prefer contact, but can result in more inconsistent feel when you *do* need to communicate in a run.

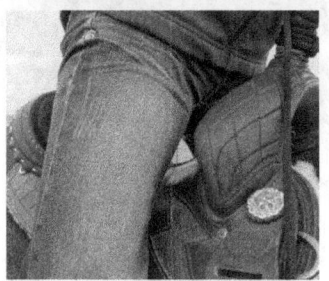

Just because you're *used to* the specific length of stirrup doesn't mean that's what's best. On average, there should be room for a hand width between you and the seat when standing. I punch half holes in my stirrup leathers for very specific adjustment. Longer stirrups help us sink securely down in our seat, but may leave us reaching when it's time to hustle. Short stirrups allow us to be more athletic and aggressive in a run, but can pop us up or cause us to tip forward. Some saddles have stirrups hung under our hips, but having our feet further forward is ideal and helps keep our rear end down in a run.

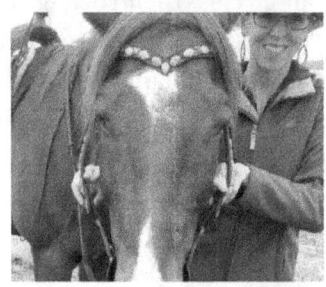

Headstall adjustment depends on many factors, but like stirrups it can make a big difference. As a general rule, I don't want a wrinkle in the corners of my horse's mouth (not even in a snaffle) because I want them to carry the weight of the bit, which makes the release even more clear. "Just right" will usually allow two fingers width on *both sides* of the headstall. Some barrel racers prefer to adjust bridles with sliding mouthpieces a little more snuggly. I also punch half holes in all my headstalls. I may make small adjustments depending on the set-up, ground, indoor vs. outdoor, etc.

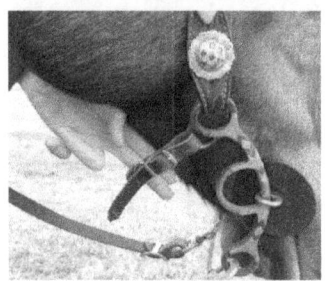

Two fingers width adjustment under a curb strap is standard. Shorten or lengthen a hole or two depending on your horse, your hands, the ground, whether you are running a big pattern or small, indoor or out, etc. The type of curb strap is important as well – leather, chain, or leather ends with a flat chain in the middle. We want our horses to respond in *any* headgear, but as we advance and get to know ourselves and our horses and run in varying conditions, we can get very specific about what our preferences and needs are, which can change over time and depending on the environment.

Is your horse ratey or a free-runner? Are they in 4-wheel drive, or does your horse lean, drop, or get disengaged? Do they need time to prepare or quick signals? Our goal is always to develop a balanced horse; but in a run, their natural tendencies will reveal themselves and the bit we choose can enhance what is good, and offer some support/lift/balance where needed. Bit selection also depends on the human – do you have impeccable timing and feel, even in a run? Or are you a little too grabby, or sometimes late? Do you need some forgiveness, such as that offered by a sliding mouth piece?

Need for Speed

If I'm going to burn images of barrel racing runs into my mind, I want them to be from the NFR or the short go of a big futurity. For this reason, unless they are breathtaking, I don't watch even my own runs more than a couple of times or even sit down and watch just any ol' barrel race. However, one day at a race last summer I paused in a coliseum hallway while waiting for my husband and caught a few runs. I watched one particularly gutsy little sorrel run his heart out. The run couldn't be faulted anywhere, but sadly the team still clocked 1.5 seconds off the mark. How could that be, I thought? It didn't seem right. The gal rode so well and the horse just *owned* his job, laying it all on the line for what was a flawless run. I suspect that the little sorrel powerhouse was perhaps cow bred, contributing to his quickness and natural athleticism. The run didn't clock fast but it sure looked fast, perhaps because that little fella was exerting himself so much. There honestly wasn't anything I could see to improve.

This situation I've shared here, is thankfully, pretty rare! The truth is, many of us never quite get to a point where our patterns are so pretty that our focus should be primarily on adding speed. Getting that last bit of speed out of a horse, in my mind, is something to focus on once the pattern is solid. And so seldom is the pattern *really* solid. Reaching potential requires "going beyond" – it requires stretching past (starting by releasing our own limited judgement) what is natural. You will have to go beyond ordinary to create something extra-ordinary! Of course, there are horses out there that legitimately don't have the athletic talent to make a run for the NFR. Some of them not only lack speed, but lack the general athleticism. Not every horse is going to make it to a highest level, obviously. But let's just not rule our horses out because of *our own* limited ability to first stamp a pretty pattern on them, *or* before we have actually taken specific steps to bring out *all* the speed they have available – because there are so many of them!

The following chapter contains exercises for leaving no stone left unturned in the process of tapping into a barrel horse's greatest potential. I'm motivated to be very thorough, because I am *a stayer*. I fall in love with my horses, and while I have bought and sold a few over the years, it's not my modus operandi. It takes a lot of time to buy, sell, train, retrain and *get with* horses. I prefer very carefully selecting them and making long term commitments. I'm not opposed to selling a horse, but that's not something I consider until I feel I've brought out all their potential and realized their capabilities aren't a fit for my goals. For example, although my gelding Pistol has been side tracked on and off with an injury in the last couple years, after getting him as a two-year-old and now having him for 11+ years, I don't feel that I have brought out *all* his potential *yet*. Just like *my own* development as a horseman, *his* development is an ongoing process!

When it comes to bringing out a horse's best, there is so much more we can do than most people realize. First and foremost, when a horse isn't cutting it in some way, there are usually some parts of their pattern that can be improved. When it comes to speed alone, there are many aspects of hoof care, bitting, nutrition, soundness, bodywork, tack, fitness and conditioning that are likely to shave off that elusive last half second. Of course, diet is an often overlooked component with speed as well – we must feed a horse to want to run! I even remember the story of one particularly sensitive mare who broke through to that elite level once she had a more comfortable fleece style cinch. You just never know how close you might be unless you fully commit and don't give up. We also can't overlook our own mental game. Limitations can be seen as opportunities with the right perspective. Instead of dwelling on the qualities you or your horse don't have, soak on the ones you do, and don't let anything get in the way of developing the ones you don't! While there *is* a time and place to move on to a horse with more speed, there's *even more* times and places to turn over additional stones in the search for it, and the following five exercises offer many!

Exercise 41 – Conditioning Game Plan

Description
When it comes to conditioning there are few timeless principles that apply across the board, regardless of where we started from and what we're working with. The challenging part that requires education, experience and expertise comes in formulating a conditioning program that meets the ongoing and ever-changing needs of our differing individual horses. The idea that "Good judgment comes from experience, and experience comes from poor judgment," certainly rings true! I have both over- and under-conditioned horses, and this has helped me find a happy medium to develop their bodies and to be strong, not stressed.

Purpose
We can assume that even if our specific goals are different, that we *all* have the intention and desire for our horses to perform as quickly, efficiently and safely as possible. Developing an effective, efficient and specific conditioning program for our barrel horses starts with understanding where we're going (our goals), and what we're starting with (our horse's current fitness level and athletic strengths/weaknesses). It also requires a firm understanding of the ingredients and action steps necessary to get there.

To clock fast and reduce chances for injury, we must understand the two qualities of speed, which are:
1. **Horsepower** – The amount of force behind a movement.
2. **Movement Efficiency** – How a horse moves, the ability to carry out movement with efficiency.

When it comes to speed, it's been proven that horses with a greater stride length are faster. So although we can train our horse to lengthen his stride, we want it to be something that comes naturally to them. One of the best ways to influence stride length is to build strength. A horse will be able to propel himself further with each stride when he has adequate strength to move his body mass.

Movement efficiency is essentially "quickness." Quickness can be defined as the measure of one's ability to move without momentum (different than being fast). Quickness is about reaction time, responding to a stimulus, or how quick your horse is "out of the starting gate." There is a genetic component in horses that move with this natural lightness and ease, meaning those with less genetic propensity for quickness will require more specifically focused effort to develop movement efficiency through training.

How-to
Build Strength – When we set out to make our horses stronger, we want *the right* muscles strong, and we want to develop them *in a way* that is specific to what we'll need from our horse in a performance. One of the best ways to condition a horse to run barrels, is to run barrels – or perform exercises that simulate running barrels as closely as possible. However, repetitive barrel runs contribute to physical wear and tear in the horse and stress the entire nervous system. The good news is that you don't necessarily have to go full speed to improve strength. Although you'll want to include some practice runs in your conditioning program, do so in moderation to protect your horse's physical and mental health. To lessen wear and tear caused by repetitive hard turns, you can: 1. incorporate straight line sprinting; 2. simulate the movements in barrel racing by incorporating small three-quarter speed circles while still requiring good biomechanics, and; 3. work on collection, perform rollbacks, transitions and other exercises that help develop strength.

Build Coordination – When training for greater efficiency and quickness, the most noticeable gains will come to horses who are young and uncoordinated. As they learn to better utilize and control their body with a rider, they become much more efficient movers. It's possible, however for an older, finished barrel horse to NOT be a very efficient mover and for a great deal of progress to be made. For the best results in improving coordination, shoot for 3-6 sessions per week if possible. Work with a horse several days in a row for ultimate learning, since frequency is important when introducing something new. As with building strength, don't overdo it; if a horse is body sore or fatigued, it will prevent him from using his body well.

It's easy to assume there's no way we can arrange our life around what would be the perfect conditioning schedule for our horses. That's a valid concern, so do your best and, most importantly, remember to give your horse recovery time in the middle of a workout, in the days in between those more challenging workouts, and also make sure they're not fatigued or sore from intense exercise in the day or two before a competitive run! Make "quality over quantity" your motto.

Equine Conditioning Schedule that Targets IMPROVING COORDINATION	
Monday	Light workout
Tuesday	Regular workout
Wednesday	Regular workout
Thursday	Regular workout
Friday	Regular workout
Saturday	Challenging workout – run/sprint
Sunday	Day Off*

Equine Conditioning Schedule that Targets STRENGTH BUILDING	
Monday	Regular workout
Tuesday	Challenging workout
Wednesday	Day off*
Thursday	Regular workout
Friday	Regular workout
Saturday	Challenging workout – run/sprint
Sunday	Day Off*

Equine Conditioning Schedule for Maintaining STRENGTH and COORDINATION	
Monday	Day off*
Tuesday	Regular workout
Wednesday	Day off*
Thursday	Regular workout
Friday	Day off*
Saturday	Challenging workout – run/sprint
Sunday	Day Off*

I've rarely personally reached a point where I felt my horses *only* needed exercise; for example, so many minutes of trotting and loping without also training and development to improve their form and therefore function (which includes a variety of circles, exercises, barrel and/or dry work, rest periods, etc.). For me, every ride is part of an on-going process of refinement. We are *always* working toward more "precision on the pattern!"

Conditioning guidelines are excerpts from 'The Barrel Racer's Guide to Speed Development'
*Denotes days off with turnout and not stalled if possible - movement is important health!

My suggestion is to reserve "exercise days" that include relatively no-brainer walking/trotting/loping for light days if you're especially short on time, tired, or not at your best. When your own mental and physical resources are limited, allow yourself a ride that is less demanding and involves primarily riding with less focus on training. It's a great way to set you and your horses up for success by not expecting more than you are able to deliver, while still making forward progress. It's estimated to take approximately seven minutes to trot one mile and four minutes to lope one mile. For a moderate four mile workout (mileage not including a walking warm-up and cool down) consider doing an "exercise ride" that includes a five minute walking warm up, seven minutes of trotting, followed by four minutes of loping on one lead, and four on the other, and another seven minutes of trotting. Cool down periods are critical and help reduce soreness by keeping circulation going long enough to remove waste products left from the metabolic processes that takes place when muscles contract. So always finish with five to ten minutes of cool down at a walk.

Exercise 42 – Fit to Fast

Description

Early in my barrel racing career, I made a disastrous error in judgement. I made a fast run on my mare when she wasn't in shape. That day she severely bowed a tendon, an injury she never totally recovered from. A couple of summers later, I took a job in a neighboring state. I returned home with just a few jackpots remaining in a local series. At that time, my mare was dreadfully out of shape again, but I did my best to catch up and get her fit enough for the last few races of the season. Had I been able to put my full attention and focus on her conditioning, she would have been so much more prepared, or so I thought. My mare was up there in years by this point, and surprisingly I ended up having my best summer ever on her and we won a high-point buckle. I realized then that the fitness program I *had been* following prior to that year wasn't fitting her needs. She would typically get sore mid-summer, and our ability to continue competing would be hit and miss. Looking back, I think she dealt with issues lingering from that tendon injury. There are two powerful lessons here. One is that we should steer clear of absolutes, such as believing that "fitter is *always* better." I know that's not necessarily true, especially for older horses or those with pathologies. The other is that just because we *can* make a run on an unfit horse and get away with it, doesn't mean we *should*. We must create a balance of physical fitness that is right for the individual horse, one that prepares them to be at their best. And at all times, we have to remember our responsibility as caretakers, which is to honor the privilege of owning and riding horses by doing everything possible to minimize risk and protect their soundness and health.

Purpose

Increasing our horse's fitness level benefits us by increasing their strength (necessary for speed), as well as their lung capacity for delivering oxygen to the muscles, improving stamina and shortening recovery times. Some folks gauge fitness by measuring heart and respiration rate. However, our horses will build their "air" the most quickly, followed by the muscles, then bone (which changes in density much quicker than most people realize), with the soft tissues such as ligaments and tendons taking longer. This makes gauging our horse's true fitness level difficult. Flexibility, agility and coordination are the first things to go during a layoff, and the last things to regain when re-conditioning. When considering the role that physical fitness plays in injury prevention, it's important that we actually have *a program*. Of course, we can't avoid all injuries and there is always some risk involved, but this is an area worthy of purposeful attention. Horses are such amazing gifts, allowing us to follow our dreams, and given to us for only a short time. We can't take them for granted by taking any unnecessary risks to their long-term well-being. Even if we're not always able to follow a conditioning program exactly, it's important to at last *have one*. That way we have a quick reference point for getting a horse legged up after a layoff or injury, or to test our horse's fitness level. The schedules I've included on the following page will help ensure you're *doing your part* for longevity, soundness, speed and success!

How-to

A second point I want to make is that your program for rehabbing a horse, getting a horse into shape to be competitive, or maintaining an already fit horse, will all be different. For example, I might take as long as six months to very gradually bring a horse back to competition shape after a serious injury and long layoff. Three months is my standard for conditioning an *already* healthy and sound, but out-of-shape horse. While I might start doing sprints and make a handful of practice runs in that third month, I'll then make adjustments to their schedule to include less speed work once I actually start making runs and competing.

Outside of bringing a horse back after a layoff or injury, I mentioned it's rare for me to get to a point where I feel I can focus on conditioning more than training. I'm always learning and improving, meaning there's always some way in which my horses are learning and improving as well, so we tend to condition as we train. Below are two example programs for those times when we are more conditioning-focused:

Traditional Program with Barrel Work		
Distance	Gait/Speed	Minutes
Month 1 - 3 Miles in 26 Min., 5 Days/Wk.		
½ Mile	Walk	7
½ Mile	Trot	4
½ Mile	Lope	2
½ Mile	Lope	2
½ Mile	Trot	4
½ Mile	Walk	7

Month 2 - 4 Miles in 32 Min., 3 Days/Wk.		
½ Mile	Walk	7 Minutes
1 Mile	Trot	7
½ Mile	Lope	2
½ Mile	Lope	2
1 Mile	Trot	7
½ Mile	Walk	7

Month 2 - 2 Miles + Training 2 Days/Wk.		
½ Mile	Walk	7 Minutes
½ Mile	Trot	4
½ Mile	Lope	2
½ Mile	Lope	2
Barrel Racing Exercises		20
½ Mile	Walk	7

Month 3 - 5 Miles in 36 Min., 3 Days/Wk.		
½ Mile	Walk	7 Minutes
1 Mile	Trot	7
1 Mile	Lope	4
1 Mile	Lope	4
1 Mile	Trot	7
½ Mile	Walk	7

Month 3 - 2 Miles + Training 2 Days/Wk.		
½ Mile	Walk	7 Minutes
½ Mile	Trot	4
½ Mile	Lope	2
½ Mile	Lope	2
Exercises + 100 yd. sprint		20
½ Mile	Walk	7

*Minutes are approximate.
Use the EquiTrack app to time rides.

Interval Program without Barrel Work		
Distance	Gait/Speed	Minutes
Month 1 - 2 to 4 Miles, 5 Days/Wk.		
½ Mile	Walk	7
½ Mile	Trot	4
¼ Mile	Lope	1
¼ Mile	Lope	1
½ Mile	Walk	7

*Each week add another ½ mile (2 min.) lope

Month 2 - 4 Miles in 29 Min., 3 Days/Wk.		
½ Mile	Walk	7 Minutes
1 Mile	Trot	7
1 Mile	Lope	4
1 Mile	Lope	4
½ Mile	Walk	7

Month 2 - Interval Workout 2 Days/Wk.		
½ Mile	Walk	7 Minutes
½ Mile	Trot	4
¼ Mile	Lope	1
¼ Mile	Lope	1
2 Mile	Gallop	6
½ Mile	Walk	7
2 Mile	Gallop	6
½ Mile	Walk	7

Month 3 - 4 Miles in 29 Min. 3 Days/Wk.		
½ Mile	Walk	7 Minutes
1 Mile	Trot	7
1 Mile	Lope	4
1 Mile	Lope	4
½ Mile	Walk	7

Month 3 - Interval Sprints 2 Days/Wk.		
½ Mile	Walk	7 Minutes
½ Mile	Trot	4
¼ Mile	Lope	1
¼ Mile	Lope	1
100 Yard	Sprint	20 Seconds
½ Mile	Trot	4 Minutes
100 Yard	Sprint	20 Seconds
½ Mile	Walk	7 Minutes

Exercise 43 – Rocket Launch

Description
Before our horses can offer every ounce of speed they have on the pattern, they must feel fresh, strong, healthy and energetic, and be confident and emotionally balanced. Sprinting confidently through the pasture without a rider is one thing, but having confidence and speed with a rider in an arena is another. My husband Craig will never forget the process of training his first rope horse, Frosty. Born a gorgeous bay roan with perfect white socks – as an own son of Lowry Star, Frosty was a legend in the making from the very beginning. He and Craig were winning saddles starting when Frosty was just five years old. But it wasn't long before then that Craig was ready to give up. Frosty would *just not run* to a steer. No amount of coaxing could convince him. Then one day, Craig says, "a flip just switched" and Frosty was a new horse. Craig still has no idea what caused the change, but it seemed as if overnight Frosty discovered how to run! He ran hard from then on, and there was no looking back. All this occurred long before I was a part of Craig life, so there's no way for me to guess what was responsible for the shift. What I *do* know is that there *is* indeed a "speed switch" that you *can* flip. I've described the process for instilling it below.

Purpose
Educating a horse to give every ounce of speed they have isn't any different than educating them to understand anything else. Take, for example, the fact that many horses aren't nearly as soft in the bridle as they could be, simply because they haven't been educated to be. While certain horses are more sensitive in general by nature, most are just a little dull just because no human has offered them "a polishing." Or consider, for example, the horse that has learned to push through bit pressure at the end of a run. That's a habit a horse learns just like anything else (albeit often unintentionally), and it can be *unlearned* as well. The meaning our communication has to a horse depends on the meaning we give it. The more we preserve their responsiveness to the things we want them responsive to, the more that level of sensitivity will be maintained. For example, if we regularly handle our horses by yanking on their lead rope and rudely slapping them, is it really fair to expect a hair trigger response when it's time to run and stop? There's a time to sensitize and desensitize, but the more conscious we are about creating, maintaining, respecting and preserving our horse's sensitivity, the more responsiveness we'll have across the board and especially when we need it most, including when we ask our horses for all the speed they can muster!

How-to
Giving our "go cues" even more meaning requires using clear, consistent and gradually increasing phases of pressure. Then it's a matter of putting an "easy button" cue in place to use when you reach that top level speed, such as a hissing or kissing sound – preferably something that doesn't require kicking, whipping or over & undering. This is because excessive and/or unnecessary movement on our part can cause a horse to tense up and actually shorten their stride. We can *all* jockey in a more balanced and streamlined way when our arms and legs aren't flailing around excessively. This process simply uses a stimulus to get a behavior, by adding a cue to create an association. To get started, let's refresh ourselves on the process for teaching GO, with an excerpt from Exercise 11 – A to B in *The First 51* (also refer to "Run & Rate" on page 64).

Saddle up with the intent to ride on loose rein. Choose a point in the distance to focus on with the goal to travel toward it in a straight line. Pick up your reins slightly without making contact to signal a coming change, then bring up the life in your body (sit taller, lean forward slightly), squeeze lightly with your legs if necessary, and the instant your horse transitions to the walk, release. If your horse doesn't initially transition forward based off your focus and energy, then use your hand, the end of a split rein, or an over & under to tap your leg first, then your horse if necessary. As you do this, you're using stages of pressure – first by lifting your reins and energy, then applying leg pressure, then tapping yourself lightly and/or your horse. Only go to the next level if necessary, then relax a bit. This teaches your horse to respond to a subtle cue to change gait and lets him know when he's correct.

When you follow these steps starting slow, you can essentially teach your horse to give you a quicker, higher quality response to a lighter, subtler cue. This is valuable because the less we have to use our legs, the more meaning they will have when we *do use them* for speed, and the better response we'll get. In my general riding, for example, I don't use my legs to go. I use them if my horse *doesn't* go. To step into a lope for example, it's as if there is a fishing line tied from my left seat bone to my horse's left hind leg. I just raise my energy, which is barely perceptible to the eye (my posture might straighten slightly) but my horse can feel it and I've trained him to understand this has meaning. Then I just lift and rotate that seat bone forward and instantly we step into an effortless lope. The more kicking and pulling we do to get a basic, low-level response, the more likely we'll run out of bit or run out of leg – meaning we can kick or pull as hard as we can and it's not enough; we end up maxing out. When this happens, it's simply a matter of the horse not having been trained to respond to subtler cues, which is a human problem more than a horse problem.

To finish installing your "speed switch," plan on doing a couple of sprints in a large space with safe footing. A groomed racetrack is ideal, but a level field or even large arena can work. Although longer distances are ideal, you can run at a diagonal, or sprint along the long side of an arena, and collect on the short end, and sprint again on the long side. Keep your phases in mind as you ask for all your horse's speed. In the moment you are asking for and getting your horse's top end speed, your energy will be intense – you'll be learned forward and fanning your legs. Just as you feel your horse reach his max, kiss or hiss to him, then tap his rear end firmly with an over & under to effectively get that extra boost of effort and create an association with your verbal cue. All it takes is a couple of times for most horses, and they'll quickly register *"what happens before what happens, happens."* The next time you make a run, the horse will make the mental connection and offer more effort in response to your verbal cue.

Keep in mind, as I mentioned in Exercise 42 – Lengthen & Shorten from *The First 51*, that either too much "go or whoa" is largely an emotional problem, because the horse's *desire* to go, or not go, is related to how he is *feeling* – which is either impulsive *or* unmotivated. Education is important as well; however, don't neglect to take into consideration that how your horse *feels* effects how he behaves, moves and responds.

Exercise 44 – Get in Gear

Description

I've shared exercises for adding speed in general, which will increase speed on the pattern, but sometimes we need to teach our horses to accelerate on the pattern itself. One common issue with the second barrel, for example, actually occurs before and after it. Namely, the fact that the speed our horses tend to demonstrate between first and second, and second and third, is often not near what is displayed to the first barrel and on the way home. It's easy to see why, considering our horses learn to anticipate blasting off to the first and they have a long stretch to gain speed on the way home. But there's a lot of starting/stopping going on in between and not nearly as much room to really let it all hang out. In their mind, why get in a rush, when they have to rate and turn right away, right? Remedying this and shaving off that last half second involves teaching our horses to accelerate and rate even more quickly with new associations.

Purpose

You might be noticing a theme: that for whatever we're missing in competition, there's a way to exaggerate it in our slow work so we'll have more of it in a run. Understanding this means we first have to be aware of what's happening in our runs and aware of our slow work, of our horse's bodies, their responses and our own position, etc. From that point, we don't even really need a book to suggest exercises as much as we need our own feel, problem solving skills, imagination and resourcefulness! Of course, experience and trial and error will teach us just how effective we are and will be in the future when it comes to making these adjustments. In my experience, it takes about two weeks to make some pretty big changes on the pattern. That might mean six to eight total sessions working on something specific. Of course, I'll work on several "specifics" in each ride, but we can expect to see significant changes on the pattern at around the two week point. At the same time, it's easy to be an over-achiever and ultimately end up with too much of a good thing! I'll never forget the time when, after being fed up with my gelding not rating at the first barrel, that in our next run we raced right in and he came to a complete dead stop at the first barrel! Again it all takes experience, awareness, trial and error, and constant on-going adjustments. If your horse just isn't snapping out of the first and second barrel like you want, I've shared three exercises below that will help turn up the intensity of your "slow work" for more fire in their feet between the barrels in a run.

How-to

Rollback Snap – One great way to set your horse up for success on the backside of the barrels is to make his departure more engaged. In other words, you want your horse's hind end to be squared more directly underneath his body weight and center of gravity so he can push off more balanced and powerfully with both hind legs. The more strung out he is behind, or the more weighted he is on one side, the less powerful he will be. If you watch closely some horses really extend their hind legs far out behind them when they push off, while others stride forward before they have extended their legs all the way back. Which style do you think is more powerful?

One way to encourage this straighter and stronger position is to come around the backside of your barrels and make a sweeping rollback-type move where your horse rotates on his hind leg. Instead of coming forward on an arc around the back side of the barrel with a subtle bend through the horse's body, you'll finish the turn far enough so that you can pivot the front end around the hind end and be lined up perfectly straight for your next turn. This helps your horse really hustle away, considering that the more bend our horses have, the more tendency a horse will have to "bind," creating a delay in forward motion. To start you can even perform this move away from the pattern, to really get the maneuver established and strengthen your horse's hind leg. Make sure you weight your seat a little more, which will cause your horse do to the same, and feel free to use a little outside leg at or slightly ahead of the cinch, or even a little outside rein (in slow work) to encourage the front end to sweep around for a straight, powerful departure.

Blow a Kiss – Use the same idea from Exercise 43, only in a specific place on the pattern where it's needed. A simple way to encourage more urgency between barrels, is to raise your life/energy and kiss to your horse to hustle him away the instant your horse straightens out after the turn (not before or during the turn!), and tap him on the rear end with a rein if their response is delayed. By using levels of pressure correctly, you can do this just once or twice to be completely effective and your horse will learn quickly. Similar to the idea that "how we start something is how we finish it," instilling a habit of hustling away from the turn is likely to result in hustling all the way *to* the next one.

Haul the Mail – Take this to the next level by increasing in speed after you finish a turn and accelerating to a gallop and going right *by* the next barrel. You can go as far and as fast as you have room for or feel is necessary, and if you like, choose to close the circle, creating a long loop of a turn to then come back to the pattern. This is a highly effective exercise, but use it in moderation so your horse doesn't lose his rate and responsibility. This is a great exercise for a horse who has become too hooked to the pattern or is going through the motions and not quite putting forward his full effort. It would be especially good timing to perform this when you'll be making runs in a small, indoor pen. Use the same concept for a horse that tends to quit running before the timer line by running all the way out of the arena (in a setup that allows for doing so safely), much faster and further than you would normally go before stopping.

Exercise 45 – Daisy Clipper

Description

Before starting my husband's rope horse gelding on the barrels was ever a glimmer in my eye, I'd put a lot of time and focus into rehabilitating him mentally and physically through movement. Navicular issues were threatening to end his career. Although exceptionally talented, he came to us with enormous white spots, not just on both sides of his back near his withers, but two more on the top of his shoulders. His scapulas were rotated forward with big, round bulges of scar tissue and protruding cartilage damage, making the atrophied holes behind them even more dramatic. The bottom of his neck was over developed while his topline was under-developed. His pelvis rotated forward, and he carried his tail high in the air, limiting his reach with his hind legs. Whenever I had him out in public, I felt the need to point out how unassuming he looked, and that he was actually very, very special and talented. I'm not exaggerating when I say that initially I was embarrassed to be seen with him. In Exercise 9 – Better Biomechanics, I explained how I started his transformation on the ground. But how I taught him to run low, flat and round instead of high, inverted and climbing happened almost by accident.

Purpose

Just because a horse *can* run and even win with poor movement patterns doesn't mean they should. When a horse moves in a high-headed, tense, short-strided and inverted way, it puts more stress on all the joints and causes more concussion to the feet because of the rough, unbalanced jarring motion vs. healthier smooth, round, balanced movement that actually provides cushion and shock absorption. When we can take their tense and inverted "climbing in motion" (although it still may be very fast) and turn it into more fluid, flat "reach in motion," it can be *even faster*.

You're probably familiar with the relief and even relaxation that comes after rounding the third barrel in your slow work. It's not really a place where we need to practice hustle when we're riding at home, at least not every time. For Dot Com, the long stretch straight home from the third, when traveling at a trot, was enough space for him to stretch out and relax into the "long & low" position I had taught him that had become so enjoyable and therapeutic. It was also where I coached and praised him, saying "good boy," as I smiled in genuine appreciation for his efforts on the pattern.

It shouldn't be any surprise then that when I started entering, although not all parts of his pattern were pretty in the beginning, that his run home from the third was breathtaking! He actually stretched out – long and round. Considering his background, it was poetry in motion. I worried that maybe all those years of performing in a bound up, inverted and high headed way would be difficult and maybe even impossible to completely overcome. I knew I could improve the habits he formerly had at speed to a large degree, but I wasn't sure I'd turn him around completely. Maybe, I thought, he ran so beautifully and efficiently all the way home from third because every time we trotted home from that barrel in slow work that we did so in "long & low" position. Sure enough, I started doing "long and low" on the way to the first barrel (where serious laterality issues in his body lent to some significant resistance at first), and little by little, his approach improved. His stride to the first was so rough and irregular, strung out, inverted and deviant of rate initially that in my desperation I considered a tie down. I'm glad I didn't, because bearing with that temporary ugliness provided just enough motivation and feedback from him to release and resolve it and replace it with better biomechanics at speed – for not only healthier movement, but a much faster turn.

How-to

To teach your horse to run and reach flat, long and low, it helps to first teach them to trot that way. To do this with Dot Com, I taught him to softly seek and reach for bit contact and also lower his head and lift and round his back in response to my "hugging" legs. He had a serious over-sensitivity to leg pressure, in part due to ulcers, but in larger part due to having been conditioned to understand that leg *always* meant go, not just respond and run, but *run away both* physically and mentally! Because of his extreme all-around sensitivity, I felt confident teaching these potentially conflicting signals to him, but I recommend doing so with care. I don't suggest going this route with a horse who already tends to ignore or push through bit pressure and it's best implemented by advanced horsemen who can quickly reroute a confused horse.

First it was important that Dot Com no longer reacted to my leg, but *responded* to it. I spent a lot of time sitting in the saddle and "massaging" his sides with my legs until he stood still and relaxed, then rewarded him by stopping (releasing the pressure) and relaxing myself when he did. He learned to accelerate and go faster in response to leg pressure *only* when my energy *also* came up when I applied it. Again, these are advanced understandings for a horse that require an advanced horseman to maintain. I also did this in motion. For example, if I started moving my legs around with no real focus, energy or intention in my body and he squirted off, I'd gently capture the excess forward motion with the reins, keeping my energy up until he relaxed, then released the reins. Eventually, when I asked him for a relaxed long trot I would hug his sides with my legs, while also asking his nose to come down with my hands, sometimes with gentle alternating pressure on the corners of his mouth with a snaffle. When he lowered his head, I'd release my legs. It took quite some time, but eventually I could use my legs to ask him to lift his back, stretch forward and lower his head. When he'd forget and squirt off, I'd smoothly block the excess forward with the reins then softly "milk" them a bit to ask for his head to lower, and when he did, I'd release. He learned to find comfort there and soon craved and sought out this position. We created some really beautiful and healthy movement this way. He would blow out repeatedly as he released tension, and still does when we practice "long & low." Outside of the initial learning stages, I emphasize that movement in this position should be very forward and not used excessively, otherwise carrying their heads extremely low can be a recipe for heaviness on the forehand. Take quality movement to the next level by gradually asking your horse to raise his head, being careful to maintain roundness over the topline and without over-flexing at the poll (nose vertical), which has the power to really transform your runs! As you master this way of moving off the pattern, simply include it in your slow work on the pattern, and watch as your horse's posture in a run changes over time, becoming a real "daisy clipper," meaning they move very efficiently and with little knee action. You'll notice your horse become longer, lower, flatter and *faster* – especially in the straightaways!

> *You know how every once in a while you do something and the little voice inside says, "There. That's it. That's why you're here." ... and you get a warm glow in your heart because you know it's true? Do more of that.*

– Jacob Nordby

In It to Win It

When I was a kid, my Mom, little brother and I would road trip with my grandparents to the Badlands near Medora, North Dakota. Words can't describe the wonder, awe and amazement of being "out West." I felt at home in that rugged landscape, like a real cowgirl. It was clear that the flat farm country of eastern North Dakota where I was raised was not where I was meant to stay. But it wasn't until college that I specifically and firmly decided I wanted to be a professional barrel racer. So although it hasn't been something I stepped into quickly or easily, it hasn't been something I wavered on either.

The more I learn about what it takes to achieve barrel racing greatness and do so consistently, and especially the more I learn about what it will take *for me* to do so, the more changes I make in my life to support that. Looking back, I see now I wasn't always making choices that aligned with what I wanted most. It's easy to do when you haven't "been there, done that" and don't yet have a realistic picture of what it takes. Sometimes I can see that what people *say* their goals are, aren't really their priorities at all. In either scenario, we're not living authentically. We have to be both aware and honest about what our values are, what we truly want (and why), and the level of commitment and sacrifice it will require. Without this clarity, the result will be a lot of repeated and unnecessary setbacks and discouragement.

Barrel racing through the summer in Texas can be exhausting. The extreme heat has a way of zapping one's otherwise seemingly limitless energy very quickly. Weekend long barrel races seem especially tiring, considering all the effort that goes in to packing and unpacking the truck and trailer for both humans and horses. When adding up all the entry fees and fuel, and the many expenses that go into helping our horses feel and perform their best, it's really amazing that so many hundreds of others volunteer for these southern, 100+ degree barrel racing weekends. I know the same can be said for the diehard barrel racers up north, because I used to be one of them. There is so much sweat, frostbite and sometimes even blood and tears that go into the preparation process alone! I feel the investment barrel racing requires is too steep a commitment *not* be at our very best. It's something worth doing well. However, it's not uncommon to set ourselves up to fail before we even pull out of the driveway, because we've inadvertently designed our life to interfere with all the ingredients that are really necessary for what we want to achieve. We have to choose. Even if our objective is to have fun at the local level, it's possible to have *even more* enjoyment as well as success, if the right steps are taken *outside* of the arena first.

When considering every little challenge that comes up in a typical barrel racing weekend, we always have a choice. Barrel racing can be frustrating or fun. It can be draining or energizing. It can be an adventure or stressful. It can be nerve wracking or joyful. We can *choose* what to focus on and think about, we can choose the meaning we attach to everything that happens, and we can choose what actions to take. It's not what happens to us, it's *what we do with it* that matters most, moment to moment, day in and day out.

The chapter that follows will take you through five specific areas with inspiration and exercises for creating a foundation that supports fun, frustration-free barrel racing achievement. Running barrels is challenging enough by itself, so if you feel called to truly maximize you and your horse's potential on the pattern, then it's important to get these supportive foundational layers in place. This ensures you'll have the time, resources and tools to make your barrel racing dreams more than just dreams, and when special opportunities present themselves you'll be ready to take full advantage of them. The journey requires radical honesty, impeccable awareness and clear cut choices. But when you *know* what you really want, and have the right systems in place and reasons motivating you to follow through, the HOW becomes easy.

Exercise 46 – Tools & Team

Description
When I first started barrel racing (in a plowed-up wheat field), some of my "tools" included a borrowed all-around youth saddle and a cheap, light-weight, solid aluminum curb bit. It was a big day when I had saved up and finally put the first set of sports medicine boots on my little mare. I remember how satisfying it was to look at her and feel that we had really made "the big time." Obviously, I was very limited in the tools I had available, but back then it wasn't that *not having* the right tools was so bad; it was that I didn't know at the time that I needed better tools, or even what kind. Now I'm not one to suggest we must have *all* the finest quality, top notch tools to be successful. I know first-hand that resourcefulness can be much more valuable than resources. However, "putting the cart before the horse" can actually limit our success so extremely in both the short and long run, that I felt it was necessary to share not just the most critical tools, but also the important *team members* that are critical to our barrel racing success.

Purpose
Having the right tools and team behind you adds fuel to your efforts, fast forwarding your barrel racing journey, helping you reach your goals faster and achieve even more. I know I'm not the only one to look at a beloved and talented aged horse, and think "If only I'd known then what I know now." There are therapeutic tools that play a huge part in supporting a barrel horse's soundness and longevity. The right tack helps us communicate more clearly and effectively with our horses, creating more understanding, and making the training process go much more quickly and smoothly. Being prepared with the right tools also translates into less stress. Without them, it will often seem hard to gain traction, in more ways than one, which is insanely frustrating. Collecting the right tools involves investing time and resources into trial and error to determine what's best for you. As strong and independent as many barrel racers are, we can't be successful all alone. Just like our tools, we don't necessarily need a large collection, but a close, quality team is critical. Your circle of team members may be small, but make sure it's tight.

Of course, it's probably most important that we fully utilize the tool between our ears! For example, even when financial resources are short, resourceful folks use their unlimited imaginations and creativity to come up with solutions for every challenge. As an example, just recently I was between saddles trying to make one work that fit my horse well but had a seat too big for me, while I waited for a new, custom saddle. My old one wasn't suiting my needs in a run, so I rigged up a temporary strap under the seat jockey to set the stirrups slightly more forward to help secure my position. I also carved a piece of black foam and attached it with double-sided carpet tape to the back of the seat to make it smaller. I went a step further and added a thicker shim under the front of the saddle, lifting it up slightly, again, to make up for the lack of security I was feeling due to the excessive seat size. We should always be forward-thinking in the sense that we don't accept or become complacent with tools that aren't effectively supporting our needs; in situations like these, there are always things we can do to "bridge the gap" in numerous ways until we have those perfect tools at our disposal. We *can* be content with what we have while working for what we want!

Your Tools
☐ **Resourcefulness** – I can't stress enough that it's not the tools you have that are so important, but how they are used. That's where resourcefulness – the ability to make the best out of what you have available – comes in. The most resourceful people are those who have lived with and succeeded despite limited options, forcing them to rely on their own ingenuity. It's a quality that will always work to your advantage.

☐ **Arena** – If I could do it all over again, I would have made building an arena with custom footing for barrel racing a top priority. Working regularly on hard or uneven ground creates excess vibration in our horse's bodies and joints, essentially wearing them out prematurely. Especially when our horses must use themselves in such a demanding way, it's important they have a safe, forgiving surface with the perfect amount of cushion and traction for the training, conditioning and speed work that barrel racing requires.

☐ **Truck & Trailer** – Most important in a towing vehicle is that it's reliable enough to get you and your horses from point A to B safely. If you've ever ridden in a horse trailer, you know how loud, bouncy and rough it is in the back. These days there are air ride options for trucks and trailers that I recommend for lessening stress and wear and tear on your horses. As a minimum, invest in foam padding to place under your rubber mats, and/or hoof boots for hauling to help absorb concussion and decrease stress on the road.

☐ **Saddle & Pad** – It's critical in these areas is that we never accept back pain as "normal." Although a sore back isn't always caused by an ill-fitting saddle (it can be secondary to ulcers, kidney, hock pain, etc.), it's important that we don't give up in the search for the perfect interface between our bodies and our horse's back. Our horses give us their all, and the least we can do is commit to finding equipment that allows us to jockey effectively, and them to perform as comfortably as possible with pain-free, full range of motion.

☐ **Bits & Reins** – The bits you choose for riding and competition will certainly have an impact on how your horse uses his body in a run. To know which to use and when, you'll need the ability to assess how your horse moves and responds, and how headgear (and how you use it) can support him in performing his best. Rein style, length, width, and type is largely personal preference, but quick communication always travels faster and more precisely over the shortest distance and through quality, approriately weighted materials.

Your Team

☐ **Veterinarian and Equine Dentist** – The veterinarian on your team should absolutely be one who specializes in equine performance athletes. In certain parts of the country, that may mean driving five hours to see the most qualified professional. Whether your horse seems to need it or not, it's ideal to see him/her at least twice a year for a lameness exam to catch any potential problems early – great vets. can do that! Just like veterinarians, not all equine dentists are created equally. Just because a high achieving barrel racer uses a certain person, doesn't mean they're not actually doing more harm than good. Educate yourself and schedule annual appointments with a trusted and qualified individual specializing in equine densistry.

☐ **Body Worker(s) and Hoof Care Provider** – You may have several equine bodyworkers that you trust, including folks who specialize in massage, chiropractic or other therapies. Every high-level barrel racer must be their own body worker to a degree; but no matter how advanced we are, it's ideal to have at least one person who has eyes to see and hands to feel what we might otherwise miss at an ideal interval of every six weeks. The same timeline goes for our horse's hoof care, make it your goal to work with the very best!

☐ **Mentor(s) and Inner Circle** – We all need one or even multiple coaches, teachers or trainers we can turn to with challenges or when we want to up our game. The role mentors play and the ones you ride with may evolve over time, but most important is that you connect regularly with the best available to you, and do so with an open mind. Your inner circle includes your close friends, family, spouse, etc. who always "have your back." They support you, encourage you, motivate and inspire you. If not, consider distancing them to your "outer circle!" Being *the best* in barrel racing requires *the very best* tools AND team!

Exercise 47 – Funds for Fun

Description

Today there are a lot of adults who are not achieving their barrel racing goals because they're still stuck believing that being a professional barrel racer is only for folks with "a lot of money." I won't argue that making a run for the NFR, for example, does indeed require hefty financial backing. But especially if barrel racing professionally is your goal, it's time to get real and get busy by creating the strong financial foundation necessary to support it. The truth is, "not having money" is a temporary condition. When this condition exists long-term, it's more due to the limitations in our minds than our bank account. Just like every other challenge, if we want something bad enough we must face the truth and take responsibility for changing our circumstances and overcoming obstacles along the way. Below I've shared five steps for firming up yet another part of the foundation that high-level barrel racing success depends on.

Purpose

It's easy to lack objectivity when it comes to our goals. Crunching numbers can motivate us to take actions that better align with where we want to go. Here are some statistics reprinted courtesy of the San Antonio Express-News sharing details on 2015 Barrel Racing World Champion Callie duPerier's expenses: "Her (2015) trip to the National Finals Rodeo had started more than a year before. DuPerier went to 100 rodeos in the 2014 season, the maximum allowed by the Women's Pro Rodeo Association. She finished third in the Rookie of the Year contest and was 25th in the world (with earnings of $44,804), but fell short of being invited to the National Finals Rodeo, which takes just the top 15 in each event." Another Express-News article shared that Callie's father, Trip duPerier estimates it cost them $125,000-$150,000 in 2014 to earn that $44,804. "To reach Vegas this year (in 2015), duPerier set a grueling pace… She competed in 87 rodeos and won $166,923, coming into the finals with the second most winnings of all rodeo competitors…" Trip duPerier estimated that qualifying for Vegas cost at least $120,000 in fuel, vet bills, travel, entry fees, and hiring a driver to at times help them haul horses thousands of miles. 'Most girls will spend $60,000 to get to Vegas. Whatever they win there is what they make,' he said." Of course this doesn't include a horse, truck and trailer, which can easily cost $200,000, or the cost of purchasing and maintaining a horse property.

How-To

Obviously barrel racing is something we don't do for the money, but because *we love it*. No matter how competitive we are, however, it's not realistic to depend on winnings alone to cover expenses. Because barrel racing professionally is a full-time job in itself, we have to be mature, honest, smart and business savvy to create a unique and specific plan to support ourselves financially, which might include flexible, passive and/or multiple streams of income. Don't add financial worries on top of the unavoidable challenges of rodeo road. If we want to compete professionally for example, a financial foundation should be in place first, before we leave for the summer run, in order to provide a cushion through the inevitable dry spells and to cover planned and unexpected expenses. The following five steps will help you get there!

#1. Get Real About Current Finances - This requires us to get organized and track our income and expenses down to the penny. You may have heard that what you put your focus on expands, and the same is true for our finances. At times it might be hard to face the facts that perhaps we're living beyond our means, but avoidance or denial is not how wealth is created. We can learn from our less than ideal financial circumstances and allow them to motivate us. It's common to inflate our income and under-estimate our expenses, so we have to get an honest and accurate picture, and pay attention to exactly how much is coming in and going out. There is no freedom in over spending. Outside of creating a budget, I recommend checking your bank balances daily to make sure this area of your life is a priority. Then create a list of the things you need to better support your barrel racing, including any tack, tools or major purchases.

☐ *I have honestly assessed my finances. I have a budget in place and closely track my income and expenses.*

#2. Incoming/Outgoing Ratio Action Plan – It's not unusual at this point to realize that your current expenses are exceeding your income. It's important to make saving a priority; and if you're barely making ends meet, something needs to change. There are only two ways to do this; to increase income or lower expenses, and sometimes both. Balance is always the best approach. For example, it's better to have one great horse that receives the best care and a modest truck and trailer, than a half dozen average horses who get mediocre care, a brand new truck and a borrowed trailer. The hard part about making a plan and carrying it out might be making some tough decisions, such as trading in a vehicle, finishing a degree, selling horses, or canceling commitments so you can focus on increasing your value and earning potential.

☐ *I made an action plan including at least three ways to increase my value/income and decrease expenses.*

#3. Slay Debt and Start Saving - A Dave Ramsey quote that I appreciate asks "What can you do with your income when you don't have any payments?" The answer is, "Anything you want." Delayed gratification is considered the mark of maturity. If we can work hard and save up for big purchases instead of taking out loans, we end up paying much less for things than if we're charged interest. There are a lot of great resources and systems out there for paying off debt. When you're not chained down by debt you have so much more freedom to do what you want, when you want. The funds left over after paying bills have a way of disappearing easily, but I suggest putting a designated amount into savings *first* to make your barrel racing dreams a true priority. You might even set up an Emergency Fund savings account and a Barrel Racing Fund account. Again, in order to pay yourself first and prioritize saving, you MUST have a healthy ratio of expenses to income. Make a plan for slaying debt, saving money, and then work the plan!

☐ *I live within my means, and I have scheduled the automatic allocation of funds to my savings each month.*

#4. Know Your Worth and Value Your Goals - Don't sell yourself short by underestimating the value you bring to your workplace, or however you choose to bring in income. At the same time, also be sure you're constantly dedicating time to learning and improving. The pay that you receive is a reflection of the value you bring to the world. Again, knowing your worth and valuing your goals means being selective in how you spend your time. In many cases, we can get ahead faster by focusing on increasing value vs. cutting expenses by always being a do-it-yourselfer. It's better to raise your value to $80/hr. by expanding your education and skills, than performing $20/hr. jobs around your home that don't require your unique and specific expertise. A penny saved may be a penny earned, but don't step over dollars to save dimes!

☐ *I value myself, my time, contributions and barrel racing goals by thinking big, and not selling myself short.*

#5. Bust Through Money Blocks - Money itself is neutral. The power it has, which can be used for good or bad, is the power *we give it*. Ask yourself, are you *truly open* to having more than enough, and plenty of financial abundance? What are your spending habits? Maybe there's an underlying fear, and things are always mysteriously occurring that set you back, keeping you in your comfort zone. Take a look at what's underneath that. Most lottery winners return to their previous financial state from before they won, because they're returning to their unconscious financial set point. To break free of this, we have to recognize the not so obvious blocks and ways of thinking that are limiting us and keeping us stuck.

☐ *I've analyzed how my beliefs and patterns around money have held me back. I'm ready to tell a new story!*

Exercise 48 – Wide Open Spaces

Description
Over the years, I've had to adopt a very strict "less is more" and "quality over quantity" approach to everything I do in order to reach my goals and keep my sanity intact along the way. Barrel racing is an all-encompassing pursuit, but I wasn't always all-in. There is no joy in being overwhelmed. There is *much less* joy in owning horses when we don't have the time or financial means to give them the very best care and attention. There is little joy in arriving at a barrel race knowing you're unprepared, or having a million things running through your head, taking focus away from your actual run. There is no joy in repetitive but avoidable frustration and distraction due to a disorganized, neglected and chaotic environment.

When I load up and head to a competition I want to be ready. I want to have plenty of mental bandwidth available to focus *only on* the runs ahead of me. If something comes up that distracts or frustrates me, I want to address it right away if possible, so I don't have to deal with it again. At every opportunity, if it's empty, I fill it; if it's dirty, I clean it; if it's broken, I fix it; if it must be done later; I write it down. That way there's less on my to-do list and less filling up my mind. Everything is prepared for the next trip upon return from the last one, so that leading up to competition, there are as few chores as possible, because they've been done in advance. I knock it all out immediately so there is *wide open space* to enjoy and focus on performing my best; that is satisfying to me. Unexpected circumstances will always come up. But when we go about things in this way, they are less likely to knock us off track because we have room for them.

Purpose
As I mentioned, when we have specific goals, we must take inventory of our day and how we spend our time and ask if our regular activities are getting *in the way* of our goals or are *contributing to* our progress? The exercise that follows is another set of questions enabling more specificity about the environments we create and surround ourselves with, to make sure they're truly supporting our horses and our own personal growth and success. When we're not being purposeful and intentional in every way we can, we're setting ourselves up for failure at worse and frustration at best. If we're not taking advantage of our ability to influence our environment, we risk becoming victims of it. There are many situations and circumstances we face in life that are completely out of our control. But the degree to which we put ourselves in these unstable environments *is* within our control. Consider for a moment how negative and fear-mongering the media has become – soak that in daily and it's just a matter of time until an anxiety disorder develops! Whether we realize it or not – the sights, sounds and energy we take in every day, whether intentionally or not, have a great impact on us. The quality efforts our horses put forth on the barrel pattern is directly related to the quality training they've been offered. The same is true for us. What we put out is only as good as what we put in, or what *we put ourselves in*. There are many aspects of our environment that affect us, and if we want to take our barrel racing to the next level, it's time to optimize our surroundings to make them as nourishing, supporting and uplifting as possible.

How-To
Similar to how binging on sugar temporarily changes our state, helping us to escape or numb out, sometimes we unconsciously create a chaotic environment out of avoidance; we don't have *to feel* if we're constantly distracted. But when our life and environments aren't cluttered with excess activities, things and "busyness," this new found simplicity creates not just physical space but mental space – space for what's really important. Decluttering our physical space(s) is a great way to start making room for more of

anything in life, from more financial abundance to a new horse. It creates margins in which to think, create and concentrate without distractions. Without all the excess, we can have a new appreciation for what we love most. The simple act of getting rid of what's unnecessary makes us feel lighter, happier, freer, and creates more mental clarity and inspiration, helping us to enjoy what we do have even more. There are so many areas in which we must become experts as barrel racers and a million ways to complicate things. This is why it's even more important for us to simplify. The questions below will get you started.

Do I use and need this? Is this useful or beautiful? Does it make me happy? Would I replace this if I lost it? To prevent clutter from reoccurring, for every item, ask: *Does this have a place? Is it easy to put away?*

Home – Having pride and respect for your home is a way to extend the pride and respect you have for yourself and your goals. Putting intentional focus toward creating a clean, simple, warm and nurturing environment helps us renew, rest and replenish after long, stressful trips, or exhausting days in the saddle.

Truck & Trailer – Your rig doesn't have to be big or expensive, but when it's well cared for you can be proud of it. Value these tools by cleaning out your truck and trailer after each trip. Wash your trailer and re-organize the living quarters or tack compartment as needed. Make regular maintenance a top priority.

Barn & Property – How would it *make you feel* to have the cobwebs dusted, the pastures mowed, the dead tree branches cut down and fences painted? It's easier to become a professional horseman, when you take great pride in your environment and treat it as a true professional would. Attention to detail is everything!

Tack & Tools – How many bits do you have that you never use? What about old or expired vet. supplies? How is your organizational system for these items? Are they quick and easy to access? The less stuff and options we have, the less time we spend making decisions, freeing up more focus for our barrel racing!

Digital Space – Tech. devices like laptops and phones run more efficiently when they're not bogged down with excess. Organize folders and files to make them quick and easy to access, saving time. Move anything you don't use to external hard drives. Do your backups, and declutter social media accounts.

Friends & Family – The people you surround yourself with are part of your environment, too! Do you need to politely create some healthy boundaries or distance from a friend or family member that drags you down? If something (or someone) doesn't bring you joy and nourish your soul, does it belong in your life?

Environmental clutter (of all kinds) that doesn't support our happiness and growth essentially slows us down and stands in the way of anything new, different or better. This isn't to say that we have to be neat freaks to be happy or successful, but that less stuff equals less work, distraction and expense, making more time, focus and funds for what matters most. Organizing and simplifying is about optimizing and improving efficiency – allowing us to *put the most in*, and *get the most out of* our horses, barrel racing and life!

Your Mind – I realized recently I had lost touch with just how connected my self-talk is to my creativity and energy levels. Our life is an outward representation of what's within. When we regularly pump ourselves up and become our own cheerleader, the more this inner dialog becomes a default way of thinking and being, and everything around us changes to reflect it as a result. We're more likely to have a winning run when we *already* feel and act like a winner! We strengthen this ability like a muscle through practice. No matter what kind of physical environment we find ourselves in, most important is that we are intentional about making *our mind* the most beautiful, supportive, uplifting and nurturing place to live.

Exercise 49 – Life Integration

Description
These days every part of our life is connected via email, text, and social media. There's little separation and our minds never seem to turn off. Our culture today has made it socially acceptable to sacrifice family time for our careers, and wear "busyness" as a badge of honor. We're not rewarded in the workplace for "balance" or satisfaction, we're rewarded for hard work. But to avoid burnout, there has to be fulfillment and joy. While consistent or complete work/horse/life balance *is* a myth, *there are* ways to avoid overwhelm and achieve harmony and happiness as we navigate it all. Many of us think about horses at work, and we spend time with our horses as a family, etc. Horses and work, then, are actually *part* of life; they aren't separate from life, and work isn't necessarily bad compared to horses. For many, it's actually *part* of what makes the horses possible. What we want then, is seamless integration or a blend vs. balance.

Purpose
The issue we run into while trying to achieve "life balance" is that while it's normal to teeter totter slightly off center, more often we find ourselves slinging back and forth in a "crazy 8" pattern between extreme states of *unbalance,* only to get frustrated and fed up, then shift gears to place our focus and attention on another area and start the cycle all over again. This occurs because we haven't been clear about our priorities from the start and realistic about the actual time commitment that achieving our goals will take. Second, we often simply haven't clarified what we *do* want most, then made adequate *space* for it. When we're clear about our values, what the investment will be, and have the resources to put toward them, the results we're after will not only be within reach, but the pursuit of them will be a lot more fun!

How-To
Whether we're fully devoted to barrel racing, or starting a business or a family, we can always expect there to be some sacrifice, especially in the beginning. There will also be phases or seasons where the focus and time commitments shift. It's my belief that we *can* have it all, just not necessarily all at the same time. When we're heavily focused on one area, some other area will suffer. It's up to each individual to decide how much, and if it's worth it. Based on what *you* value most, you might drop certain goals or priorities completely, rearrange their order, or you might extend your timelines. In any case, the first step is getting clear about what those highest values, goals and priorities are. Until we do this, we'll be bouncing back and forth, living in conflict. To interrupt this cycle, answer the questions below:

- **What areas of life are most important to me? (Such as: health, family, friends, love, learning, relationships, faith, fun, financial freedom)**
- **WHAT do I want more of? Again (and again), ask WHY? Get to the core!**
- **Go deeper - WHY do I care? What does having this mean to me? WHY is it important?**

When we don't know where we're going, all the roads look good. If we don't purposefully choose where our time and attention goes, life will choose for us; and we may look back one day and not be happy with where we've ended up. With clarity, we don't have to feel anxiety and frustration when some area isn't getting enough attention, when it's not actually a priority anyway. We can let it go, simplify, and focus only on what matters most. As we do, we compound our efforts and remain much happier and more content. Everyone is different and has different priorities. When we have clarity, however, that's where our power, focus, fulfillment and contentment is comes from!

Below are additional tips and questions for mastering your work/life/horse integration:

- **Your Goal Roadmap.** Once you have answers to the previous questions, you can intentionally map out a plan for the days, weeks, months and years ahead that will take you to your desired destinations. Set up the structure, schedules, and incremental achievements that will get you where you want to go. Along the way, remember that having true work/horse/life integration means having some flexibility as you go. Most people over-estimate what they can do in a year and underestimate what's possible in five years. Allow for margins and shifts in seasons to ensure each area of life that you value most gets adequate time, focus and attention.
    - **What are my short and long-term barrel racing goals?**
    - **Considering these goals, what would a "balanced" day, week, month, year, etc. look like?**
    - **What are the current time/schedule challenges that interfere with this and why?**
    - **What action steps must I take to change this, now and in the future?**
- **Say No.** When life already feels full, every additional opportunity or commitment we say "yes" to, no matter how seemingly small, means saying NO to something else. When you must decline invitations, simply say you have previous commitments and are unable to give the project/opportunity the full focus and attention it deserves at this time, without guilt, without apology. We have to invest in *ourselves* before we can give our best to our family, horses, goals, career, etc. Honoring and using the passions and gifts God gave you can actually be a powerful way to inspire and *serve* others.
    - **What responsibilities, commitments or relationships must I let go of?**
- **Reduce Distractions and Invest Time Wisely.** Maybe it's obvious what drains your time the most, such as TV or social media. If it's not obvious, keep a "time suck journal." Distractions are goal stealers. We are most productive when we can focus in one area for 90-120 minutes at a time. Ruthlessly protect your time! Set boundaries with others. Be disciplined. To be wishy-washy about the value of your time is to be wishy washy about *your own* value, and that of your barrel racing dreams. We can devote ourselves to things that add value to our life, things that don't add value and that are neutral. Make it your goal to invest time in ways that *add* value to your life. For example, maximize every minute with uplifting and educational podcasts and audio books while driving, turning your vehicle into a university on wheels. Avoid activities (and people) that drain your energy or bring you down. Complete tasks *now* when you have the opportunity, to make space for when other areas will demand more of your time. Investing time is all about preparing for the future!
    - **How am I spending time each day that's not related to my goal (e.g. Facebook, TV, etc)?**
    - **What can I replace it with? How can I better invest time to receive a return? What's my motive?**
    - **Where and how must I set boundaries, or make changes to eliminate distractions?**
- **Optimize Productivity and Progress.** The best way to do this, first and foremost, is to treat your body like the high performance machine it was designed to and has the potential to be. If we don't want limits on our goals, it's important that we care for our body in ways that don't limit our mental and physical energy. Daily dedicated time to exercise, nutrition and rest must be high priority, not an afterthought. The more we want to achieve in life and the more demanding our goals become, the more maintenance our bodies and mind will require. Optimization also means that we don't do this alone. There is only so much we can do by ourselves. Get help and ask questions – success takes a village!
    - **What action steps are necessary to create more natural energy and focus?**
    - **How can I get more support? (outsource house cleaning, lawn mowing, etc.)**
    - **How can I optimize and maximize everything I do? (delegate, hire an intern, invest in coaching)**

Exercise 50 – Heart & Soul

Description

Like me, Theodore Roosevelt was immediately impressed with the breathtaking beauty of western North Dakota's colorful hills, buttes and gorges. For him, it was the prospect of big game hunting and the opportunity to build the stamina and endurance he'd been lacking as a sick boy raised in New York City that lured him out West. In the rugged landscape, Roosevelt threw himself whole-heartedly into the wild Badlands life, and developed quite a reputation as he transformed from a frail, tender-foot the locals called "four-eyes" to a respected big game hunter, rancher, cowboy, author, and eventually the 26th President of the United States. After suffering the loss of his wife and mother, both on Valentine's Day in 1884, it was also where he went to grieve, heal and refresh his soul, once saying it was where "the romance of my life began." Understandably, after developing such a reverence and appreciation for it, Roosevelt was deeply concerned by the destruction of big game species and the overgrazing of grasslands in 1800's Dakota Territory, and conservation became one of his primary focuses. The harshness, freedom and beauty of the country challenged him, changed him and molded him into a strong and courageous leader.

Purpose

Roosevelt was the ultimate Badlands badass. He answered life's calling, showed up as an amateur, yet outmuscled a serious health condition, overcame tragic loss, ignored nay-sayers, fell in love with life, conquered strenuous circumstances with discipline born of enthusiasm, and fiercely protected what he held dear to become an uncompromising man of action, and essentially take the world by the horns!

His example inspires us to fearlessly pursue and stand for what we know to be true in our hearts. That we must embrace what we love most without hesitation; to run at it with enthusiasm, and most importantly take great care to *preserve* and *conserve* what we value. To protect the horses and sport we love, and *our love for them*, means making intentional decisions to structure our lives so that we never lose the wonder, fascination and connection that ignited our spark to begin with; to hold onto everything that is wild and beautiful and amazing. We won't always get it right, of course, and distractions will get in the way, sidetrack us and threaten it all. So we must stay on high alert, ready to thwart such threats in an instant.

I always knew that horses would be at the center of my life but never wanted riding, training and competing to feel like a job. My initial love for them was so strong that I knew I had to protect it. After pouring my heart and soul into launching BarrelRacingTips.com, then finally transitioning back to rodeoing last summer, my mind and heart was just as full of inspiration and awe and genuine love for it as when I was a starry-eyed youngster looking out the back seat window of my grandparents car, as we cruised through the rugged and beautiful Theodore Roosevelt National Park – and I *just knew* I was born to be a cowgirl. While reaching big barrel racing goals requires serious commitment and time investment, I've found that having a sense of balance or "life integration" to be the best way to keep that fire burning inside. The intense and unwavering enthusiasm I have also stems from the fact that like Roosevelt, the lifestyle I was born *for* wasn't quite the same one I was born *into*. I had to go out of my way and pursue it. As a result, it's been easy to feel like I'm behind at times, but truthfully the gift of gratitude it's brought has been a much bigger blessing, and means I never tire of going the extra mile.

Although I won't claim even a fraction of ol' Teddy's toughness, I resonate with his story, and not just because we share an appreciation for western North Dakota's landscape. His love affair with the country reminds me of that sense of aliveness I'm sure *also* overcomes you, when witnessing a grand entry for example. The promise of wild west, fast paced, exciting action, and the thrill of the unknown, the gratitude and patriotism, and anticipation built up by the careful crescendo of the announcer's voice; it gets my heart racing and eyes teary every time! We're *inspired* when we step into an environment or a *state of mind* that connects us to our core. The original meaning of the word inspire is "in the spirit," or to "breathe life into." Whether you feel that in nature, in the rodeo arena, or both – it's a sign, I believe, of what God *made us for*.

The barrel racing life, also with its long journeys, dry spells, challenges, twists and turns, mental highs and lows, critics and judgements, self-doubt, wins and losses, trips through "buttes and gorges" (in *and* out of the arena), wrong turns, right turns, the discovery of new rodeo grounds and navigating tight 90 degree corners along the way – it's the ultimate adventure, and not for the faint of heart. It too, will challenge you, change you, and shape your character.

How-To

Just recently I typed out favorite scripture I had bookmarked in the Bible app on my phone. In the process, I noticed several lines that seemed to be repeated over and over. One that especially stands out is "all your heart," which is mentioned 24 times. One is Deuteronomy 4:29, *"But if from there you seek the Lord your God, you will find him if you seek him with all your heart and with all your soul."* When you look up this verse, it's obvious God wants us to love, obey, follow, seek, serve and trust with *all our heart*. Now if we were to let this flow over into our barrel racing, I'm confident we would *seek* and *find* there as well. He died for us to *be free*, to live and love and follow the very passions He put *in our heart*, with *all our heart*.

Once you've sought out and confirmed what is near and dear to you, next is to take massive action to pursue it whole heartedly, including *removing obstacles* in the way of doing so, whatever they might look like. I've shared a few tips for doing so in this chapter. Really take time to ask yourself: What dangers have the potential to rob my barrel racing joy and take my heart out of the game? What circumstances have ever caused barrel racing to lose its luster? What's frustrating? Be honest. What legitimate or *perceived* limitations are blocking your success? What *seems* to be in the way?

If competing at a higher level is your goal, then get clear and take the necessary steps so you can *be free* to put, *and keep* the fun in running barrels, to compete without limits and run without holding back. If your goal is to pursue barrel racing full-time, there are ways to go about it that keep your passion alive for a lifetime. It doesn't matter where we start, or that we fail at times the way. What matters is that we keep daring greatly and facing uncertainty by running enthusiastically toward what we love, without guarantee – knowing that even when we learn more than win, that giving our personal best, no matter how it compares in competition, is *always more than* enough.

What an amazing honor and privilege it is just to have *the opportunity* to *ride* horses, let alone compete on them. *The point* is to thoroughly enjoy the whole journey. Think of it like music; we don't *work* the piano. We *enjoy* an entire song for the inspiration, the emotion, *the way it makes us feel*. Training a barrel horse can be like making art. But we have to create the foundation and *space* for sustaining the fun and fascination over the long haul. Our horse's development and performance is an extension and representation of the love we have for them. Relentlessly care for and protect these passions by eliminating what threatens them, whether imagined or real. Keep the life, the enthusiasm and the energy intact by *falling* and *staying* in love with the process. Cherish every ride. Make each run like it was your last. Most importantly, seek with *all your heart* by staying connected to *why you started*.

> *I cannot teach you anything.*
> *I can only help you learn.*
> *The real learning comes within.*
>
> – Tom Dorrance

About the Author

Little did she know where such humble beginnings would lead. Today Heather Smith is living her dreams. She can be found in the arena developing her barrel horses, on the road competing with them and sharing what she's learned with others, *or* in her home office writing about it all!

Over the years, Heather has overcome numerous obstacles that stood in the way of barrel racing success. Lessons were often hard-earned, which is why she's enthusiastic to pave a smoother path for other barrel racers. Although she has successfully trained for and competed in reining, and has experience with starting colts and rehabilitating troubled horses, barrel racing continues to be Heather's primary focus.

Perhaps what sets Heather apart is her unbridled enthusiasm for continuing education. This passion has inspired her to create and take advantage of opportunities to learn from the best in the industry. Heather has worked closely and ridden with many leading professionals, whose guidance has no doubt influenced and shaped her integrative style of horsemanship and teaching.

In addition, Heather has invested a great deal of time and resources in developing her education on the specific topics of equine bodywork and therapy, nutrition and hoof care. She holds an Associate of Applied Science Degree in Veterinary Technology and is licensed as a Veterinary Technician.

Heather's experiences have led her to realize that achieving success in barrel racing, or any other discipline, is really more about personal development than horse training, and that only when we reveal the best in ourselves, can we do the same with horses.

Through her own experiences, she's become determined to make the *secrets to barrel racing success* more understandable and readily available to barrel racers around the world. Today, she does just that through her website, **www.BarrelRacingTips.com**, where she offers quality, original how-to articles and videos as well as a collection of resources designed specifically for barrel racers who are ready and willing to take their competition to the next level.

A North Dakota native, Heather spent fourteen years in Wyoming before she and her husband Craig, became Texans in 2013. They make their home in the central part of the state between Waco and College Station.

Be sure to visit **www.BarrelRacingTips.com** to receive free winning tips and stay updated on opportunities to learn from Heather.

For even more barrel racing tips and encouragement, connect on Facebook at **www.Facebook.com/BarrelRacingTips** and Instagram at **@BarrelRacerTips**

Photo by Kirstie Marie Photography

www.ingramcontent.com/pod-product-compliance
Lightning Source LLC
Chambersburg PA
CBHW081359290426
44110CB00018B/2419